MAKING THE ALLIANCE WORK

CORNELL STUDIES IN
SECURITY AFFAIRS

edited by Robert J. Art
and Robert Jervis

Making the Alliance Work

THE UNITED STATES AND
WESTERN EUROPE

GREGORY F. TREVERTON

Cornell University Press

ITHACA, NEW YORK

First published 1985 by Cornell University Press

International Standard Book Number 0–8014–1822–4
Library of Congress Catalog Card Number 84–046177

Printed in Hong Kong

Library of Congress Cataloging in Publication
Treverton, Gregory F. Making the alliance work.
Bibliography: p.
Includes index.
1. North Atlantic Treaty Organization. 2. Europe—
Foreign relations—United States. 3. United States—
Foreign relations—Europe. I. Title.
UA646.3.T74 1985   355′.031′091821   84–46177
ISBN 0–8014–1822–4

Contents

List of Tables

Preface

It is striking that politicians and those who work for them, men and women whose careers are made and whose lives are comprised of bargaining, compromise and detail, frequently are transformed when it comes to foreign policy. Then, talk switches quickly to great quests and concepts, new charters, directions or partnerships. There is a stubborn sense that foreign policy is different, or ought to be. Surely some sense of purpose and direction is necessary; without it, it becomes diffficult to relate one issue to another, and everything becomes simply a deal.

Yet too often grand efforts grandly stated ignore, or run against, or are substitutes for the task of managing the grubby details on which success will depend. It is to that task that this book is addressed, in the context of relations between the United States and the nations of western Europe hitherto regarded through shared purposes as allies, and by common agreement as friends as well. It is a task for those whom Michael Howard once called in another context "those grey inconspicuous ranks of specialists, writers and officials who are in all countries gradually incrementally working towards minimizing the danger facing mankind, even if they cannot eliminate them altogether".[1]

The tendency to talk of foreign policy as different encourages us to think about it as different as well. That accounts for the neglect of – or even disdain for – domestic politics which so often characterizes writing on foreign affairs. It also accounts for many of the wild oscillations in commentaries about the US–European alliance: for most of its existence in the post-war period that relationship has been, depending on the commentator, on the brink of ultimate crisis or merely passing through another ruffle in basically stable arrangements. Of the two, crisis-mongering has been more notable probably because it is more noteworthy.

Yet we are accustomed in the Western industrial world to considerable stability in domestic arrangements despite periodic turmoil.

Indeed, we would worry if that stability seemed called into question by changes of government or by periods of economic bad weather. Hence it would be surprising if the trans-Atlantic alliance were liable to change dramatically from one year to the next, for it as much as any aspect of foreign affairs is an extension of those domestic politics and arrangements. By the same token, however, we would equally be surprised if long-term changes in our societies did not produce considerable change in domestic arrangements, changes which crystallized at particular moments. So, too, should it be surprising if the Western alliance remained forever unaltered.

The problem is assessing what has changed, and by how much, and what has not. That is the first set of questions to which this book is addressed, across the range of central issues in European–American relations: the nuclear issue, defense and detente in Europe, security issues outside Europe, and economic dealings and their impact on basic alliance arrangements.

The tendency to treat foreign policy, and the Atlantic alliance, as a thing apart has another effect. It breeds the temptation to conjure a "golden age" of the alliance when common purposes were clear and leadership strong, and to judge current travails by light of past successes as they are now remembered. Yet in a cursory look at the history of the alliance it is striking how often the allies have disagreed, even on issues that appeared central to their common purposes. That raises the second set of issues that are my concern: assuming the allies will continue to share some common purposes, even if their differences are greater, how common do their policies on particular issues need to be? Put the other way around, to what extent are different policies on major issues tolerable in light of shared purposes?

That leads directly to the third set of questions. The tendency to talk and write of alliance relations as different leads to curiously – and unhelpfully – abstract analyses. Most treat both the United States and its allies as unified governments – what modern political analysis borrowing from economics would call "rational actors" – making calculations of national interests, examining various alternative policies in light of those interests and choosing accordingly. That model of international relations, to the extent it ever approximated reality (especially for the United States), has long been a fiction. A few other discussions, ones written by Europeans or by those sympathetic to Europe, try to understand the political currents around, say, the emotive nuclear issue that make it difficult for any government in Bonn to take forthright positions on nuclear deployments. Yet those tend to do less well at comprehending American politics; they often treat inconsistencies in US policies as an aberration, and frequently end with strong calls for more "coherent" approaches.

Thus, my third task is asking how much space there is in the domestic politics of the allies, and the alliance politics among them, to fashion policies that reflect an adequate degree of unity in pursuit of shared purposes. That means bringing together an understanding of politics and interests on both sides of the Atlantic. Long-term changes in American politics – the shift of power away from the East or the gradual enfranchisement of large Latin populations – will bear on US relations with Europe. Some inconsistency in American policy may be a fact of political life, and it may not be all bad: it reflects the range of domestic groups interested in foreign policy and the intensities of those interests. It also reflects the fact that most Americans have been and continue to be little interested in foreign affairs and probably lag in realizing why they have reason to be more interested.

It is impossible for an American writing on these issues to escape the tendency to talk of the "Europeans" (or "Americans," for that matter) as though they existed, to understate differences within countries and among them. I do not escape that tendency. Nor do I escape the obverse: seizing those "European" attitudes that confirm my analyses or my prejudices. If there is a justification for occasionally referring to the "Europeans" in shorthand, it is to sharpen differences from the "Americans" where those are important. I do try to point out differences among Europeans when those are critical.

As usual, this book accumulated, in seminars, conversations and drafts for related purposes, more than it was "written." That means I owe intellectual debts to many who will not recognize their paternity for ideas expressed here (and indeed might reject it if they recognized it). But I single out Richard E. Neustadt and Robert E. Klitgaard, friends and colleagues, who offered help and criticism of many different sorts at different times, and Francis Bator, Derek Leebaert, Ernest May, Iris Portny, and Raymond Vernon, whose comments enriched the book. I also happily acknowledge my debts to Bert van Barlingen, for his patient research assistance during the latter stages of the writing, and to Caroline Coleman, for doing the endless revisions of this last of the pre-word-processor era manuscript.

Also as usual, I owe a number of more tangible debts: to the Fritz Thyssen Foundation, which sponsored the early part of the project; to the Rockefeller Foundation, which provided early support and a stay in that most conducive of research settings, the Villa Serbelloni; to the

Ford Foundation, whose grant to Harvard's program in European security provided financial support and a focal point for interested colleagues; and finally to NATO, whose Fellowship I held during the latter stages of writing the book. To these good institutions and their staff I give my sincere thanks.

The debt I am happiest to record is the least tangible – a clean index aside – but the most pervasive. It is to my wife, Glen.

Needless to say, I alone am responsible for what follows.

G.F.T.

Cambridge, Massachusetts

1 The Nature of the Alliance

The absence of agreement on major policies is striking . . . The United States-British view with respect to disarmament is rejected by France and greeted with distrust and fear by the Federal Republic. . . . Basic issues of strategic doctrine have gone unresolved.

The issue of nuclear control threatens to divide the Alliance. . . . No European government, with the possible exception of the United Kingdom, is likely to be convinced that its security is jeopardized by events in another part of the globe.

Henry A. Kissinger, 1965[1]

The most urgent crisis is the impending collapse of NATO. In all of Western Europe, a wave of public opinion that favors unilateral nuclear disarmament is gathering force. The governments oppose it, but even more feebly and ineffectually. We deplore it, while consoling ourselves that it is a passing spasm of the kind we have lived through before. But it is not a spasm. It is a tidal wave that will sweep all before it, leaving NATO in ruins.

Irving Kristol, 1982[2]

Judging by these commentaries and many others like them throughout the postwar period, the North Atlantic alliance* is about to collapse, and always has been. Crisis-mongering about the alliance has been an avocation not just of columnists and leader writers, but of scholars as well. By these accounts, the alliance has been in "crisis" at almost every point in its three-plus decades of existence. Indeed, by one analyst's label, alliance relations are "the enduring crisis."[3]

Yet the opposite view, less dramatic, has been nearly as common.

*By alliance with a small "a," I mean not just the NATO Alliance but the web of relationships linking the United States and Western Europe. With a capital "a," alliance means NATO.

By its lights, what others see as "crises" are in reality just minor flaps in a basically solid set of relations; those flaps are family fights, often sharp but contained in a web of common interest. The adherents of this view are most visible within governments; for them, the rhetoric of alliance – partnership, common interest, shared tradition and the like – is in part a professional duty. But this view is shared by analysts outside government as well. For one, alliance relations reflect not an "enduring crisis" but an "enduring balance."[4]

In this view, the task for policy facing the United States and Western Europe has changed little in the postwar era. Writ large – in substance – it has been to manage the relationship so that disputes over the few conflicting interests do not undermine the more important common interests. Writ small – in process – the classic form of the policy-making problem, neatly described by Richard Neustadt, is recognizing, then assessing, then dealing with the effects of one nation's actions on the politics of an ally.[5] National leaders are busy and distracted by the press of national governance. The presumption of friendship which alliance often implies may mean both that they presume understanding hence spend less effort worrying about what is going on in allies than they would with adversaries, and that they expect more. Leaders of one nation thus may remain ignorant of, or deny the effects of their actions on allies, or assume that allies easily can cope.

What is clearly lacking in discussion of trans-Atlantic relations – and in their handling by governments – is some framework of common assumptions. That lack bedevils judgments about the two sharply different views of the alliance. Two decades ago a basic framework was widely agreed, even if it did not lead to identical assessments of particular episodes: security concerns predominated and the threat resided in Europe, economics were both secondary and seen as largely cooperative, and strong American leadership, if frequently resented, still was taken for granted. None of these assumptions fully holds any longer, yet no alternative set of assumptions has replaced them. There simply is no agreement on the structure of the relationship. As a result, individual episodes, such as those over the neutron bomb or enhanced radiation warheads (ERW) during 1977–78, are interpreted in sharply different ways: either as minor ruffles in a basically solid and consistent alliance, or as the latest evidence that the relationship is changing beyond recognition. Absent some sense of framework, it is hard to decide between those interpretations.

Assembling the pieces of a framework for thinking about – and making policy within – the alliance is the purpose of this book. This chapter sets down benchmarks for later analysis, reminders of why nations make alliances and how they are tempted to behave as allies. Then the next four chapters examine four sets of major issues in alliance relations. Those issues are central questions the allies have confronted and will continue to face: the nuclear question, policy toward the Soviet Union in Europe, security issues beyond Europe, and the interaction of economics and security.

Across the four sets I ask the same questions: how different are the interests of the United States and its allies, and how divergent are their domestic politics? How common do the policies of the allies need to be? And how much room is there, given politics within the allies and among them, to fashion the requisite degree of common policy? The concluding chapter puts those rough answers together, and it draws lessons for the making of policy by the United States and by the European nations.

WHAT HAS CHANGED?

So much has changed in the postwar era. The relationships between the United States and Western Europe seems a far different affair than it was in the 1950s. Perhaps we delude ourselves by holding to the traditional formulation of the problem: managing a few divergent interests so they do not undermine the many common ones. Perhaps the crisis-mongerers are right this time. It may not be just, as Macaulay put it: "Every man who has seen the world knows there is nothing so useless as a general maxim." The extent of change may have undermined whatever guidance the maxim did provide. It is not easy to believe that the changes merely make the policy problem trickier, calling for new forms of consultation across the Atlantic or of "leadership" within the alliance.

Even if, in general, the traditional formulation still holds, what does managing alliance politics require when divergent interests may be more salient than in the past, and when even the nature of the stakes held in common may have changed? Whether the interests and politics of Europe and the United States are growing apart, how much, in what areas and to what effects: these are my central questions.

The changes in trans-Atlantic relations need not be rehearsed in detail here, but noting some will suggest the need to be clearer in assessing their implications. Most obviously, the alliance no longer is a rich America shepherding a collection of tired, war-ravaged economies. In 1950 the economies of Western Europe together amounted to about half the size of the United States economy; by 1980 they were a quarter larger. In 1950 the American economy accounted for 33.9% of the world's production; by 1980 that had fallen to 23.3%.[6] The implications of these numbers are not self-evident. It is worth remembering that Europe's time of maximum economic weakness in the dark days of the early postwar period was precisely what gave it the "leverage" to elicit the Marshall Plan from its American ally. Even now the United States remains, in economic terms, as big as the western European nations together and much larger than any of them singly. But the change means that the Europeans now have large economic stakes of their own, will articulate and defend those interests and will expect the United States to acknowledge them.

The shift in the balance of economic weight across the Atlantic has played a part in producing a change in the political balance of power within the alliance. That change is more elusive of description and harder to assess than the economic shift, but it is certainly as important. American political dominance has diminished. The European states are more able to define their own interests and act to advance them, although there remain sharp limits in most areas of foreign policy on how far the European states can go without the United States. When, for example, West German Chancellor Schmidt met with Soviet President Brezhnev in June-July 1980 and again in November 1981, he could not produce movement in the Soviet–American talks about theater nuclear forces. But he did do nuclear business in those meetings – putting indirect pressure on his ally by pressuring his adversary – in a way that would have been hard to imagine as little as a decade earlier.

If the European states are more able to define and defend their interests, they also have some stakes that do not coincide with those of the United States. That has always been true. But it is at least more apparent now, and the number of interests that diverge surely seems larger. Relations with Eastern Europe and the Soviet Union are the clearest case in point. It is commonplace but no less true to say that East–West detente worked for Western Europe in a way it did not for the United States. The web of economic and humanitarian contacts that has been constructed between the two halves of Europe is not paralleled for the United States.

Since the early 1970s, some 300 000 ethnic Germans have been allowed to emigrate from Eastern Europe and the Soviet Union, but about 3 million still remain, hostages to the state of East–West relations in Europe. While trade with the East is still relatively small for most European countries and has been declining since the mid-1970s as a percentage of total trade, it is still much more important for them than for the United States. American exports to the Soviet Union in 1980 amounted to 0.9 billion dollars; in contrast, West German exports were 4.4 billion dollars.[7] In 1979, some 6% of EEC exports were channeled eastward, about the same percentage that went to the United States. Even if these exports are not crucial to the over-all economy, they may be to particular sectors with political clout. Witness the disputes in the early 1980s over West European participation in the Soviet gas pipeline: between 1973 and 1979 half of West German exports of large diameter steel pipe went to the Soviet Union, thus helping to sustain factories and jobs during a glut on world steel markets.

Energy is another area in which differences of interest are apparent, a subject of Chapter 4. Western Europe is more than twice as dependent on imported oil than is the United States; it accounts for some 45% of their total energy supplies, compared to about 20% for the United States.[8] As important, they are much more dependent than the United States on imports from the Persian Gulf. Three-fifths of German, two-thirds of French, and three-fourths of Italian oil imports come from Arab OPEC members. The implications of those numbers are easy to overstate: to say, as Americans sometimes do, that the United States could suffer a complete cut-off of Persian Gulf while Europe could not, may be true in technical terms. But politically, it is to assert that America would be prepared to sit by while the basic structures of its postwar commitment to the Western Alliance were undermined. Still, Europe's greater dependence is bound to induce it to make assessments of the costs and risks of particular strategies in the Middle East that differ from those of the United States. Europeans will be more tempted than Americans to insure oil supplies in the short run, even at cost to longer-term strategic interests.

Similarly, European participation in the Soviet Urengoy gas pipeline project, discussed in more detail in Chapter 3, reflected different calculations rooted in different interests. By 1990 that pipeline will mean that the Soviet Union provides about 25% of the Federal Republic's natural gas and slightly over 4% of its total energy, up from 17.5 and 2.7%, respectively, in 1980. It was easy for Americans to see the project as a trend toward dangerous European dependence. To Europeans, by contrast, it looked like a sensible diversification of supply, preferable to yet more dependence on even more unreliable energy sources in the Middle East and Gulf.

Only in the military realm do things seem relatively unchanged.

True, the Europeans provide 75% of the ground forces, 65% of the air forces, and 75% of the armor for the defense of Europe. But the aggregate defense budgets of the European NATO members total only that of the United States. British and French nuclear forces notwithstanding, the extent of the American nuclear monopoly within the Alliance did not diminish between 1965 and 1985. Certainly, the changes in other areas affect patterns of decision-making on military issues; theater nuclear forces (TNF) is a case in point. But it remains true that a Western Europe as populous and twice as rich as the Soviet Union is unable or unwilling to defend itself without the United States.

What has changed in the security area is the nature of the security concerns and their place in the trans-Atlantic relationship. Europeans echo Americans in repeating that the most likely threats to Western security no longer reside in Europe but rather outside it, in the Persian Gulf for example. Yet exactly what that means is unclear, and so are the implications for existing security arrangements. Europeans are more dependent on oil from the Persian Gulf than are Americans yet the United States provides the great bulk of military forces for contingencies in that region. The diversion of half the American Sixth Fleet from the Mediterranean to the Indian Ocean is likely to be permanent. Yet does that mean that the threat to which the former stationing responded has been reduced by half? That proposition hardly would command agreement on either side of the Atlantic; the new military situation, at least, deserves strategic reassessment.

Within Europe, there is a paradox: Soviet forces threatening Western Europe continue to improve, but the real threat of an attack seems less, certainly than the dark days of the early post-war period. In part that is the result of the relative success of detente in Europe. In part it is a commentary on the success of NATO in deterring the uses of Soviet military power against Western Europe; at least, happily, we have no cases to the contrary. Yet it means that in times of East–West tension, Europeans will fear for Europe's relative stability; that, in turn may make them nearly as concerned about what the United States does as how the Soviet Union behaves. It certainly colors their responses in crises – the Soviet invasion of Afghanistan in 1979, or the Polish crisis of the late 1970s and early 1980s.

On both sides of the Atlantic economic concerns now rank ahead of security, as traditionally defined. Public opinion polls demonstrate that clearly. It may be that it will be harder to insulate basic security arrangements from economic issues; addressing that question is a central theme of Chapter 5. At a minimum, security and economics will become mixed in ways that were unheard of two decades ago. The anti-nuclear protesters of recent years have been motivated as much by economic as by nuclear insecurity: not only has the world seemed a more dangerous place, but it has also been hard to find a job.

A final change affects both the Western European nations and the United States, though in different degrees. On both sides of the Atlantic the making of foreign policy, even on traditional security issues, is more and more bound up with domestic politics. That is more obvious in the United States, and probably true to a greater degree as well. The post-war bipartisanship in foreign policy, itself limited, is no more. When a rough consensus develops – for instance in support of more defense effort in the late 1970s – it is general and fragile. Special interests are more and more able to have their way on specific issues: witness the Reagan Administration's lifting of the grain embargo on the Soviet Union in 1981.

What is true in the United States is also the case in Europe. Although old traditions and bureaucratic habits that insulated foreign policy from domestic politics remain, they have weakened. Anti-nuclear protest washes across nuclear power and nuclear weapons alike. Special interests often have their way in Europe no less than America – for instance, heavy industries and their unions which depend in considerable measure on exports to the Soviet Union. Policies and their consequences create new constituencies: witness the need of a German Chancellor, especially one from the Social Democratic Party (SPD), to demonstrate that relations with the East are not frozen. In many countries, the politics of uneasy coalition governments make decisions hard to take or especially vulnerable to special interests.

THE NEED FOR A FRAMEWORK

Analysts and policy-makers nod in the direction of these changes but seldom seek to draw their implications. Instead, they retreat to the familiar caricatures: the "end of the alliance" or "nothing has changed." That is so for at least three reasons. One, the analytic task is hard. In a set of relationships as stable as those across the North Atlantic, conclusions suggesting radical change from current patterns are bound to be wrong. Separating what has changed from what only seems for a period to have changed is almost too hard.

Second, asking hard questions threatens assumptions that are as comfortable for analysts outside government as for policy-makers within: indeed, the line between the two often seems to blur. That is particularly so with regard to the most sensitive issue, the role of the Federal Republic. Not only are radical departures from current practices unlikely, they would be deeply threatening to happy assumptions. And so they become too delicate even to raise – even by analysts outside government.

That suggests a third reason why hard questions about the alliance so seldom are seriously addressed. From an American perspective, current arrangements within Europe and between it and the United States are a pretty good "second best." The division of Germany has, on balance, proved a factor for stability, not instability, in Europe. The division, and particularly the continuing US responsibility in Berlin, gives the United States role in both Germany and Europe a legitimacy it might not otherwise have. Economically, Europe is united enough to facilitate trade but not enough to be a still more formidable competitor. Politically, the existing degree of cohesion in Europe make some trans-Altantic dealings easier without threatening American pre-eminence.[9] And if asking hard questions threatens happy assumptions, the answers might threaten a relatively happy status quo, forcing still harder questions about the implications of a "third" or "fourth" best if the "second best" cannot be sustained.

For all these reasons, thinking hard about the changes in European–American relations is both hard and uncomfortable, its consequences awkward. But throwing up hands and assuming that things have changed beyond recognition surely is wrong; even if the changes are far-reaching, the United States and its allies in Western Europe will remain central to each other's purposes in foreign affairs, albeit to a degree and in ways different now than earlier. By the same token the opposite reaction is equally inappropriate. The time is past when the allies could manage issues by avoiding them, when differences of view could be smothered in rhetoric backed by appeals to alliance solidarity.

For example, it is hard to believe that the debate over nuclear issues in the Federal Republic after 1979 would have been worse if the real alternatives had been more explicit. After all, the real alternatives are few and hard: continued reliance on the American nuclear umbrella; more independent or European arrangements, both of which would eventually mean a nuclear Germany; or no serious attempt at defense. German leaders, and Germany's partners, do the debate a disservice by letting the impression remain that there are easier choices – for instance a cheap conventional defense of Germany. What has changed in the nuclear realm and what has not is dealt with in Chapter 2.

The lack of a framework afflicts both discussion of the alliance and the making of policy. It leads policy-makers to avoidable mistakes; it produces confusion and misunderstanding of each other's actions and motives. And it leaves policy-makers as uncertain as outside analysts whether particular mishaps were avoidable mistakes or the inevitable result of divergent interests. In some instances the problem seems straightforward and traditional. The Carter Administration, for example, took a number of initiatives early in its tenure, in non-proliferation, arms transfers and human rights. These, more functional than regional in character, all bore heavily on politics in Europe and of the trans-Atlantic relationship. Some of the ensuing political strains were predictable, some not, but most were not well-understood, by Americans either in or out of government, even if rhetoric seemed to suggest otherwise.

In that sense the policy-making problem seemed to run in the traditional form articulated by Neustadt: one nation had difficulty recognizing, then sorting out, then dealing with the implications of its actions for the politics of its allies. Had it made better calculations about allied politics, the United States might have gotten more of what it sought substantively, created less adverse political spill-over in the relationship, or both.

Yet in other instances the policy problem seemed to run deeper; it seemed primarily political, not one of assessing the politics of allies. It is not clear in these cases that the United States would have, or even could have acted much differently had better assessments of European politics been drawn and understood by senior political leaders of government. President Reagan's lifting of the grain embargo on the Soviet Union in April 1981 is an obvious example. The dollar is another. For much of the last decade the dollar has been the overriding issue in European–American relations, with Europeans worrying either that the United States was letting the dollar drop, thus forcing on Europe more expansive monetary policies than its leaders desired, or pushing the dollar up, with the opposite effects on Europe. Yet American policy-making with regard to the dollar hardly has been driven by European–American relations, or even foreign policy considerations at all. Domestic factors have been paramount. Even if officials had been better at recognizing the implications of their actions for their allies, they appeared to have little space in which to accommodate those assessments.

Cases like the dollar slide into a third set of instances. In these the problem for policy-making seems not one of assessment or even of politics. Rather it seems rooted in concrete interests of America and Europe which are growing apart. European policies toward the Middle East and the Persian Gulf that differ from those of the United States may make sense, especially in the short run. Europe's greater dependence on Arab oil argues for cozying up with the Arab states, and doing so is cheap since the United States can be relied on to guarantee Israel's security. Giving pride of place to political and economic, rather than military approaches to the Persian Gulf makes sense both because Europe has relatively little to contribute in military terms and because political approaches are less likely to unsettle existing arrangements.

A clearer sense of framework would aid policy-making in all three instances, though in different measure. It would, first, provide some guidance to busy foreign policy managers on both sides of the Atlantic in discerning which kind of instance they confront. In the first set of cases it would suggest how much room they have to turn better assessments of allies' politics into better policies in their own governmental machines.

In the second and third cases, a better sense of framework would at least provide keys to assessing the importance of particular instances, and their relations to other concerns of allies or to other issues in the alliance; and it would give hints about how deeply embedded in domestic politics specific issues were likely to be. As a result, policy-makers might decide that the best they could do was to try to insulate particular tensions in the alliance, for instance over economic issues, from other alliance business, and a framework might suggest how likely they were to succeed. And it would also provide clues to when different policies among the allies could be tolerated, and when they would be dangerous – either in substance or in alliance politics. Finally, failing all else, a clearer framework should at least diminish wasted effort and mutual recriminations when inter-allied differences matter and cannot be managed, thus diminishing the chances that allies would view their partners' actions as craven or treacherous.

PERSPECTIVES ON ALLIANCE

In trying to be clearer about the framework of the trans-Atlantic alliance, it is easy to forget old truths about alliance. Alliances are – for most countries but perhaps especially for the United States – unnatural acts. They imply cessions of national autonomy and authority, always unwelcome. For that reason, enduring alliances have been a historical rarity, at least when the alliance was real – that is, resulted from consent among the allies, not the imposition of superior force.[10]

For the United States, George Washington's advice in his Farewell Address to "steer clear of permanent alliance" and only to "safely trust to temporary alliances for extraordinary emergencies" goes deep into the political fabric.[11] More than a quarter century ago an astute observer, William Lee Miller, pointed out how unusual an alliance like NATO is in American historical experience. The United States cannot command its allies; instead the alliance plunges Americans into "an interallied politics of a most complicated kind." The task of alliance management is intensely political for a people that have not been accustomed to thinking politically. For Miller: "We Americans are not oversupplied with the kind of 'historical' or 'political' wisdom our situation now requires."[12]

Peacetime alliances are not only unusual and uncomfortable for the United States. Since Washington's time, they have seemed faintly · illegitimate. So it is today, especially to those on the ends of the political spectrum, an undertone that runs through the pages to follow. Liberal internationalists have been wary of alliance because it smacks of the evil "old" system – balance of power. For their part, conservative nationalists disdain alliances because they are entangling, a constraint on unilateral American action. And the two groups find common ground in a number of attitudes. Both want to act in a single, "pure" way. Both are prone to treat the world as they wish it were, not as it is – the one by consulting only ideals, the other only images of national glory.

A second fact of alliance is also frequently overlooked. Nations make alliances, informal or formal, because they regard themselves as sharing some set of purposes. That set of common purposes may be broad or narrow; it may be buttressed by common language, tradition and shared history, or it may be more limited in roots. But allied nations are not likely to have common interests across all or even most issues. And their interests, even when roughly common, are more likely to be parallel than identical. Even the most basic of common interests between Europe and America – deterring a Soviet attack on Western Europe – reflects parallel interests, rather than interests that are identical in all respects. Plainly, in their heart of hearts Americans would prefer strategies of deterrence which did not compel immediate American responses, especially nuclear ones, that might put the US homeland at risk. Needless to say, the preferences of Europeans, who live on the real estate to be defended, are somewhat different; they want the surest deterrence possible, never mind the risk to the United States.

It is also easy to lose perspective in a third way. We surely mislead ourselves in addressing the central questions if we compare present disarray with a memory of earlier times when the alliance was solid in all respects. Historical memories are notably short; current issues have historical tails that are easy to neglect or discount, especially for Americans. The nuclear debate of the 1980s shares much in common with that of the 1950s and 1960s. Inter-allied dealings over the non-European interests of the European nations in the early post-war period cast a shadow over American entreaties with respect to the Persian Gulf now.

More generally, it is easy to cover past episodes with a rosy glow of allied unity that has everything but the ring of truth.[13] That tendency is almost inescapable: after all, past crises, no matter how severe, are now past; alliance arrangements survived them, and so those past crises must look easier in retrospect than those that lie ahead. But how united was the NATO Alliance over Suez? How willing was it in the 1960s to back British efforts, bipartisan but vain, to fund a military presence East of Suez – the presence whose lack NATO now laments and the United States improvises at a far higher cost? How able was it to take and sustain strong positions in the wake of Soviet invasions of Hungary in 1956 or Czechoslovakia in 1968, when its relatively military position, *at least as we now perceive it*, was much stronger? Those examples at least should make us wary of too much "back-casting," too much temptation to dismiss past episodes as somehow easier than those we now confront, or to impute more unity in the past than we see in the present.

ALLIANCES AS COLLECTIVE GOODS

In making alliances, nations judge that they share important purposes. Yet once allied, their interests partly coincide, partly overlap and partly conflict. Sorting out that mix – in interests, domestic politics and perspectives on particular issues – in the instance of the trans-Atlantic alliance is the task of this book. As a benchmark in that effort it is worth pausing over the incentives the allies confront *as nations*. Armchair analysis confined to that level of abstraction is still the rule in studies of international relations.[14] It is inadequate for my purposes;

by excluding the claims of domestic politics or the vagaries of public opinion or the peculiarities of governmental machines and the quirks of their leaders, it leaves out too much.

But it also provides powerful insights whose effect is sometimes visible beneath the hurly-burly of politics or the popular fascination with individual leaders. At least it can suggest that the fact of alliance gives a logic to the actions of particular allies. The logic may not in any direct way "determine" the action; indeed national leaders may be ignorant of it. But actions that are frustrating, even look disloyal, to a nation's allies, need not be irrational given its position in the alliance. That is a useful reminder to both analysts and policy-makers, one I return to over and over in this book.

By the abstract analysis of an economist, a principal reason nations make alliances is to capture the benefits of collective goods. Security is one such good. The system of economic interchange among Western industrial nations, to which the European–American relationship is so central, is another. In banding together after World War II the states of Western Europe made the decision that in doing so each could have more security than any could enjoy through its efforts alone. In joining that alliance the United States reached a similar judgment, overturning two centuries of history and inclination.

Yet security, once provided, shares many characteristics with other collective or public goods, like clean air or police protection or public parks.[15] The first is that once the group is constituted and the good "produced," it is not easy to exclude group members from the benefits. If I enjoy security, it is not easy to deny that security to you. In the NATO Alliance, if the United States is prepared to threaten nuclear war to defend Germany, it is not easy to withdraw that "nuclear umbrella" from Italy. The nuclear case is a stark one, but much the same logic holds for conventional defense as well. France's withdrawal from NATO's integrated military command in 1967 hardly led anyone – French, American or Soviet – to believe that France was excluded from Western security arrangements.

However, if it is difficult to exclude, it is also cheap to include. That is a second defining characteristic of collective goods. For a pure collective good, the additional cost of including an additional member of the group is near zero: if I breathe clean air, there is no additional cost if you enjoy it as well. In the case of NATO, the cost of including additional members is low: once (some level of) security is provided for the Federal Republic, extending it to Holland is relatively cheap.[16]

The rub created by the difficulty of excluding is the problem of "free riding," again familiar from the economic theory of collective goods. If it is difficult to deny security to one member of an alliance if it is provided to others, *every* member will have an incentive to have its cake and eat it, too, to enjoy the benefits of the common good of security while paying as little as possible to provide it. That temptation is present for all members of the alliance; all would like their partners to pay the cost of providing security. It is, however, stronger for the smaller members of the alliance, for good reason.

A small member knows that his contribution to the public good is small; if he does nothing, he will continue to enjoy nearly the same public good. Thus, while it may be frustrating for Americans, it is hardly irrational for Denmark or Belgium to spend less of their GNP on defense than does the United States. There is in fact a significant positive correlation between the economic size (GNP) of NATO members and their spending on defense as a percentage of GNP. The large countries do spend more, not just absolutely (which would be obvious since they are bigger) but *proportionately*.[17]

A logic akin to this runs through the discussion of the nuclear issue in the next chapter. From the perspective of the European NATO members, nuclear deterrence provided by the United States is both protective and endangering – protective if it deters the Soviet Union and endangering if it threatens to involve them in Soviet–American crises from which they might prefer to remain aloof. Since once the nuclear umbrella is extended, it cannot easily be withdrawn from a particular Alliance member, the European states have an incentive to put some political distance between themselves and the United States, "free riding" of another sort. As Hans Morgenthau put it as far back as the 1950s: "If there is a chance for the nations of Western Europe to survive in an atomic war, it may lie in not being too closely identified, or perhaps not being identified at all, with the United States."[18]

So, as Morgenthau observed, some distancing by the Europeans from the United States is not necessarily weakness, or neutralism; as a result of Europe's position in the alliance, it may be an effort to hedge Europe's bets, sensible to them even as it is frustrating to Americans. Moreover, the logic may run further in parallel to that about defense spending. Smaller NATO nations further from the division of Europe may have more incentive to distance themselves from the United States, both because they know they will have little leverage over their superpower ally in a crisis and because, small and less strategic, they might have some greater hope of being exempted by their superpower adversary. The anti-nuclear protest in the Federal Republic in recent years makes plain that this logic is hardly determinative, but the logic may underlie the policy of Denmark and Norway not to accept NATO nuclear weapons on their soil in peacetime.

From the perspective of American policy-making, the free rider problem is even more frustrating. As the largest member of the Alliance, how much the United States provides of the public good directly affects how much it enjoys. If Belgium does less, it gets about the same; if the United States does less, it gets less. That means that if security arrangements in Europe actually do provide a collective good, the United States can only make itself worse off by doing less, almost no matter what its allies do. Retaliating against free riders only ends by making the United States worse off. That means that American threats to, say, withdraw US forces from Europe if the Europeans do not spend more on defense are not very credible. At least they are not very credible in analytic terms; to carry them out would be to cut off the nose to spite the face. They may be more credible in political terms, to the extent tht Europeans perceive that the collective good of European security arrangements is not equally valued by the American Executive, Congress and public opinion.

Since all members of a group would prefer to be free riders, the result, also familiar from the study of other public goods, is that as a group they will under-invest in the particular good. All may wish that all had invested more, but none will do more alone for fear that its partners will not follow suit. Notice that this is the problem nations face in raising money for most public goods and services. Despite appeals to duty and patriotism, no nation has been able to raise money for national defense by voluntary contributions. If they tried, citizens would free ride, understating their preference for the collective good, since their individual action would have little affect on the amount of good they enjoyed. Since the same would be true of all citizens, the result would be too little spending on defense.

Nations rely on taxes or some other form of coercion to solve the free rider problem. Lacking the authority to tax, it is not so easy for alliances of sovereign nations. They try mutual exhortation or negotiated agreements. In NATO those agreements typically have taken the form of loose promises by all (or most) nations to increase *existing* defense efforts by a given percentage: witness the "three per cent" pledge taken by NATO leaders in May 1977. That at least assures members that the collective benefits of their increases will not simply be pocketed by free-riding partners. It does not, however, change the pre-existing distribution of shares, hence does not provide any incentive for nations to make clear their true preferences for defense.

In contrast, alliances might agree first on each nation's *share* of total defense spending, with the level of total spending determined only afterward. Analytically, that should diminish the incentives toward free riding that cause the Alliance to under-invest in defense, and it might also bring the smaller nations' proportionate shares closer to those of the larger nations. Spending on NATO infrastructure (supply depots, pipelines, and the like) provides a qualified test of these propositions. There, the allies do agree on percentage shares first, then decide on projects. And it turns out that the smaller nations pay, if anything, disproportionately large shares.[19] That conclusion, however, is qualified because much of the infrastructure is located in the smaller countries who thus make large private gains by possessing the facilities and receiving the economic benefits of their construction. Moreover, since the infrastructure program is a small fraction of any nation's defense budget, there may be incentive for small nations to try to buy prestige (or diminish criticism of over-all defense spending) through bearing disproportionately large shares.

It hardly needs to be said that NATO has never come close to more general agreements on defense spending along the lines of the infrastructure program. The negotiating problems would be awesome, since any nation's defense spending produces private goods of value primarily to it as well as contributing to the collective good (and any attempt to agree on shares for "NATO-related" spending would only give nations the incentive to juggle the categories to meet "NATO" commitments). Moreover, agreements would have to be implemented through national parliaments, some of them perpetual coalitions, which might not share the preference for defense implied by the agreement or which might themselves be tempted by free riding.

The implications of these analytics are not always obvious, and sometimes they border on the perverse. Defense effort, even by members of an alliance, produces private goods of value mostly to the provider, as well as contributing to the public good of alliance defense. Portugal's colonial wars in Africa, for example, induced it to spend much more on defense during the 1960s and 1970s than the analytics of public goods would have predicted. In that case, the additional spending no doubt was a purely private good, since Portugal's NATO partners regarded it, at best, as a pure diversion, at worst as a deep political embarassment. But other cases may mix private and public benefits: Britain's residual responsibilities in the Persian Gulf, for example, while a colonial remnant, have value to NATO members in responding to security threats beyond the NATO area. By contrast Britain's increased defense effort on behalf of the Falklands/Malvinas Islands in the wake of the 1981 war looked to Britain's partners like a mostly private good even though it probably slowed the decline of British military sea and air transport; for the Falklands/Malvinas simply are in an area of low threat and little interest to Britain's NATO's partners.

A perverse implication is that some degree of antagonism among members of an alliance may not be bad. Greece and Turkey, for example, both spend more on defense than their national incomes would suggest. An obvious reason they do so is that the spending produces a private benefit: defense against each other in the context of historic rivalry. Militarily, that may induce the wrong sort of military preparation from NATO's perspective; and politically it hardly seems healthy for an alliance to have members who fear each other more than they worry about the Soviet Union. Yet since the essence of NATO is preparation against a Soviet attack that is a very low probability, the alliance may, within broad limits, prefer that its members do more, rather than less by way of military preparations almost irrespective of why they do more.

ECONOMICS AT ISSUE AMONG ALLIES

Economic interchange among the North Atlantic nations, and international trade more generally, exhibit many of the same analytic features as security. Those features underlie my discussion in Chapter 5 of "West–West" economics in the alliance, and its implications for security. The set of international agreements and practices that have been created since World War II, the "international economic system," constitute a public good. Members of the system are all made better off through the kind of cooperation the system entails. Once the "system" is in place, it is difficult to exclude new participants if they are willing to play by the rules. Similarly, the cost of extending the system to new participants is small. Your use of the opportunities for trade created by the system does not diminish mine (though your exports of a particular good may compete with mine).

Further, the international trading system is a "positive sum game." By trading, nations can produce a larger "pie" – more goods and services – than they could in the absence of trade. All can be better off. Nearly two centuries ago the English economist, David Ricardo, demonstrated the principle of "comparative advantage."[20] If nations specialize in those economic activities where they are best, all nations can be better off through trade. That is true not only when one nation is more efficient in producing one good (say grain), while another is more efficient in producing another (say computers). It also is true when one nation is absolutely more efficient in producing both grain and computers. Even then, trade among nations specializing in the production of what they do best will constitute a positive sum game – all can have more than they would in the absence of trade.

Notice, however, that comparative advantage says only that nations can be better off through trade. It says nothing about how those additional benefits will be distributed. That is a separate issue. One nation could take all the extra benefit, the other none. While the game is positive sum it is still a game: nations, even allies, have cooperative interests in having more through trade than they could otherwise, but their interest in the distribution of that surplus remains competitive. Every nation can be better off through trade, but not every nation will necessarily be better off, even in theory. Some may merely be no worse off, and they will, to boot, suffer the discomfort of seeing their trading partners become richer.

Moreover, while in the logic of comparative advantage no nation need be worse off through trade, that is not true of every citizen of every nation. The United States and its allies may be able to make the transition, with little economic loss, from older industries in which they have lost the comparative advantage to Asia or elsewhere. But that transition will be painful for the domestic "losers" – declining industries, their workers and the regions where they are located. Those losses will become issues in domestic politics; losers will seek, and sometimes receive redress from their governments. Often that redress will take the form of restraints on the operation of comparative advantage – that is, restrictions on trade. Those restraints will then become issues among the allies as trading partners. Economic logic points to the working out of comparative advantage; domestic politics makes that working out problematic.

Both these differential effects – the fact that some nations will gain more than others and that some citizens of some countries will lose – produce strong incentives toward free riding in economic dealings among allies, akin to those in the realm of security. Each nation would like to benefit from the system but not have to precisely play by its rules. Worse, as in the security realm, free riding is more attractive the more of one's partners play by the rules. For example, all nations would like the international eonomic system to be sustained, but all may be tempted to manipulate the value of their currencies artifically – either to undervalue them to increase their exports, or overvalue them to reduce the cost of imported raw materials.

To cushion domestic losers, and to protect themselves from the political effects of those losses, governments will be tempted to engage in the forms of restraint on trade that have become so familiar: quotas on imports, price discrimination against imports (or in favor of domestic products), subsidies to exports, either directly or through subsidies to research and development or energy, and so on. The list is long, the forms ingenious. And all these kinds of manipulations are more attractive the more other nations play by the rules – that is, the more the free rider has the benefit both of a tidy system and of its own manipulations.

These incentives to free riding give rise to problems analogous to those in the security area. Free riding may be rational, particularly for smaller nations; their own manipulations do not much affect the openness of the system but may yield significant (private) benefits. Yet if the United States retaliates in kind, it will only hurt itself. The United States has played and contines to play the major role in sustaining the international economic system. The dollar is the world's pre-eminent reserve currency, and that role has increased, rather than diminished in the wake of the oil price shocks of the 1970s.

That means that if the United States chooses to free ride, it may bring the entire system down. Something like that happened with the American devaluations of 1971 and 1973, though the pieces were put back together. Yet in international economics, as in security, the effects of the United States deciding to behave "like other nations" and free riding are much greater than for those "other nations." (This is not to deny that there may be special benefits as well as special responsibilities to America's pre-eminent role: in the 1950s and 1960s, and to some extent today, the United States could run large balance-of-payments deficits, with the other nations simply compelled to build up large dollar balances and the United States spared the painful adjustment measures that would have been required of "other nations.")

Since free riding is tempting for all the trading partners, all may try it, particularly during economic crises. That may be all the more likely because free riding in the economic realm takes so many forms that is magnitude is hard to judge; hence the transgressions of other nations will look worse than those of one's own. Americans, for example, often talk as though they are the world's only remaining free traders, with the Europeans and Japanese sunk more or less deeply in the sins of protectionism.[21] That may be true, in part for the reasons outlined in the previous paragraph, but virtue seems unlikely to be distributed so unevenly.

In the security area, temptations toward free riding are likely to mean that less of the collective good – security – gets produced than would be the case if the partners had no incentive to hide their true preferences. In the realm of economics, however, in the extreme free riding may bring the entire system down. That occurred in the 1930s. Then, many nations tried to be free riders, all seeking to devalue their currencies to increase their exports. Those competitive devaluations, in turn, destroyed the trading system, prolonging the depression and sowing the seeds for the radical politics that led to World War II. There was great risk that the oil price shocks of 1973 and 1979 would touch off another catastrophe of competitive devaluations, for most nations of the world except the OPEC states were confronted with enormous payments deficits. Had they all tried to cope with them through restricting imports, stimulating exports and devaluing their currencies, the international economy would have collapsed. Only delicate management and some luck prevented that outcome.

Finally, the logic of collective goods suggests both why the United States in particular will feel both tempted and frustrated by the prospect of somehow linking economics and security. That issue of "linkage" in alliance relations, sometimes nearly as fashionable as "consultation," is a subject of Chapter 5. The temptation is obvious. The United States, as the alliance's pre-eminent partner, will feel, partly fairly, that it bears a disproportionate share of sustaining both security and economic arrangements. It will thus argue that it cannot do both – that the allies must do or pay more, or be less protectionist lest the United States feel compelled to draw down its military forces in Europe; or that the twin burdens of economics and security threats outside Europe mean that the Europeans must bear more of the share of security arrangements in Europe. These calls by the United States have recurred in alliance history.

Allies other than the United States will be less tempted by these forms of linkages: lacking pre-eminence in either security or economics, they have less wherewithal for them. Yet even for the United States, linkage will be frustrating, for exactly the logic of collective goods. In both security and economics, the United States can only hurt itself by retaliating against free riders. Any threat to do less in either domain if the allies do not do more would be self-defeating if carried out, hence it will not be very credible to the allies. The logic suggests, and alliance history demonstrates that direct linkages for such tactical purposes will be rare. Linkage will be more likely to arise if the American government is divided, when the "national" logic of collective goods visibly is not operating. Congress may, for example, credibly threaten to compel the United States to withdraw troops from Europe even if doing so would be irrational by that national logic. Congress may act in frustration or pique, perhaps not expecting that the threat will have to be implemented, or particular political considerations may be overriding, or a majority in Congress simply may not believe that carrying out the threat would hurt the "national" interest.

IMPLICATIONS FOR POLICY

These observations about the logic of alliance hardly define a framework, but they do suggest benchmarks for both discussion and policy making. First, they amount to the reminder that not all frustrating behavior by allies should wisely be regarded as profligate or irrational. Much of it reflects real interests. By the same token, many of the ways the United States might respond to the malfeasance of its allies would be irrational. Whether the US likes it or not, it makes sense for Holland and Belgium to do proportionally less in defense than the US does. For the United States to retaliate by doing less itself would only be to damage its own interests. There is no easy escape from those hard facts.

Moreover, these analytics bear on alliance issues well beyond who pays for defense and how trading arrangements are sustained. Something akin to free riding, for example, may run through inter-allied dealings over political issues. For Western European states to flirt with the radical Arab states or groups, including the Palestine Liberation Organization (PLO), in a way the United States does not may be conceived as free riding. The Europeans know they can count on the United States to safeguard collective interests – a counterweight to Soviet military forces or the maintenance of Israel's security, for example – and so are free to seek the private benefits of closer relations to the Arab states. Again, such European policies are not necessarily irrational, at least in a medium term perspective. For American policy they raise both substantive and tactical issues: how much unity among

the allies really is necessary, and how much pressure it makes sense for
the United States to exert on a particular issue to try to bring deviants
into line.

However, American urges to denounce European behavior as free
riding should be tempered, on two grounds. First, as with defense,
foreign policies driven primarily by the desire for national gain may
also produce collective benefits. For instance, close French relations
with Iraq, motivated in a great measure by narrow French national
interests, may also produce benefits to the alliance in the form of
limited Western leverage or an alternative to Soviet pre-eminence in
Iraq.

Second, what looks to Americans like free riding may not be.
Europeans may be motivated to frame policies not because they know
the US is unlikely to follow suit – the essence of free riding. Rather,
they may hope that the US will follow. The more forthcoming
European attitude toward the PLO smacks of free riding to Americans, but it may in fact reflect simply a different view. Europeans
probably think they are right and the US is wrong, and wish American
policy would change.

To the extent that specific trans-Atlantic differences are fairly
described as free riding, the logic suggests several lines of response.
One, especially when money burdens are to be shared, is the attempt
to devise schemes that apportion costs according to negotiated shares.
That is the case with NATO infrastructure projects (supply depots,
pipelines, etc.) A nation whose share is five percent knows that in
agreeing to a new project it will also receive the benefits from its
partners providing the other 95%. There is no gainsaying the difficulty
of negotiating and implementing these agreements. But they may be
possible more widely than they now exist, especially when, as with
NATO infrastructure, the spending produces substantial private
benefits to indivdual nations as well as collective goods. And at least it
should be no surprise when costs shared in other ways than by such
agreements give rise to temptations toward free riding.

A second line of response is that more cohesion among the
European allies, or even groups of them, should be in the American
interest. If, for example, the Benelux countries were a union for
defense purposes, they would be sharing defense costs with more
nearly equal partners. That should reduce their incentive to free ride.
In 1970 the European NATO members save France organized the
so-called Eurogroup, at the time an explicit effort to come up with
additional defense measures in order to persuade the American

Congress not to withdraw US forces from Europe. The logic suggests an American interest in encouraging such groupings.

These larger groupings can also be in the American interest on political, as well as money, issues. They should increase responsibility by increasing stakes. For example, temptations toward political free riding should be diminished when the Europeans coordinate action toward the Middle East within the EEC, rather than acting individually. The model of consultations developed during the Conference on Security and Cooperation in Europe (CSCE) – Europeans first coordinating within the EEC, then with the US – seems to have served the West's interests. For Europeans it had the clear benefit of compelling the United States to take into account the "European" view when Europeans were agreed. The strongly held view in Europe that arms control should continue notwithstanding tension between the superpowers, for example, induced a reluctant American Administration to agree, in the Madrid CSCE review conference in the autumn of 1983, to a follow-up conference on disarmament in Europe. Of course, the process inevitably is frustrating to Americans: it is slow, or looks like an attempt to gang up on the United States, or produces what seems a least common denominator result.

Finally, how closely allies cooperate is bound up with how decisions are taken. Allies debate not just who pays and who benefits, but also who decides. Bargins about control are implicit in many NATO arrangements. So-called "dual key" nuclear systems are an example. The European ally on whose soil the system is based pays for and controls the launcher, while the nuclear warheads remain in custody of the United States. What the ally "buys" in paying for the launcher is an explicit veto over the firing of the weapon. By contrast, as Chapter 2 discusses, many other NATO nuclear arrangements are pure sleight of hand, intended to give the Europeans some information and some access to planning without diluting American control. The NATO Nuclear Planning Group (NPG) and arrangement for stationing European officers at Strategic Air Command headquarters in Omaha fall into that category.

This desire of smaller allies for a voice in decision-making can serve as a counter-weight to their temptations to free ride. Europeans frequently observe that they must "do more" in order to be taken seriously by the United States; a recent example has been the argument that if Europeans do not contribute to the effort to structure military capabilities for the Persian Gulf they will lose claim to participation in decision-making with regard to contingencies there.

Free-riding may take allies out of the game. They thus may be cajoled into supporting policies they dislike lest they lose influence to prevent still more distasteful ones in the future.

The interest in control can be an incentive to cooperate even if the situation does not contain what may be fairly described as temptations to free riding. That is a theme of the chapters to follow. If the United States wants, or feels it needs more cooperation from allies than it is likely to get, it can elicit more by conceding a measure of real influence over decisions. The December 1979 NATO decision on intermediate nuclear forces (INF) can be seen as a departure in that direction, although the jury is still out on whether the outcome will judge the process one to emulate or one to avoid. The Western Contact Group (the US, Britain, France, the Federal Republic and Canada) seeking a negotiated solution to the Namibian conflict is a less publicized example of such real sharing of decisions.

The United States will confront this choice – achieving more allied cooperation but at the price of diluting American control – more and more often in the future. The reasons, some of them sketched earlier, run through this book. The United States is less pre-eminent in political and economic terms by comparison to its partners. In many areas of policy – the Persian Gulf and Middle East, or economic dealings with the Soviet Union, for example – American initiatives will depend for their success on some degree of European cooperation. For other issues, European cooperation may be less important in substance, but American administrations may fear the backlash in public and congressional opinion if Europeans are not seen to be "doing their share." As with dual-key nuclear arrangements, the United States may be able to "buy" cooperation by conceding a measure of real influence over decisions. Arranging the politics of these implicit bargains will not be easy; the bargains run against ingrained habits on both sides of the Atlantic. But they are likely in many instances to be better than the alternative. At least that proposition is one I test in the discussion to follow of major sets of issues in alliance relations.

2   The Nuclear Dilemma

NATO's nuclear dilemma is nearly as old as the Alliance itself.[1] It is rooted in the fundamental paradox of geography: most of NATO's ultimate deterrent, American strategic nuclear forces, resides an ocean away from the likely point of attack or political pressure. The dilemma is also an anomaly: it crystallized the exceptional situation of the 1950s and with it the military dependence of Europe on the United States. Western Europe has become a confederation, its nations past the point of fighting with each other. In the decades after World War II the Western European states came to possess all the attributes of sovereignty save one: responsibility for their own defense.

Yet NATO's nuclear dilemma has persisted for three decades, through periods of serious questioning, doctrinal evolutions and marked change in the Soviet-American nuclear balance. So is anything now different? Even the language of the current debate sounds like that of two decades ago. Is the concern, on both sides of the Atlantic but especially in Europe, anything more than the latest bout of nuclear jitters which strike us once a generation? Unhappily, things *have* changed. That is the first argument of this chapter. The nuclear question will continue to be sensitive. It is hard to imagine a period of relative quiet like the fifteen years between the demise of the Multilateral Force (MLF) proposal in 1964 and the debate surrounding NATO's December 1979 decision to deploy 572 American cruise and Pershing II ballistic missiles in Western Europe.

The images of dilemma and anomaly connote the inevitability of sharp change: dilemmas seem to cry out to be broken, and anomalies to be resolved. Yet sharp change will not occur. That is this chapter's second proposition. Dramatic changs in existing nuclear arrangements in and for Europe are, for the foreseeable future, either unwise, or impossible, or both. The solution would be worse than the problem. The dilemma may grow sharper. But it cannot be resolved. No result growing out of the December 1979 decision will do so. There are no once-for-all solutions to the nuclear dilemma. It can only be managed.

Yet if the dilemma can only be managed, it *can* be managed – the third argument in this chapter. Part of the reason is that the dramatic alternatives are so unattractive, hence protest against the nuclear status quo will ebb for want of something better with which to supplant it. But the nuclear issue can also be managed for reasons that derive from the politics, domestic and alliance, surrounding it, reasons that are paradoxical from the perspective of anti-nuclear protest of the mid-1980s. Governments will retain more control over the nuclear agenda and its connections in domestic politics than they will have for other issues in the alliance.

DILEMMA AND ANOMALY

The paradox of geography inevitably means that Europeans and Americans have different interests in nuclear arrangements. For Europeans who live on the potential battlegound, the imperative has been "pure" deterrence. Lacking faith in conventional defense, "pure" deterrence implies the certainty of early resort to American central nuclear systems as *the* way to deter the Soviet Union from beginning *any* war. Europeans' lack of faith in conventional defense is reinforced by lack of interest: if the Soviets believed a conventional attack would be met with wholly conventional defense, they might be more tempted to try; even if NATO's calculations were correct and the invaders were thrown back, Western Europe would still have incurred the appalling damage of conventional war – for Europe a living memory. In that narrow but important sense, the distinction between "nuclear" and "conventional" blurs for Europeans.

American interests are different. If conventional defense of Europe is possible, it is preferable. Similarly, if nuclear weapons must be used, battlefield systems look better to Americans. In any event, American stakes run to delaying as long as possible any resort to central US systems. Any use of American nuclear weapons would risk Soviet retaliation in kind, and no one could be sure that the Soviet Union would not respond even to the use of battlefield systems with strikes against continental America. But central systems would seem positively to invite that Soviet retaliation. Thus, it is scarcely an accident that Americans continually have exhorted Europeans to provide more conventional force in Europe; nor that American leaders occasionally scare Europeans by observing that a nuclear war might be limited to Europe.[2]

These differences of interest are real. They are not new. But they were not inevitable. The kind of European dependence on the United States enshrined in existing nuclear arrangements was no part of the security discussions in the early post-war period. Originally, the Europeans sought an automatic mutual assistance treaty, on the model of the 1947 Anglo-French Treaty of Dunkirk, while American thinking first ran to some sort of unilateral American guarantee as a backstop to defense arrangements established by the Europeans themselves.[3] In the result, the Atlantic Treaty, signed in 1949, the parties agreed that an "armed attack against one or more of them . . . shall be considered an attack against them all." The signatories pledged to come to each others' assistance, but that assistance was less than automatic: each party would "take such action as it deems necessary . . . in accordance with (its) respective constitutional processes."[4] At the same time, atomic bombs scarcely figured in the considerations of the Truman Administration: what good would it do to drop them on allies after the Soviet Union had attacked, and, in Truman's reported words, "Russia was too big to occupy."

In the 1950s, nuclear weapons became a way to have deterrence on the cheap. NATO never came close to meeting its conventional forces goals established at Lisbon in 1952, and the American nuclear monopoly, then superiority, seemed to make doing so unimportant. And so the anomaly was created. It has grown sharper in the ensuing three decades.

The consequences of the anomaly are corrosive. For Americans, it is a constant temptation to look for technical "solutions." That temptation is increased by the frequency of new administrations, their politicians and senior civil servants invariably on the lookout for problems to "solve."

For Europeans, the consequences are more far-reaching. It is hardly surprising that Europeans periodically doubt American commitment to their defense. Dependence is grating to European elites and occasionally terrifying to people in the street. In the 1950s, Europe had little choice; dependence was, if not desirable, at least unavoidable, and so European leaders adjusted their actions accordingly. However, as Europe has become the political and economic equal of the United States, dependence has become more uncomfortable, for both leaders and publics. Leaders have been more tempted to vent their anger at the United States, and sloppier in calculating the effects of their actions of their ally. Examples of both anger and sloppiness run through this chapter. Publics have been more prone to fear that the superpower that is their ally is nearly as dangerous as the superpower that is their ostensible adversary. European temptations to "equidistance" between the two superpowers have been abetted.

The anomaly of European dependence exaggerates the role of nuclear issues, sensitive enough in their own terms, as barometers of the European-American relationship. That is a central fact in managing the nuclear dilemma. The general state of trans-Atlantic relations will bear on the adequacy of nuclear arrangements as much as the specifics of military hardware. When Europeans are tolerably confident of American purpose and leadership, nuclear matters will be less salient; when they are not, specific issues, like the Soviet SS-20 missiles, will heat up as surrogates for concern about the ultimate reliability of the American nuclear guarantee.

At the bottom of both the dilemma and the anomaly is the position of the German Federal Republic. Alliance arrangements in the early postwar period reflected European fears both of and about Germany. If Germany was to be rearmed, better to embed those armaments in alliance. And even if Germany was to be rearmed, it still had to remain non-nuclear. Germany accepted those limitations, even sought them, as a reasonable price to pay for re-joining the West and rebuilding its economy. So long as Germany was consigned to non-nuclear status in the alliance, it literally had no alternative to dependence on the United States – a fact which is much of the reason why the anomaly has been prolonged. In the last three decades the concerns of Germany's neighbors about the German role have become less in evidence, but they are still present beneath the surface. The same is true of German sensitivity to those concerns. And so limitations that have prolonged the anomaly will remain.

Thus, all efforts to manage the nuclear dilemma will bear especially heavily on the Federal Republic. It is twice exposed: as the most important state on the front line, it is the most vulnerable; as the largest non-nuclear state in the Alliance, it is the most dependent. The nuclear issue thus evokes the rawest nerves in the Federal Republic's relations with both West and East. German leaders will remain attentive to the symbolism behind specific proposals: will more German involvement in nuclear decision-making lead to less American commitment to German security? By American lights, this attentiveness will often seem beyond reason, but it is built into existing arrangements.

WHAT HAS CHANGED?

The circumstances of the 1980s strain those arrangements. What has changed does not derive from any single Soviet force deployment. In particular, the Soviet SS-20, a three-warhead intermediate range missile deployed against Western Europe and China, is as much a symptom of the problem as a cause. Rather, it is the range of Soviet force improvements that put pressure on NATO's nuclear dilemma and cast doubt on the credibility of NATO's strategy: from the continuing improvement of Soviet conventional forces in Eastern Europe, to the deployment of the new short-range nuclear systems, to the new intermediate-range systems like the SS-20, to the attainment of over-all strategic nuclear parity with the United States.

Of these, the emergence of strategic parity (some would say worse) is the most critical. In purely military terms it can be argued that not much has changed, at least not in the last decade and a half. As long ago as that the United States lost "superiority" by the clearest and most significant definition: it lost any credible threat to "disarm" the Soviet Union in a nuclear first strike. The United States homeland had become vulnerable, and the Soviet Union had achieved a kind of "minimum deterrence." Then, as now, deterrence in Europe rested on the confidence that the United States would respond with nuclear weapons if need be, despite the risk to its own cities.

Yet, more recent implications of strategic parity do matter in militry terms. One is the theoretical vulnerability of American land-based intercontinental ballistic missiles (ICBMs) to a Soviet first strike. This is vastly overrated as a general problem for American strategic forces; it is, however, a specific concern in extending deterrence to Western Europe. In an escalating nuclear exchange, the United States may want to make selective strikes against military targets in the Soviet Union. ICBM forces, despite their vulnerability, would be attractive for this role, given their accuracy, flexibility in re-targeting and relatively secure control. Yet their use for such missions would compete with the need to withhold warheads of all types for the ultimate deterrent – assured destruction of the Soviet Union. ICBM vulnerability sharpens that conflict of interest, and an American President might therefore be reluctant to spend these forces for a European contingency, especially early.

More generally, assuming the vulnerability of ICBMs, the United States might be reluctant to resort to the use of nuclear weapons based in the continental United States lest the Soviet Union retaliate by destroying (remaining) ICBMs. That poses the risk that the United States might try to contain a nuclear war in Europe without committing its strategic forces, or even that NATO might never use American nuclear weapons at all, even in a losing conventional war.

The strictly military considerations slide into political and psychological ones. Somehow, Europeans felt that so long as the United States

TABLE 2.1:   *Soviet and American strategic warheads plus intermediate-range nuclear missile warheads, 1955–82**

	1955	1960	1965	1970	1975	1980	1982
US Strategic	2310	4362	4002	3689	7725	8018	9268
Plus INF Missiles, incl. British and French forces	0	105	0	144	258	290	290
Soviet Strategic	0	294	381	1403	1875	6156	7300
Plus INF Missiles (excludes SS-N-5)	0	200	705	598	598	940	1236

SOURCES: Robert P. Berman and John Baker, *Soviet Strategic Forces: Requirements and Responses* (Washington: Brookings, 1982); and International Institute for Strategic Studies, *The Military Balance*, various issues.

* Warhead estimates are rough at best. The bomb loadings of strategic bombers can vary, and missiles, especially Soviet missiles, of the same type can carry different numbers of warheads. The SS-20, for instance, has both one- and three-warhead variants. This accounting generally assumes all missiles of a type carry the most warheads that type is known to carry.

remained superior in nuclear terms to the Soviet Union, by however loose a definition, they could be tolerably confident that it would respond to a Soviet attack on Western Europe with nuclear weapons if need be. It did not matter much that Europe became in some sense "hostage" to Soviet intermediate range missiles targeted against it – some 700 SS-4s and 5s by the early 1960s. Now, with parity, they can no longer be so confident. That surely was the meaning of Helmut Schmidt's words in 1977 to the IISS in London: "SALT neutralises . . . strategic nuclear capabilities. In Europe this magnifies the significance of the disparities between East and West in nuclear tactical and conventional weapons."[5]

Nuclear "parity," by some definition and label, will be a continuing fact of life. A number of nuclear modernizations, of both American strategic and NATO theater forces, are necessary. It will be important to recognize the extent to which apparent problems with American central forces, such as the vulnerability of land-based ICBMs, are driven by the need to extend deterrence to Europe, and to frame decisions accordingly. That has both a military and a technical dimension. Technically, for example, it is the vulnerability to pre-emption of the ICBMs that matters and needs to be remedied. There is no comparable need for the capability against hardened targets, like Soviet missile silos, that is embodied in the new American MX missile. Politically, American decisions about US-based forces will wash over European choices: if the US is unwilling to base new central systems on land in the United States, its allies will use that as an argument against accepting the cruise and Pershing missiles on European real estate.

Yet important as nuclear modernizations are, they will not restore an American "superiority" that is psychologically reassuring, let alone militarily significant. NATO's nuclear dilemma will continue to be sensitive. It is an exaggeration, but not much of one, to say that Europeans care less about the precise technical details of the nuclear balance than about whether Americans are tolerably comfortable with that balance. There are analytic grounds for that: Europeans can do little about the technical details of the balance, and they are dependent, finally, on American decisions. So American confidence is critical. With continuing parity, Americans will not be tolerably confident; in European eyes, American analysts will continue to worry about this or that technical deficiency in the nuclear balance. The worry will be vocal; politics may make it more so. Europeans, in turn, will hear that lack of confidence and make it their own. NATO's existence as an institution matters: if the German chancellor does not voice concerns on Europe's behalf, NATO's supreme commander (SACEUR), an American, will do it for him. (The American debate over nuclear issues, technical in character, may feed the European debate in more specific – and often unfortunate – ways, a point developed below.)

NO RADICAL ALTERNATIVES

There are no radical solutions to the nuclear dilemma, even as that dilemma becomes sharper. Solving the paradox of geography runs directly into the problem of nuclear weapons for Germany. Now, as in the 1960s, the logical alternative to existing arrangements is a dramatic increase in European nuclear cooperation, or even the creation of a European nuclear force. On that score, General de Gaulle's logic is compelling: if Europeans fear that America will not push the button, then they need buttons of their own with nuclear weapons to match.

If the logic is both familiar and compelling, so are the obstacles: the political difficulty of Anglo-French cooperation, and the much greater problem of how to include Germany. A European force would hardly be credible without a German finger on the button, but will continue to be politically impossible with it. Half-way measures such as existing NATO "dual-key" arrangements – Europeans controlling the launchers and Americans the weapons, thus insuring both must agree in order to fire – will not suffice. If Germans doubt the willingness of the United States to use its force in their defense, even with dual keys, they could hardly believe that Britain or France would commit their much smaller forces. Talks in the early 1980s between France and Germany about increasing their military cooperation illustrated the difficulties: the French sought to convince the Germans that French nuclear weapons protected them, while the Germans were more eager to beef up the French conventional presence in Germany. European interst in "European" defense arrangements will increase, but the obstacles to dramatic change will remain for the foreseeable future.[6]

Nor can NATO move in the opposite direction – toward nuclear defenses that economize on manpower. Again, the logic of nuclear defense is as old as the Alliance: NATO could have broken its dilemma by acknowledging frankly that no conventional defense was possible within foreseeable levels of spending, given Soviet conventional capabilities. The Alliance would then have built its defense around the threat to use nuclear weapons at the very start of any conflict. Its forces would be structured accordingly, and might be much smaller and cheaper than at present.[7] Such strategies would explicitly decouple the American strategic arsenal from the immediate defense of Europe. They would aim to deter attack by presenting unacceptable odds on the ground, not by the risk of escalation.

NATO has never accepted such strategies, and they were specifically abandoned when the doctrine of flexible response was formulated in the early 1960s. Yet they persist. The growing Soviet arsenal of short-range systems, coupled with the conclusion that NATO could well be worse off after an exchange of battlefield nuclear weapons would appear to make such strategies less and less attractive on military grounds. However, a nuclear defender dispersed for nuclear combat could retain some of the advantages of the defense, and a variety of means of making the early use of nuclear weapons credible have been suggested, for instance by creating or preparing to create in time of crisis a de-populated border zone on the intra-German frontier.

However, responsible political leaders in the West simply will not authorize the use of nuclear weapons early in a conflict (unless the other side fires them first), or delegate responsibility for firing weapons to *anyone else* (much less to field commanders). Politics in NATO Europe are strained enough by current nuclear issues. They could not bear the weight of strategies that relied on the early and extensive release of nuclear weapons, even if those strategies had the virtue of a clarity that current NATO doctrine does not.

That conclusion is not fundamentally altered by the impact of new technology. Technology will not solve NATO's nuclear dilemma. The most that can be said about enhanced radiation warheads, for example, is that under certain specific, and transitory, battlefield conditions, they would be marginally more effective against Soviet tank formations than NATO's existing tactical nuclear weapons.[8] That marginal gain hardly outweighs the problems with their use. ERW are, after all, nuclear weapons, with all the inhibitions surrounding their use. To make a military difference, they would have to be used early and in large numbers. Even if we could convince West Germans that ERW could be used on *their* territory without devastating it, they could not be convinced that the Soviet Union would play that game. Indeed, the Soviets would have reason not to do so. And given the fragility of command and control arrangements, especially in Europe, no one could have any confidence that a nuclear war could be contained once dozens of even "small" nuclear weapons were being exchanged.[9]

If dramatic nuclear alternatives are beyond the pale, the opposite possibility, greater reliance on conventional weaponry, merits more consideration. Again, the logic is compelling: if deterrence through the threatened resort to nuclear weapons is less and less credible, then raising the nuclear threshold through better conventional defense is preferable.

Unhappily, however, conventional defense will not be a way out of the nuclear dilemma, though NATO can and should try to do better. Part of the reason is that NATO has preached its inferiority in conventional forces for so long it has come to believe it, hence confidence, especially among defense analysts and attentive publics, that NATO can rely less on nuclear weapons will be slow in coming. Moreover, given the uncertainties that surround any reckoning of the balance in central Europe, prudent military planners can hardly avoid making worse-case estimates, and those will never be comforting. Improvements in conventional defense are not only costly, but they also run up against the shortage of personnel which most Western armed forces will experience in the latter part of the 1980s, especially as commitments beyond Europe expand to make more demands on fewer men of age for military service.

Nor will new technologies – like precision-guided weapons for deep interdiction strikes behind the front lines – or new tactics – such as recent enthusiasm for maneuver defenses – sever the dilemma.[10] They will turn out either not to be cheaper than existing arrangements or to imply changes, such as a NATO posture with more "offensive" capabilities for counter-attack, that are politically unacceptable.

Even if NATO could markedly improve its conventional forces and convince its publics that it had, it would still confront the abiding European horror of a conventional war in Europe: in European eyes, if better conventional defenses make a resort to nuclear weapons less likely, the Soviets may in a crisis be *more* tempted to risk such a conventional war. More generally, Europeans will cling to the *status quo*: after all, happily we have no proof that current arrangements have not worked. Changes look either risky in substance or costly to implement through domestic political processes. That is true whether the change is deploying 572 new American missiles or contemplating radical changes in conventional tactics.

THE MUDDLE OF TNF

No dramatic resolution of NATO's nuclear dilemma is on the horizon. At the same time, however, existing arrangements are hardly reassuring. The point of greatest strain is the role of American (or dual-key) nuclear forces based in Europe, NATO's theater nuclear forces (TNF). There as elsewhere in trans-Atlantic relations, old decisions cast long shadows on current issues. The process that produced NATO's existing theater nuclear posture was haphazard at best.[11] The NATO Council made the initial decision to introduce tactical nuclear weapons in 1954, but the actual weapons choices hardly were driven by clear determinations about the role of nuclear weapons in NATO doctrine. The total number of 7000 warheads seems to have been as much related to the production capabilities of the American weapons laboratories as to anything else. The arsenal that resulted was a grab-bag of yields, ranges and types of weapons, but it was, and is, heavily tilted toward short-range systems. The 6000 warheads that remained in the inventory in 1982 were many more than NATO had systems to deliver; many of them were so obsolete as to be essentially unusable.

Decisions about longer-range TNF appear especially haphazard.[12] NATO deployed medium-range American nuclear missiles in Europe in 1959 – 60 Thors in Britain and 45 Jupiters in Italy and Turkey.

NATO's Supreme Commander at the time, General Norstad, advocated a force of NATO medium-range ballistic missiles (MRBM) in addition to the Thors and Jupiters, and for the next few years there were a variety of schemes for some form of NATO nuclear force. Of these the most famous, now infamous, was the Multilateral Force (MLF), which was to be a fleet of 25 NATO surface ships, manned by sailors of different NATO nations and carrying nuclear missiles whose firing was to be under American control.

The debate over NATO's nuclear role, especially in longer-range theater forces, subsided rather than ended with the withdrawal of the Thors and Jupiters by 1964 and with the demise of the MLF in 1965. The strategic rationale for those actions was that land- and sea-based missiles from the central American strategic arsenal could by then cover all targets of interest deep into the Warsaw Pact, including the Soviet Union. In the 1950s the United States had given equal emphasis to the development of intercontinental ballistic missiles (ICBMs), to be deployed in the continental US or at sea, and of intermediate range ballistic missiles (IRBMs) for deployment in Europe. Yet from the start, the IRBMs were viewed by Americans primarily as a hedge against technical problems in the ICBM program. By that logic, the sooner ICBMs could cover all the Soviet targets of interest, the sooner the need for IRBMs would fade.

The debate at the time recognized some of the arguments for European-based forces – they would disperse the retaliatory forces and provide more flexibility for limited wars, in addition to whatever value they had in providing political reassurance to Europeans. However, the counter-arguments seemed over-riding, in American eyes at any rate: politically, the interest in centralized command and control seemed imperative, as Americans worried about independent European nuclear forces; moreover, effective ICBMs were at hand, while a second generation of more survivable IRBMs appeared to be years away.[13] Psychologically, the rapid American build up of strategic forces of the early 1960s and the attainment of clear "superiority," never mind that it was hard to know exactly what that meant, were critical in reassuring Europeans.

Yet as that "superiority" eroded, in the context of the range of Soviet improvements in European nuclear and conventional forces, NATO's TNF posture came under increasing strain. At the lower end of the range spectrum, the preponderance of existing TNF is of very limited range: some 1850 US and European artillery pieces capable of firing nuclear rounds, but with ranges under 10 miles, compared with under 200 Pershing IA missiles, 400 miles in range. In many cases the nuclear yields are relatively large. Aircraft are vulnerable to preemption, all the more so if their ranges require them to be based forward. Even the existing Pershing missiles, in form mobile, are cumbersome to move and must be fired from a limited number of pre-surveyed sites, thus raising questions about their survivability.

Worse, most of NATO's 6000-odd tactical warheads in Europe are stored at some fifty sites; according to a recent estimate, NATO presents no more than 70 TNF targets in peacetime and only 200–300 once weapons are dispersed for war.[14] Storing tactical warheads in the United States, as the Reagan Administration decided to do with enhanced radiation warheads in 1981, solves some problems but creates more. Moving them to Europe in a crisis would compete for scarce airlift and would be likely to be regarded by political leaders as provocative, only deepening existing doubts about whether NATO would actually use to advantage what warning time of an impending attack it could expect. Much of the current NATO posture does, as one analyst put it several years ago, beg the Soviet Union to pre-empt, and perhaps even makes it possible to do so with conventional weapons.[15]

Procedures for securing release of weapons, dispersing them from stockpiles to be mated with launching systems, and applying the codes to unlock the weapons would take hours, even days in the case of the older weapons. The development of so-called Permissive Action Links (PALs), now generally electronic rather than mechanical as in the past, to activate warheads diminishes the risk that terrorists could detonate a bomb even if they could steal one. Still, there is inherent tension between interests in storing weapons in a small number of very secure sites to protect them from terrorists and dispersing them widely to make them less vulnerable to pre-emption; and between making weapons hard for terrorists to activate but quick for NATO forces to make ready in the event of war.

Any NATO TNF posture would put a tremendous burden on arrangements for command, control, communications and intelligence (C31), but those arrangements are particularly dubious for the existing posture and doctrine. In the customary scenario of a tactical nuclear response to a losing conventional war, it is not clear that NATO would be able to use nuclear weapons at all; the imperative of control collides with the requirements of timely use for military purpose. By the time the American President authorized release and approved targets, presumably in consultation with his fellow NATO leaders, and the weapons were physically prepared and triggered, they could well have been overrun or their use have otherwise become inappropriate. Moreover, Soviet strikes on some ten C31 centers in Europe could "blind" the Alliance.

The problems at the longer-range end of the TNF spectrum have been the focus of recent attention. As Table 2.1 illustrated, before the deployments of Pershings and cruise missiles began in December 1983, NATO had no land-based missiles in Europe with range to reach the Soviet Union, with the exception of the 18 French SSBS S-2 missiles (and France remains outside NATO's integrated military command). NATO's intermediate range systems were, and still are, mostly aircraft: American F-111s based in Britain, carrier-based A-6s and A-7s, US and European F-4s, British Vulcan bombers and French Mirage IVs. Many of these are aging – the Vulcans are being rapidly retired – they are vulnerable to pre-emptive attack, even on fifteen-minute alert; they will have increasing difficulty penetrating Soviet air defense; and they are badly needed for conventional missions in any event.

The submarine-based component of NATO's longer-range TNF presents a different set of difficulties. None of the systems – the French MSBS M-20 submarine-launched ballistic missiles (SLBMs), the British *Polaris* force or the 400 American *Poseidon* warheads assigned to NATO and targeted by the Supreme Allied Commander, Europe – has anywhere near the accuracy imputed to the Soviet SS-20, although they are certainly accurate enough to strike "soft" military targets in the Soviet Union, like airfields, of which there are a great many.[16] Each *Poseidon* missile carries between 10 and 14 warheads, which would make "small" attacks difficult, and single missile launches could reveal the location of the boat. These problems are reinforced by the difficulty of communicating quickly with submarines underwater, by the inability to re-target SLBMs rapidly, and by the fact that if French and British systems are to have any meaning as independent national systems, they would have to be withheld for last-ditch retaliation, not used for NATO purposes earlier in a war.

THINKING ABOUT TNF

To some observers, these problems with TNF signify that NATO's doctrine of flexible response, formally adopted in 1967, has come to the end of the road. The doctrine says that NATO will resist an attack with the lowest level of violence practicable. It explicitly contemplates using nuclear weapons *first* if the Soviet Union is about to overrun Western Europe in a conventional attack. It implies a ladder of nuclear escalation: the first nuclear weapons to be used would be short-range battlefield systems; these would be followed by deeper strike theater systems if need be; and eventually, in the extreme case, the Alliance would resort to American central strategic systems.

Yet since the doctrine can mean all things to all people, it means little to any of them. From the start, it was as much a political compromise as a military strategy; in Lawrence Freedman's phrase, flexible response involved "an inadequate conventional defense backed by an incredible nuclear guarantee."[17] In the realm of TNF it has amounted to little more than the hope that the Soviet Union would be deterred because it would be at least as uncertain how NATO would behave in a crisis as the Alliance itself was.

The existing muddle of flexible response may in fact deter the Soviet Union, but it can no longer reassure us. It may deter because, in the first half of the theorem attributed many years ago to Denis Healey, even a small probability that the United States might come to Europe's defense with nuclear weapons probably is enough to deter the Soviet Union. The second half of Healey's theorem was that even a large probability of such a response would not suffice to reassure American allies in Europe. Now, it should be added, specific arrangements designed to increase the credibility of that response may look distinctly frightening to those European allies they are intended to protect.

The current TNF posture reassures neither American hawks nor European doves. It does not reassure hawks because they insist on looking at ladders of escalation in a purely mechanical way: for them, deficiencies at the top of the ladder, for instance ICBM vulnerability, make any use of nuclear weapons – or even military force at all – unthinkable. Worse, current arrangements are the opposite of reassuring to doves because those arrangements look both mindless and unpredictable, making the West seem as likely to ignite nuclear catastrophe as the East, hence as dangerous. And hawks and doves coincide, and thus reinforce each other on a number of points: growing East–West tension increases the risk of a confrontation between the superpowers, new technology will unsettle the strategic balance, and the security interests of Europe and the United States are not identical.

There is no question that the weakest point in the doctrine of flexible response is the first use of nuclear weapons. That is so because the doctrine brought together but could not integrate two different concepts of deterrence. One was deterrence through denial, physically preventing the Warsaw Pact from occupying Western Europe, the classical strategy of defense. In accepting flexible response, the European NATO members genuflected in the direction of conventional defense but remained unwilling to improve forces to match intentions.

The other concept is deterrence through punishment, the threat to wreak unacceptable damage on the other, not necessarily in areas adjacent or related to the point of aggression, the kind of threat that has been at the center of nuclear deterrence since nuclear weapons were invented. This notion of deterrence can be rational only if the side making the threat is superior to its opponent in the sense of being more able to stand punishment. It can be credible though not rational if the other side believes the stake which occasions the threat is so important that the threat might actually be carried out despite the irrationality of doing so. In this sense, the Soviet Union may believe that western Europe is so important that the United States and its allies would go nuclear to prevent it being overrun even if doing so was tantamount to committing suicide.

TNF stand right at the intersection of these two notions, with Europeans and Americans looking at them through the lenses of different concepts of deterrence. It is harder and harder to escape the conclusion that, with respect to the specific question of the role of TNF, Europeans have been right and Americans wrong, even if the Europeans have been unwilling to accept the implications of their own analysis. Nuclear weapons, by their nature, can deter through the threat to punish, not by their role in physical defense. In a time of nuclear stalemate between the two superpowers, that means that nuclear weapons primarily can deter other nuclear weapons. They may also have a role as last-ditch uppers of the ante. That latter threat may be credible if the Soviet Union believes our stake is so important to us, yet since the threat is irrational, there will always be doubts about its credibility, perhaps more to us than to the Soviet Union.

Both these roles for TNF are essentially political, not military. Indeed, to push the point further, it is hard to conceive of any strictly military role for TNF in the defense of Western Europe.[18] That underscores an old lesson, too easily obscured in the technical debate: the role of TNF in NATO strategy is primarily a political question. Weapons matter but politics are decisive. Put differently, the political arrangements in which weapons are imbedded count for more than the weapons themselves. The credibility of NATO strategy – and of the role of TNF in that strategy – turns, finally, on political confidence and cohesion, an awareness of shared stakes backed by the presence of 300 000 American GIs in Europe.

At the same time, NATO can no longer afford to be so vague about TNF, on the argument that somehow the mere presence of the weapons will be politically reassuring. Most presumptions about how NATO would use nuclear weapons in Europe simply are wide of the mark. Suppose, to use the hardest case, NATO actually were losing a conventional war and its leaders decided the time had come to face the great abyss of a first use of nuclear weapons. It is hard to imagine that battlefield weapons actually would be used, for a number of reasons. Most obvious, the Soviet Union now has an array of short-range systems of its own, from nuclear artillery up through the latest generation of shorter-range missiles, the SS-21, 22 and 23. More than a decade of NATO studies have shown that if NATO used short-range weapons and the Soviet Union responded in kind, it is far from obvious that NATO would be the net gainer in purely military terms.

Second, using short-range systems in a losing conventional war would mean using them on NATO's own territory. A German Chancellor who agreed to an American use of nuclear weapons – and it is hard to conceive that the United States would use them, at least initially, without such agreement – surely would add a condition to his agreement: not on German territory, West, and probably East as well. NATO's Carte Blanche war game in 1955 had a lasting impression on Europeans, for good reasons. That game, held in Germany, the Low Countries and northeastern France, simulated the use of 355 atomic bombs and resulted in 5.2 million prompt civilian casualties, leaving aside longer-term effects.[19] A German Chancellor or British Prime Minister who agreed to use nuclear weapons might also add a second condition: not fired from German or British territory. That is reasonable enough: who wants to invite nuclear retaliation on their own heads?

Finally, there would be no automatic decision to go nuclear, far from it; the decision would be the most agonizing one political leaders have ever made, and they would give great emphasis to those nuclear systems which are most controllable. The US President certainly would want to approve every release of a nuclear weapon and every single target; he could hardly do less. Yet that suggests that he would be extremely reluctant to release short-range weapons for battlefield use at the subsequent discretion of commanders on the scene.

So where would that leave NATO a few minutes after its leaders began to face nuclear war? A strike on the Soviet Union itself probably would be ruled out for the time being as too escalatory, and NATO leaders would be likely instead to look at targets in Eastern Europe.[20] They would look no doubt at military targets, but the intended effect would be more political than military. And they would quickly move to discussion of "offshore" systems as the best launch vehicles. No one could be sure that the Soviet Union would respect *any* categories in framing its response, but using "offshore" systems at least would make more difficult the Soviet decision about how, and where, to respond. Thus, for NATO a limited, demonstrative *Poseidon* strike against targets deep in Eastern Europe could turn out to be not one of the last "rungs" on some notional escalation ladder, but the first.

NATO's customary assumptions may be more tenable in the contingency of a selective Warsaw Pact nuclear attack on military targets in Western Europe. In that case, NATO would want to have a broad range of nuclear options with which to respond and to select the most limited option commensurate with the attack. Yet given that even a "limited" Soviet attack would cross the nuclear threshold, with all its awesome implications, it is hard to imagine such a strike except as part of, or as an immediate prelude to a Soviet conventional attack. NATO might then want to respond with TNF, but the same inhibitions on the use of short-range weapons would apply.

There is no escaping the conclusion that NATO needs to sharply reduce its nominal reliance on short-range systems. That reliance distorts military planning and the large numbers are handy objects of anti-nuclear protest. At the time of the December 1979 decision, NATO agreed to withdraw 1000 warheads – and then withdrew them so quietly it got no public credit for having done so – and in October 1983 NATO leaders pledged to withdraw 1400 more. It should be possible to go even further, though NATO needs to retain some short-range systems – in part as a deterrent to the use of comparable Soviet systems, in part to insure that Soviet conventional forces cannot concentrate as they might if there was no risk of nuclear weapons being used against them.

Moving away from such reliance on short-range systems would have several happy consequences for the Alliance. In military planning, it would free nuclear-capable aircraft and, to a lesser extent, artillery pieces which are badly needed for conventional roles in the defense of Europe. More important, by reducing numbers of nuclear weapons, especially those that seem in popular image the weapons most likely to be used, it should diminish opposition to nuclear weapons among publics in Western Europe. It now looks to many Western Europeans like NATO is simply piling up weapons beyond reason, and is dangerously trigger-happy to boot. Fewer total numbers of weapons and more clarity about their purpose would hardly satisfy all the nuclear critics in Europe, but it would help.

The aim would be to provide NATO with a TNF posture comprising many fewer weapons than at present but with a much larger proportion of longer-range systems. The December 1979 decision went in the right direction. It may be necessary to go further. Longer-range systems are less vulnerable to pre-emption because they can be based further back in NATO Europe even if their targets are not deep in the Warsaw Pact.

In particular, there are grounds for avoiding too much preoccupation with land basing. From a military perspective there are strong arguments for sea-basing: mobility, hence relative invulnerability to pre-emptive destruction, and the lack of obvious retaliatory options against European territory inherent in land-based systems. Command and control of sea-based systems will remain a problem but not an over-riding one. Moreover, some of the political controversy that surrounds the stationing of nuclear weapons on European territory could be avoided, and the escalatory distance to strategic sea-based systems reduced. Almost unnoticed in the public debate over the December 1979 decision, the Reagan Administration accelerated previous plans to deploy hundreds of cruise missiles aboard attack submarines and surface ships, in both anti-ship and land attack missions.[21] It should not be beyond the wit of the Alliance to give many of those a theater mission, and to concoct ways to connect them with Europe, for instance by assigning them to NATO and perhaps basing a portion in Europe.

THE DECEMBER 1979 DECISION

Because the nuclear dilemma can only be managed, not resolved, *how* the alliance reaches decisions matters nearly as much as *what* is decided. The most recent nuclear episode, events surrounding the December 1979 "double decision" – to deploy 572 cruise and Pershing missiles but simultaneously to pursue Soviet–American arms control talks in the hope of rendering the deployments unnecessary – underscores that fact.

Military concerns about TNF were one strand in the discussions leading to the decisions. Allied defense ministries had been discussing the problems of longer-range TNF – now called intermediate nuclear forces (INF) – since the mid-1970s.[22] In May 1977 the NATO heads of government agreed on a broad program of defense improvements, the Long-Term Defense Program, one part of which was devoted to TNF. The task force that took charge of TNF, the so-called High Level Group (HLG) of NATO's Nuclear Planning Group (NPG), quickly focussed on longer-range TNF. Thus, in one sense, Schmidt's October 1977 speech in London only went public with concerns that Alliance officials were already at work on behind the scenes.

However, a second strand to discussion, and to Schmidt's concern, was the progress of SALT II, then being negotiated by Washington and Moscow. By the autumn of 1977, the United States returned to an earlier position of a three-part formula for SALT II – a treaty, a protocol of limited duration, and a statement of principles for SALT III. Cruise missiles were relegated to the protocol, with other issues that were too important to defer yet too difficult to solve definitively in the treaty. As initially conceived, the protocol was to ban deployment of ground or sea-launched cruise missiles (GLCMs and SLCMs) with ranges of more than 600 kilometers, with air-launched cruise missiles (ALCMs) limited to 2500 kilometers. During 1977 European uneasiness with the provisions of SALT II increased as it became clear that the Soviet SS-20 would be excluded but that the protocol would ban GLCM and SLCM deployment.

Throughout 1977 and 1978 the United States frequently repeated the same reassurances. GLCMs and SLCMs could not be deployed during the period of the protocol in any case, and so the ban on deployment had no effect. Testing of those systems would be permitted, however. The United States would not consider the **provisions of the protocol a precedent for future negotiations, and** the Senate would not permit the protocol to be automatically extended.

None of these efforts was entirely successful. Europeans turned American arguments around. If the protocol was so inconsequential, why bother with it? And why had the Soviet Union seemed to cooperate? If Europeans, West Germans in particular, sometimes sounded overly legalistic by insisting that the protocol would constitute a precedent even if it expired, they were correct that it would not only put cruise missiles on the agenda for future SALTs but would also suggest one possible way to treat them. When, in June 1977 the US made the decision to add ALCMs to the bomber component of its strategic triad, it seemed to be saying that cruise missiles were good for the United States but not for Europe. For example, a 1977 American briefing paper on cruise missiles was regarded by European defense establishments as more a brief for SALT II than an analysis of the weapon. These European concerns were expressed at a special meeting of the NATO Nuclear Planning Group (NPG) in October 1977 and again at the NATO winter meetings of foreign and defense ministers in December 1977.

In this context, Schmidt's October speech ws primarily a reflection of his concern about the course of SALT II. Europeans like Schmidt had more qualms about the political symbolism of the emerging SALT II treaty than about specific provisions. Measures that were agreed upon before or during the SALT "breakthroughs" in September 1977 – when it was decided that the United States would include cruise missiles in SALT while excluding the Soviet SS-20, would treat air-launched cruise missiles differently from those that might be based in Europe, and would include provisions for the Backfire that would ensure its use exclusively against Europe – all seemed to suggest to the Soviet Union that the security of the United States and that of Europe could be treated separately.

A third backdrop to INF was the debacle over enhanced radiation warheads (ERW) – or "neutron bombs" – of 1977–78. The ERW itself was not new. It had been designed in 1958, tested in 1963, considered for anti-ballistic missile systems in the 1960s, and revived in the 1970s as an antitank weapon once the nuclear threshold had been crossed. It was hardly a great secret before the summer of 1977. It had proceeded easily through the Alliance negotiations at the technical level, buried within defense ministry relations. It apparently was discussed at Nuclear Planning Group (NPG) meetings at least as early as 1974, but communiqués from those meetings mentioned it only once, in 1976, and then only indirectly.[23] Neither the NPG nor any other alliance instrument served to provide early warning of the possible political impact or pressed the issue on political leaders of allied governments. By the time the issue emerged from the NPG for decision, opportunities to shape the domestic politics surrounding it no longer existed. In 1977 a US newspaper article described the ERW as "the ultimate capitalist weapon, destroying people but leaving buildings intact."[24] However compelling the NPG's technical analysis might have been, it had little effect.

Once ERW became public, Washington painstakingly put together a scenario, to be ratified by NATO, whereby the United States would announce the production of components for the enhanced radiation warheads and the European NATO countries would assent to their deployment *after* the United States first offered not to deploy them in exchange for measures of Soviet restraint.[25] The process drew European leaders into explicit support for a nuclear decision, to their discomfort. Bonn, for instance, said it would not be the only continental NATO member to deploy the neutron warheads, and that put enormous pressure on Belgium, the only country in which deployment made military sense and politics might permit it.

President Carter evidently did not realize, and was not so informed by his advisers, that clear-cut support from European heads of government for deploying neutron warheads in Europe simply was not likely to be forthcoming. It ran directly against practice in NATO and the reluctance of European leaders to take the lead on nuclear issues. Once President Carter understood that, he declined to press forward with the planned scenario and announced in April 1978 that the issue would be deferred. That was sensible, but it produced bad blood on both sides of the Atlantic: Carter felt let down, and European leaders, especially Schmidt, felt the rug had been pulled from beneath them. All drew the lesson that, having backed away from one hard nuclear decision, they could not afford to flinch a second time. INF became that second occasion. And the shadow of ERW increased pressure on alliance leaders to deploy new "hardware" rather than to hope that innovations in consultation would suffice.

Once active discussions of INF began in NATO, the High Level Group (HLG) quickly reached a consensus in favor of deploying new systems, a proposal first expressed at a meeting in Los Alamos, New Mexico in February 1978 as "evolutionary upward adjustment."[26] At this point the United States remained somewhat ambivalent. The Department of Defense was prepared to join the HLG consensus, but other parts of the government were wary, their initial reaction dominated by two concerns: that the issue should not further complicate SALT II, and that the Alliance was not ready to reach decisions on issues that touched basic NATO nuclear doctrine and practice.

By 1979 the official US view had shifted toward accepting the NATO consensus of the previous spring, a sign of the seriousness of the United States in addressing allied concerns as much as an indication of clear US preference. But with the United States aboard, the train was down the track. In the spring of 1979 the HLG reached agreement of a total force size of 200 to 600 warheads, and in the summer the US suggested 572, apparently expecting that NATO discussions might reduce that figure and that subsequent arms control negotiations might pare it further. The ultimate decision was bound to be political: too many new warheads would suggest the capability to fight a nuclear war limited to Europe, while too few would not be credible or worth the political trouble of deploying.

With numbers agreed, choices of weapons were fairly straightforward. Land-based missile technologies were at hand: shorter-range Pershings were already deployed in Germany and were due to be modernized in any case, so it was merely a matter of extending the range of the new systems. Since the United States was developing cruise missiles to be launched from its strategic bombers, that technology could also be adapted to basing in Europe. In deciding between land and sea-basing, cost was crucial: sea-based systems would have been more expensive, either directly if new submarines (or fast surface craft) had been built as launch platforms, or indirectly, if existing submarines had been converted to the cruise missile role.

Which countries would host the new systems was more complicated. NATO sought an *Alliance* decision, underscoring shared risks, thus the more countries participating, the better. Greece and Turkey, in difficult political times, were uninterested; Portugal was too far away; the Scandinavians do not permit nuclear weapons on their soil in peacetime; and France does not participate in NATO military decisions. That left the five countries that agreed to deploy the new systems: Germany, Britain, Italy, Belgium and the Netherlands.

In the late spring of 1979, NATO formed a foreign office counterpart to the HLG – the so-called Special Group (after the December 1979 decisions renamed the Special Consultative Group) – to look at arms control. It operated on the same basis as the HLG, with experts from national capitals and under US leadership, not the NATO consensus principle. In form, the United States decided on negotiating approaches, although after consultation in detail with the allies and on the presumption that clear European desires would not be overridden.

Yet it was all too plain that the second track of the December 1979 decision, the negotiating track, was driven almost entirely by political concerns. If they were to deploy new nuclear weapons, the Europeans had to convince their publics that they had first done everything they could to avoid the need to do so. On military grounds, however, the negotiations were unpromising in the extreme. Soviet systems like the SS-20, which were the subject of first concern, were deployed in large numbers (350 SS-20s at the middle of 1983) and increasing in number rapidly, while NATO would not begin to deploy its 572 missiles until the end of 1983. NATO was thus in the position of bargaining intentions, and questionable intentions at that, against weapons in place. It was clearly too much to expect arms control negotiations to produce balance from an existing imbalance. There was also a host of more technical problems: what to do about British and French nuclear forces; whether to include aircraft, and which to include and how to count them if they are included; how to count Soviet forces facing China but which are mobile; how to ensure adequate verification; and so on.

MILITARY SENSE AND POLITICAL PURPOSE

These latest nuclear episodes illustrate the lesson that runs back to the Multilateral Force (MLF) misadventure of the 1960s: military measures designed to serve political purposes will fail to do so if they do not make sense on technical grounds to the ostensible military experts.[27] MLF failed for several reasons, but critical among them was the fact that it was unconvincing to the military experts, which made it unsaleable to party groups and publics inclined against it on other grounds. In the end, that combination made it unattractive to politicians. It was too "gimmicky" to persuade.

NATO's December 1979 decision may yet have a happier outcome than MLF, but there are disturbing parallels between the two. The military rationale for the December 1979 decision was stronger than the case in the 1960s for the MLF, but that rationale was neither obvious nor simple, a fact which bedevilled the public debate in Western Europe. The number of 572 new missiles was a rough compromise between military desires and political constraints, and no rationale could be convincing about why 572 was the needed number. To hard-line civilian strategists in the Reagan Pentagon, the 572 seemed too few, and of too dubious survivability, to be worth the bother.

The most straightforward rationale for the new deployments was simple modernization – the need for new means to carry out an existing mission. While by 1979 NATO had few systems based in Europe capable of striking the Soviet Union with nuclear weapons, it did have some. However, excluding submarine-based systems, all those were nuclear-capable aircraft. Those planes, badly needed for conventional missions in any case, were more and more dubious in their ability to survive on the ground and penetrate Soviet air defense. Hence the need for modernization.

The second line of rationale for the new systems raised nearly as many uncomfortable questions as it answered. It invoked all the esoterica of strategic analysis – escalation ladders and control, sanctuaries and thresholds – fundamentally inconclusive. Is an American president more likely to fire American cruise missiles based in Germany than American *Poseidon* submarine-launched missiles assigned to NATO and parked in mid-Atlantic? If he is not, new weaponry looks irrelevant. If he is, that raises the European nightmare of a nuclear war confined to Europe. To be sure, the new missiles in Europe would increase Soviet uncertainty by providing additional options, and thus make NATO a more difficult beast with which to deal. But that argument was hard to make, harder still to make compelling. Thus it let loose the feeling in Europe that, at best, NATO was simply piling up more nuclear weapons without reason, at worst, that the new missiles would be more endangering than protective by providing more targets for Soviet missiles.

In the circumstances, there was a temptation, understandable enough, to focus on the Soviet SS-20. Politicians and public opinion were aware of it, and concerned. Yet the focus on the SS-20 misposed the issue, since it was a small part of the argument for new NATO deployments. It focused on what *they* had rather than what *we* needed. It handed the Soviet Union easy opportunities to make arms control proposals intended to undermine European support for the NATO deployments. As SS-20 deployments reached what no doubt had been the original Soviet target for them, it was child's play for Soviet leaders to tempt Western public opinion with various proposals to freeze or reduce its SS-20s.

Other details of the December decision also left a long political trail. For instance, the United States was willing in principle to deploy the new systems under the "dual-key" arrangement – launchers owned by the host country and the United States retaining control over the warheads. Given NATO practice, that meant that the host country would have bought the launchers, an additional attraction from the US point of view. The German government decided early that its political problem would be lessened if the systems could be advertised as completely American, but other countries were interested in the dual-key arrangement. In the end, however, cost seems to have been an overriding factor for all countries, and all opted for a "single-key" plan with the United States providing both launcher and warhead. That made financial sense at the time but complicated future politics. It made the new deployments appear to be an American scheme, and it provided an opening for arguments by opponents that the European countries might be dragged into nuclear war against their will. In fact, with or without the dual-key plan, no US president would fire nuclear weapons from Europe without consulting his European counterpart in the host country. British Secretary of State for Defence Francis Pym made that implicit understanding explicit in discussing the new deployments, with the argument that the British government would in any case have an effective veto over firing weapons.[28] Italy made similar pronouncements. From the perspective of managing the nuclear debate, it was in the US interest to let these assertions stand.

The decision against sea-basing of the new systems was also driven mostly by cost. But there was, too, the widely held view that only the visibility of deployment on land could demonstrate NATO's resolve to the Soviet Union, reassuring Europeans that the American President would not be tempted to fail to respond to a Soviet attack on Western Europe. Alas, there is more than a hint that Europe and America were caught in a game of mirrors, with the US arguing that only ground-basing would assuage European fears and the Federal Republic in particular sensing an American preference for land-based systems.

At points in the process, domestic politics of one of the allies ran directly against sensible inter-allied handling of the issue. For Chancellor Schmidt, for example, taunted by the conservative opposition for lack of nerve and facing deep divisions within his own governing coalition, it made eminent sense in 1977 and again in 1979 to say that Germany would not be the only continental nation to deploy new nuclear weapons. His predecessors also had used the principle of "non-singularity" to manage nuclear issues.[29] Yet in 1977 that put tremendous pressure on Belgium; again in 1979 it would have put similar pressure on the smaller NATO members, precisely those that had reason to be most tempted by free riding, save for the surprisingly prominent role of Italy.

(Italy's role owed to the conjunction of three factors. Bureaucratic and cabinet politics offered some insulation for "defense" decisions. More important, the principal opposition party, the Communists, all but acquiesced in the deployment for calculations based exclusively on domestic politics: it sought to prove its respectability and fitness to govern. Finally, for Italy, unlike the Federal Republic, the issue was symbolism, not high political and military purpose; history and tradition reinforced a difference geography suggested. Also, much of the symbolism for Italy was gaining a seat at the high table, so the fact of a "NATO" decision mattered and being left out was hardly thinkable.)

The irony of the process by which the December 1979 decisions were taken is that it looked, and was, painstaking in detail. It looked like a model of nuclear consultation. The NPG's working-level group, the High Level Group (HLG), and its two years of deliberations meant there was time for a consensus to form on the emerging technical choices. Its key participants were defense officials from the NATO capitals. Yet for all its detail, the process did not pose, clearly and in time, the central political issue: would Europeans and Germans in particular, want the missiles when the time came? Instead, it turned the deployment plan into a "made in America" scheme for dealing with a European political problem as (mis) perceived by Americans.

NATO's machinery for dealing with nuclear issues, the Nuclear Planning Group (NPG), was itself the product of the last bout of trans-Atlantic nuclear strain – events surrounding the MLF proposal in the 1960s. From 1963 onward the United States assigned submarine-launched missile warheads from its central strategic arsenal to NATO for planning purposes, and officers from NATO countries became participants in targeting at the Strategic Air Command headquarters in Omaha, Nebraska. These gestures did not suffice. Beyond them, the attention of the allies was directed to hardware "solutions," culminating in the MLF. When that initiative was reversed by President Johnson, the outcome was more political than technical – the creation of the NPG in 1966. Initially with a rotating membership that always included the alliance's major members (now with a permanent membership), it provided Europeans with access to US nuclear planning.[30] It built confidence without changing weaponry or procedures for its use.

In the 1960s the NPG managed to lay nuclear matters to rest in part because the East-West climate improved after about 1963, and also because European confidence in the United States grew – hence nuclear matters were less sensitive. Yet the process solution, the NPG, was adequate in the mid-1960s in part because the hardware alternatives made so little apparent sense.

By contrast, the "model" process of the late 1970s, for all its detail and for its apparent "success," still raises disturbing parallels to the MLF – an American "solution" to a European problem based on slender European intimations. Once the American governmental machine had convinced itself that European concerns required new nuclear hardware, that approach gained all the momentum of the machine. Once State Department and White House officials convinced themselves that cruises and Pershings were not an "MLF," planning for deployment shifted to the Pentagon, to colonels who had been captains or junior majors at the time of MLF and probably had never heard of it. Once momentum developed, it could not easily be diverted. Certainly Bonn could not renege, and certainly not in negotiations among defense ministries. That would have confirmed the worst American fears of its unreliability. In substance, the December deployment decision made more sense than the MLF. Yet, after all, 572 missiles hardly were decisive one way or the other; they were not worth a major rift in the alliance cohesion on which deterrence ultimately depends.

Chancellor Schmidt reportedly came to regret his October 1977 speech. Certainly he had reason to. If he was indulging his anger at the course of SALT II, he was sloopy in reckoning the effect of his words. Or he may have expected, then and later, that once SALT II was ratified, SALT III could include INF, thus sparing him need to deploy missiles in Germany. In any case, he miscalculated, ultimately fatal to his government; he did not recognize the juggernaut effect within the Washington machine once it is seized of a problem.

The course of the ERW was similar. It proceeded through the NPG at the technical level. Until too late, no political warning flags were raised. There was no way to drive home the central political fact, true for ERW in 1977 and in 1967, and in the end true for MLF: neither merited the trans-Atlantic row both caused; both were marginal military gains that were bound to be purchased at high political cost.

There are several reasons why the NPG seems unlikely to play a role as timely signaller of domestic political hazards and interactions. First, as a defense ministry operation, the group is not one that can make decisions involving sensitive political considerations, so has little incentive to examine them. Moreover, its ministerial participants may share with their bureaucracies an interest in not sounding warning signals that would affect new weapons on which national budgetary decisions were being made. Third, the emphasis of the NPG on security, appropriate enough, has limited the range of officials in any government who know of the issues that come before it, and are thus in a position to draw implications, especially when it matters most, early on.

At a minimum, the NPG needs to be broadened and opened more to foreign policy considerations. Since crucial nuclear decisions will inevitably be made by heads of government, there might be a case for infrequent summit meetings of NPG members, perhaps in tandem with NATO summits. However, the problem is less one of ensuring that attention is paid to nuclear issues at the top of government than of getting that attention at the right time and in the right form. In the case of the neutron bomb, attention at the highest levels came too late. In the instance of TNF, high-level attention – in this case Chancellor Schmidt's speech at the IISS – came too early, before staff work began to pose the issue coherently.

Finally, the arms control side of the December decisions also illustrates the difficulty of keeping political needs and military logic tolerably in step. INF arms control negotiations were from the start extremely doubtful, for reasons mentioned earlier. The so-called "zero option" – President Reagan's offer in the autumn of 1981 to forego the INF deployments if the Soviets dismantled all their SS-20s[31] – only compounded the problem. It was good short-term politics but bad military logic. Since the reason for NATO's deployments had only partly to do with the SS-20, there would have been an argument for some deployments even if there had been no SS-20s. The zero option thus eroded whatever justification for the deployments NATO leaders were able to articulate, even as it seemed to serve their short-run political purposes.

The zero option only underscored the "iffiness" of the original deployment plans. NATO had bad luck: without the Soviet invasion of Afghanistan and with the ratification of SALT II, INF negotiations in SALT III might not have been so unpromising. Still, if the politics of deploying the 572 missiles was such a close-run thing that it first depended on unpromising arms control negotiations and then was advanced by a questionable arms control proposal, that should have stood as a danger signal to those who took the December 1979 decision.

MANAGING THE NUCLEAR DILEMMA

These recent episodes bespeak the hazards in managing the nuclear dilemma. The fact that there are no once-for-all solutions is uncomfortable for leaders and publics on both sides of the Atlantic. For example, given strategic parity as a continuing fact, American strategists will continue to worry about this or that technical imbalance between American and Soviet forces. That will contribute to European jitters, but it also will play into the nuclear debate in Europe, often in the unhappiest of ways. Presidential Directive 59, signed by President Carter in July 1980 was an obvious case in point. It was the latest step in a decade-long evolution of American doctrine; by

American lights, its emphases on limited nuclear options, and on the durability of command and control were logical responses to the problem of sustaining the credibility of nuclear deterrence in a time of strategic parity.[32]

Yet when Americans talked of "limited options," Europeans heard "limited war." And so the NATO alliance had come full circle: the missile deployment plan that grew out of European, and specifically German concerns over the strength of the link between Europe's defense and American's strategic deterrent – concerns first expressed publicly in Chancellor Schmidt's October 1977 speech – now appeared to many in Europe to do just the opposite, to raise the specter of a nuclear war limited to Europe. Those concerns were compounded by loose statements from President Reagan and Secretary of Defense Weinberger early in the Reagan Administration suggesting that limited nuclear war might be possible.

The gap is growing between how strategists, so-called, think about nuclear issues and how those issues are perceived by people in the street on both sides of the Atlantic. The former will continue to worry about technical details in the balance; that is their business, and it is important. Yet with nuclear arsenals on both sides approaching ten thousand warheads, those concerns will continue to strike ordinary citizens as irrelevant at best, a kind of weird game, and, at worst, as smacking of Dr Strangelove, hence dangerous. That gap is most obvious between American strategists and European publics, but it also separates European defense establishments from their own public opinion. And, as the American anti-nuclear movement of the early 1980s showed, it also divides Americans. That makes it particularly perilous to talk of "Europeans" or "Americans."

In the end, the nuclear dilemma can be managed mostly because the radical alternatives are worse than the existing state of affairs, even if experts and publics do not always realize that. Americans and Europeans will continue to share overriding objectives – deterring *all* war and *any* use of nuclear weapons – even they will differ over how best to accomplish those ends. But it can also be managed because governments have relatively greater control over the nuclear agenda and its connections in domestic politics than is the case for other issues between the allies. For example, the nuclear freeze movement in the United States in the early 1980s resulted only in congressional resolutions exhorting the President to negotiate a mutual and verifiable freeze with the Soviet Union. The Administration might have pre-empted even that had it indulged in less loose talk about nuclear "war fighting" or "war winning" and had it acted to counter the deep public skepticism over its commitment to arms control. Fewer loose words and some progress in arms control would have done much to undercut anti-nuclear protest in Europe as well.

Despite the protest, for most people the threat of war, and with it the salience of security issues, has remained low. Fear of war did increase in the early 1980s but not by much. When Germans, for example, were asked what problem is most important to them, economic and domestic isues continued to receive over 80% of the nominations.[33] Among "foreign policy" problems, "maintaining peace" consistently has been held to be most important, but over-all the percentage of Germans citing it declined during the 1970s.

In that context the apparent paradox in public attitudes on security issues is more understandable. Polls recorded both large majorities in support of NATO *and* considerable opposition to particular defense arrangements, especially nuclear deployments like INF. Given that security issues are for most people not at the top of their concerns, what seems likely is that people react in a generally favorable way to the notion of buying some security insurance through participation in the NATO alliance. Yet when pressed further to contemplate unpleasant scenarios which they had not previously thought much about – like using nuclear weapons in their defense or having them stationed in their neighborhood – people retreat from the prospect. In that light, the paradox is more apparent than real.

These and similar results make it difficult to know what the "public" on nuclear issues is, and how much its "views" matter. The anti-nuclear movements of the 1980s are best seen less as grass-roots phenomena than as the result of contending elites competing for public support. Leaders of anti-nuclear protest now constitute a rival elite; it frequently has been observed that they are fully capable of arguing nuclear strategy with the commander of the Strategic Air Command. The contention between elites probably means that efforts to improve "public" understanding of nuclear issues, while worthy, are not hopeful; the debate will remain as it has been – passionate but frequently ill-informed. It will be more promising to see if a greater consensus among elites and experts can be patched together.

The 1982 proposal by four eminent former American officials to foreswear the first use of nuclear weapons by NATO testifies to how difficult it is to address political concerns over nuclear weapons. The case for such a no-first-use pledge is substantial.[34] If changing military circumstances have made a first use incredible while retaining the doctrine makes NATO look reckless, why not change the doctrine? Renouncing first use would provide the need, and should increase the political willingness, especially in Western Europe, finally to make adequate arrangements for conventional defense. Finally, since the Soviet Union never could fully believe in a no-first-use-pledge, the effect on deterrence of renouncing first use might well be small in any event. The purpose of the change would lie more among the allies than between them and the Soviet Union; it would aim at a doctrine in which Western publics had confidence.

Substantial as those arguments are, NATO should get its force posture right first by reducing its reliance on short range nuclear systems, and only then consider a change in declaratory policy. For the near term, we will remain prisoners of the lack of public confidence in NATO's conventional forces. In that circumstance, there is the risk that Europeans, especially Germans, would read a renunciation of first use as a sign that the US was abandoning them. As a first reaction from governing elites that was predictable; it is the ritual – and from a European perspective, reasonable – opposition to any change in the status quo, a pattern alluded to earlier.[35] For its part, the peace movement in Europe initially paid little attention to the idea; for it, no doubt, the change would have been pure rhetoric, scarcely worth noticing. Thus, no first use – a proposal explicitly intended to increase public support for NATO doctrine and defense arrangements – was worrisome to governing elites and ignored by the nuclear opposition. It was a kind of political "MLF": a made-in-America solution to a European political problem as misperceived by Americans.

If there is political space to manage the nuclear dilemma, that is no guarantee that it *will* be managed. Recent history is hardly encouraging on that score. The first requisite for United States administrations, easy to state but hard to accomplish, is to discipline their rhetoric – about PD 59 or limited nuclear war. Careless statements undercut reams of reassurance. It cannot be said too often that the purpose of NATO weapons and doctrine is to ensure that the weapons will not be used: the objective is deterrence.

Better public rationales for particular decisions will not convince opponents and may not, given the relatively low salience of nuclear issues, educate publics. But at least the Alliance can avoid conveying the impression that *it* does not know why it is acting. Again, the December 1979 decision drives home the lesson. It was not easy to fashion a compelling three-sentence rationale for the new weapons. Yet the elements of such a rationale were at hand: emphasis on the missiles as a modernization of a capability NATO always had in some measure, and on the argument that the new systems would tighten the link between Europe and American strategic weapons, thus strengthen deterrence. Instead, spokesmen appeared to use virtually any argument that led to the conclusion that new weapons were necessary.

Second, arms control will remain essential to managing the nuclear dilemma. That is as true of "strategic" negotiations, like SALT or START, as of talks dealing specifically with TNF or INF: the former are as much about the management of inter-allied politics as of the Soviet-American relationship.

Suppose, for example, that in 1981 or 1982, the Soviet Union had accepted "deep cuts" – sharp reductions in the strategic forces of the two sides – but only on the condition that NATO forego deployment of the 572 long-range theater missiles. That would have tempted a US administration, particularly one like the Reagan Administration that made "deep cuts" its central negotiating objective. Yet such a deal would have sacrificed European interests to achieve American ones, in appearance if not in fact.

With the Pershing and cruise deployments underway, it will make sense to merge the START and INF talks, the form of negotiation originally expected for SALT III.[36] That approach would not solve the daunting technical problems of the INF, but, despite the complications of enlarged negotiations, it would have several advantages. The large imbalance in the Soviet favor in INF would be less dramatic, hence more manageable, in talks comprising both strategic and INF systems. Similarly, Moscow insisted on counting British and French nuclear systems in INF, which NATO resisted. Those systems are by mission and configuration strategic; they would also be easier to handle in expanded negotiations in which they would be only a fraction of the total warheads under discussion. Most important, merged negotiations would underscore the unity between NATO's TNF and American strategic forces. In any case, arms control negotiations will confront the US and its allies with uncomfortable trade-offs between TNF and strategic forces; better to confront those directly in merged negotiations.

For the time being, existing arrangements within NATO – Washington engaged in bilateral negotiations with Moscow, though after consulting its allies in detail – will suit both Europeans and Americans. They will provide Europeans a reasonable guarantee that their interests will be taken into account but spare them direct involvement with choices that might be uncomfortable in their internal politics – a modest form of free riding. If the negotiations go slowly or badly, the Americans will come in for most of the blame. For the immediate future that will suit American interests as well, by giving the United States somewhat more freedom for maneuver – to make zero option or deep cuts proposals. Yet if at some point Europeans want to participate more directly, the United States should not resist.[37] It surely would complicate the negotiations, and it would give Europeans a more explicit veto on issues where European and American interests differ. But over time it would begin to build European responsibilities commensurate with their increasing stakes, diminishing temptations to free riding.

A final requisite in managing NATO's nuclear politics is, when possible, to anticipate the *next* nuclear issue. For example, neglecting shorter-range TNF was one of the dangers of NATO's preoccupation with the SS-20 after 1977–78. Just as SALT II dramatized the SS-20 by excluding it, so the risk of the INF talks was that they would underscore the threat posed by the shorter-range systems they left out. NATO could find that it had "solved" its SS-20 problem only to have it replaced with an SS-21, 22 and 23 problem. These latter systems could threaten Western Europe from bases in Eastern Europe the same way as do SS-20s based in central Russia. The SS-22, for example has a range well over 500 miles.

Anticipating the issue of shorter-range TNF will require a combination of arms control and sensible public statements. Any negotiated limits on INF should be accompanied by collateral constraints on at least those systems, like the SS-22, that could be used to circumvent limits on INF systems, like the SS-20. If the Soviets respond to NATO's deployments of Pershing and cruise with increases in their battlefield and very short-range TNF forces in Eastern Europe, the allies' response should be steadiness, especially in public. After all, if NATO judges short-range TNF to be of declining value for it, some increase in comparable Soviet systems is hardly cause for alarm.

Managing NATO's nuclear dilemma depends on understanding the purpose of nuclear weapons in the alliance: those weapons are political symbols; they cannot by themselves provide the substance of cohesion. Recognizing that there is no acceptable alternative to something like current nuclear arrangements is a first step. Arranging NATO's nuclear forces, both strategic and TNF, in a way that makes sense, particularly by moving away from such reliance on short-range systems, is a second. But to pretend that these measures will provide a "solution" is to misunderstand the problem. American support for Europe's security is rooted in continuing political cohesion more than specific military arrangements. On that score, General de Gaulle was right, though he was careful not to put it that way.

3 Defense and Detente in Europe

In a speech in Brussels in September 1979, Henry Kissinger asserted that he and his colleagues had perpetrated a dangerous delusion in the Harmel Report of 1967. That was the notion that NATO was in the business of both defense and detente, the twin pillars of the Alliance, faithfully recited at every NATO meeting since. "In 1968, at Rekjavik, NATO developed the theory, which I believe is totally wrong, that the Alliance is as much an instrument of detente as it is of defense. I think that is simply not correct. NATO is not equipped to be an instrument of detente."[1]

The remark is a caricature of NATO, but it does evoke enduring problems in trans-Atlantic relations. One is what combination of carrots and sticks is appropriate policy toward the Soviet Union. The second, harder still, is whether the allies can manage the appropriate mix. Will their separate policies make sense in combination? How common are their interests? What degree of common policy among them is necessary; and what degree is politically possible?

These questions are not new. They are sharper now because differences in real interests seem more apparent and because the United States is less able to impose its conception of policy toward the East. Here as elsewhere in alliance relations, however, it is tempting to overstate the degree of unity among the partners that existed in the past; memories are good except, as the saying has it, most of what we remember best never happened. There have been differences even on this most central of issues. De Gaulle's efforts in the 1960s to play a "mediating" role between Moscow and Washington are the most obvious sample. But they are by no means the only one.

Consider, for example, the sequence of events which brought the Federal Republic into NATO. The original NATO allies realized that any effective defense of Western Europe should be "forward"; thus West Germany would fall within the defense perimeter. If Germany was to be defended, what better way to defend it than with German troops? As early as the autumn of 1950, a scant five years after the end of World War II and at the same time as the United States first agreed to re-commit troops to Europe, the North Atlantic Council agreed in principle to rearm West Germany. Over the next five years NATO searched for ways to do it. One ambitious proposal for European defense cooperation, the European Defense Community, was defeated by the French parliament in 1954. It was substituted by a clever sleight of hand, the Western European Union (WEU) which served as a framework for German rearmament, and the Federal Republic subsequently joined NATO.[2]

These decisions look easy and logical in retrospect but were not so at the time, especially not for the Federal Republic. The Soviet Union did not arrive at a settled approach to the Federal Republic until after the WEU and German accession to NATO, the Warsaw Pact was not formed until 1955 and East Germany was not incorporated into it until 1956. Thus, at the time, for West Germany to decide to join NATO was to ratify the division of Germany, particularly painful for the Federal Republic, and with it the division of Europe. Those facts were obscured, and still are, by ritual rhetoric about German reunification as the goal of the NATO partners. But the sequence of events underscores the point that differences of interest among the allies run back to the beginning of the NATO alliance, and that even common policies have different costs and benefits for different nations.

HOW DIFFERENT ARE THE INTERESTS?

Yet if some differences among the allies in policy toward Moscow are of long-standing, other differences of interest are now more and more obvious. A decade and a half of detente in Europe did have benefits for Western Europe that were not paralleled for the United States. The web of economic and humanitarian contacts built up across the East-West divide in Europe did not have effects only on the East. It created stakes in Western Europe as well. If it produced strains in the Eastern alliance – of which Poland is the most vivid recent evidence – it also led to some loosening in the Western alliance.

Trans-Atlantic differences are obvious in economics, and most stark between the United States and the Federal Republic. In 1979 some six per cent of total Western European (European Community) trade went to the East, about the same percentage as to the United States.

For the European NATO members, trade with the communist countries (including China and Cuba) amounted to 4.5% of exports and 4.6% of imports in 1979. For the United States, by contrast, the figures were 1.2 and 4.1%, respectively. Only in 1975 and 1976 did US machinery exports to the Soviet Union exceed a half billion dollars. In percentage terms, European imports from the East have remained fairly constant, while exports have declined in importance (from 5.4% of total exports in 1976). Of course, since trade overall by the Europeans was growing rapidly, even constant shares meant rapid increases in the volume of the trade; in dollar terms, for example, imports from the East by European NATO members increased by some 70% between 1976 and 1979.[3]

For the Federal Republic, trade with Eastern Europe (including East Germany) amounted to 4.5% of all German trade in 1981; this share also had declined, from 5.8% in 1975. About half that West German trade with the East was with the Soviet Union, the Federal Republic's largest Eastern trading partner.[4] Germany is much more dependent on foreign trade than is the United States. In 1981, for example, exports came to 25.6% of German gross national product, but only 8% of American. And expectations about future trade have been nearly as important as the current numbers. Given highly competitive Western markets, German (and other European) traders have been tempted to look east despite the fact that trade with the Eastern countries has grown more slowly than trade overall. Given the prevailing pessimism in Europe about the continent's ability to match its main competitors in the industrial West, the interest in exporting east will only grow.

Still, it is easy to overstate the importance of the aggregate figures. Two thirds of West German's trade is with its Common Market partners, and its trade with the West is ten times its trade with the East. Germany's trade with the East in 1981 was only 9.5% of its trade with its fellow EEC members, or only slightly greater than its trade with Switzerland and only two-thirds of its trade with the United States.

At the same time the aggregate figures may disguise as much as they reveal. If, for example, German exports to the East are not particularly important to the overall economy, they are to particular sectors, ones with political clout. For example, the German steel industry has been second only to Japan in its dependence on exports, and it, like its competitors, has been badly hurt by the global glut of steel production capacity. In those circumstances, the importance of exports to the East for maintaining jobs and industries has been far out of proportion to

TABLE 3.1: *Importance of East–West trade, 1965–81*

	1965	1970	1975	1980	1981
United States					
Exports to E. Eur. and USSR* (millions of $)	152	334	3067	4949	4804
% of total exports	.6	.8	2.9	2.3	2.1
(exports as % of GDP)	4.0	4.4	7.1	8.5	8.0
France					
Exports to E. Eur. and USSR* (millions of $)	316	745	2501	4303	4335
% of total exports	3.1	4.1	4.7	3.7	4.1
(exports as % of GDP)	9.6	12.8	15.6	17.7	18.6
Federal Republic					
Exports to E. Eur. and USSR* (millions of $)	833	1590	5839	9151	7608
% of total exports	4.7	4.6	6.5	4.7	4.3
(exports as % of GDP)	15.6	18.5	21.4	23.5	25.7
Italy					
Exports to E. Eur. and USSR* (millions of $)	355	757	2331	2878	2623
% of total exports	4.9	5.7	6.9	3.7	3.5
(exports as % of GDP)	11.5	13.1	18.1	19.7	21.4
Britain					
Exports to E. Eur. and USSR* (millions of $)	476	858	1836	3346	3391
% of total exports	3.4	4.4	4.1	3.0	3.3
(exports as % of GDP)	13.8	16.0	19.2	20.9	20.5

* Exports are f.o.b., international transactions basis.

SOURCES: Special Table O, *1981 Yearbook of International Trade Statistics*, vol. 1, (New York: United Nations, 1983); International Monetary Fund, *International Financial Statistics*, various years; and *International Financial Statistics Yearbook 1983*.

the aggregate figures for the economy as a whole. Between 1973 and 1979, 50% of German exports of large-diameter steel pipe went to the Soviet Union, constituting 12% of total German-Soviet trade and the largest single export item in that trade.[5]

The importance of particular exports to a particular sector of the economy – and the political significance of that importance – are hardly phenomena limited to the Federal Republic. If all American exports to the Soviet Union stopped, that would barely register on the economy as a whole. But it would be a disaster for the grain sector, which accounts for over three-quarters of those exports.[6] Because of its concentration and its prominence in relevant committes of Congress, the American farm lobby is a factor to be reckoned with out of all proportion to the number of farmers in the United States. In that light, President Reagan's decision in April 1981, to lift the grain embargo on the Soviet Union is less surprising than it might seem in the context of an Administration otherwise committed to a tough line toward the Soviet Union. Nor should it surprise that particular sectors of European economies also have a political importance well beyond their numbers.

The specific content of European trade with the East also constrains European policy choices. Most of American exports to the East are commodities; by contrast, the Western Europeans are heavily involved in selling capital and other industrial goods. The latter have long lead times, all the more so given the centralized planning of the Eastern countries. Thus, for the Europeans to apply sanctions is to break contracts. For them, the sanctions instrument is particularly blunt, and the long-term implications of using it especially serious. The difference between European and American trade patterns with the East is less a result of structural factors than of past policy choices – the Europeans also sell considerable food to the East, and the United States could export industrial goods if it chose. But in European perception at least, it is harder for Europe than for the United States to implement modulated economic sanctions against the Soviet Union and its allies.

Moreover, while European exports east are critical for some industries, over-all, imports from the East have grown more rapidly than exports to the East. While the United States imports virtually nothing from the Eastern countries that it could not do without or buy elsewhere, that is not the case for the Europeans. Energy imports from the Soviet Union are critical to current and future economic well-being in Western Europe. That was illustrated sharply by the trans-Atlantic debate over the gas pipeline linking Western Europe to Soviet gasfields.

THE PIPELINE DISPUTE

That pipeline, the Urengoy project, will provide seven European countries with additional Soviet natural gas, beginning in the mid-1980s. By the late 1980s the Soviet Union will earn about seven billion dollars of hard currency annually from those gas sales.[7] The pipeline will gradually increase the importance of Soviet natural gas in the energy balances of the West European nations. By 1990 the pipeline will mean that 25% of the Federal Republic's natural gas comes from the Soviet Union, or slightly over four per cent of its total energy supplies; for 1980 the figures were 17.5% and 2.7%, respectively. In 1980 the Federal Republic also imported 6% of its oil, amounting to slightly over 3% of its total energy, from the East, but given the Soviet Union's oil problems, those imports are not likely to increase. The pipeline will mean that Soviet natural gas comprises about 5½% of France's, and over 6% of Italy's total energy by 1990.

There is no need to rehearse in detail the European–American row over the pipeline. On 30 December, 1981, three weeks after the imposition of martial law in Poland, the Reagan Administration imposed an export ban on all American-made parts for the pipeline. That was part of an effort to prod the Europeans to economic sanctions of their own against Moscow, but it had little effect. Six months later, however, immediately after the Versailles Western Summit, the President extended sanctions to cover not only American suppliers but also their subsidiaries and licenseholders abroad. That was triply discomforting to Europeans.[8] Most of them disagreed with sanctions against the pipeline in substance, especially since contracts already had been signed. The "long arm" – not to say "strong arm" – effort by the United States to compel European subsidiaries of American firms raised the issue of "extraterritoriality" – an old European grievance against Washington.

Finally, the decision seemed to have been taken in pique. In preparations for the Versailles Summit the United States gave the Europeans to understand that it would treat European participation in the pipeline as a *fait accompli* provided the allies committed themselves not to give further credit subsidies in trade with the Soviet Union. At the Summit the seven Western leaders agreed on the need for "commercial prudence" in trading with the Soviet Union in light of their common "political and security interests." In a classic misunderstanding, the Europeans apparently thought they had bought off the United States with declarations of good intentions, while President Reagan left the session feeling he had extracted a firm commitment against further subsidies. When French President Mitterrand made clear at a press conference immediately after the Summit that he regarded himself as having given no such commitment, President Reagan felt betrayed, angry. By all accounts, that made him readier to heed the counsel of those in his Administration who favored an extension of sanctions.

In the end, however, the United States retreated, but not before a major row in the alliance. On 13 November, 1982 the Administration lifted its restraints in exchange for what seemed a relatively bland European commitment to review all East-West trade issues. It was hard to assess the impact of the affair on the Soviet pipeline; at most it probably delayed the pipeline slightly, although the extension of the sanctions – if successful – would have hurt more since it threatened to close the last source of turbines which were an American monopoly. Yet whatever the harm done to the Soviets, it was nothing by comparison to the damage of open bickering among the allies themselves.[9] As cynics had it, Moscow could hardly have done better if it had designed the episode itself.[10]

As so often in trans-Atlantic debate, there were too many debater's arguments. When, for example, Americans argued that Soviet gas sales would provide the Soviet Union with foreign exchange, Europeans countered by observing that the foreign exchange thus earned would just about cover Soviet grain purchases from the United States; for Europeans, grain sales and European participation in the pipeline were symbolically equivalent. American arguments against the pipeline were something of a moving target, sometimes focussing on the long-term peril of energy dependence on the Soviet Union, sometimes concentrating on the need to respond to martial law in Poland. And the United States invented a kind of "grain drain" theory: by this notion, Soviet gas sales were bad and American grain sales good because the former earned, but the latter cost, the Soviet Union foreign exchange. Whatever that argument's attractions in the debate, it made little economic sense. The Soviet Union, a notoriously inefficient grain producer, probably was better off to buy grain and use the resources thus "saved" to produce high-value energy for export.[11]

The pipeline issue had a long historical tail, which American policy ignored at its peril. Many of the arguments, within Europe and between Europe and America, had been played out two decades earlier. After 1959 the Soviet Union became the largest single purchaser of West German steel pipe.[12] On 5 October 1962 the three leading German producers signed a contract with the Soviet Union to sell 163 000 tons of large-diameter steel pipe in exchange for crude steel; the pipe was to supply the so-called Friendship Pipeline connecting the Baku oilfields to Poland, Czechoslovakia and East Germany. The next month, on 21 November, the NATO Council adopted in secret an American proposal opposing the export of large-diameter steel pipe to the Soviet Union. Then, the main American argument was that the pipe network inside Eastern Europe and the Soviet Union might be used to supply the Red Army.

Then, as two decades later, a major row in the alliance ensued. Apparently, the United States had used the Council instead of COCOM, the allies' customary machinery for limiting exports of sensitive technology, in part at least because the Europeans had resisted using COCOM. What emerged from the NATO Council was a recommendation, to be implemented at the discretion of national authorities. The Federal Republic immediately accepted the recommendation, in the hope that its European partners would do likewise. It also decided to apply the ban retroactively to the October deal, though it did so in considerable secrecy; the firms did not learn of the NATO decision until 19 December, and the final decision to deny export licenses was not made until 15 March 1963.

In this instance, Germany was the odd man out, as Britain, France and Italy were prepared to continue exports of large-diameter pipe to the Soviet Union, a fact which intensified the internal debate in the Federal Republic. Yet many of the arguments were precursors of those heard two decades later. The steel industry and labor complained bitterly, arguing that six to nine months of full-capacity work had been lost.[13] Members of the Bundestag from the governing parties but with steel industry constituencies were under great pressure to toe the government line. Opposition figures argued that the ban was both bad politics and bad business; in particular they stressed, as did their counterparts two decades later, the danger of repudiating international agreements. In the end, the Adenauer government prevailed, and the ban held. But it did so at great cost, both internally and externally within the alliance, given an image if not a fact of sharp American pressure.

As two decades later, the effect on the Soviet Union was probably minor, at least by comparison to the fuss within the alliance. The Soviet Union did acknowledge some delays, though the embargo also served as an incentive to the Soviets to increase their own production of large-diameter pipe even if that pipe was inferior to the German product. Moreover, the United States never was able to persuade Japan to join the embargo, and so the Soviets were able to circumvent much of its effect through purchases from Japan, Sweden and elsewhere.

Most important, however, both episodes, and especially the latter, demonstrated the different perspectives borne of different interests. What looked to the United States like a trend toward dangerous European dependence on Soviet gas seemed to Western Europe like a sensible diversification of supply. To the latter, some increase in reliance on Soviet sources seemed preferable to yet more dependence on even more unreliable energy sources in the Middle East and Gulf. And if alliance history tells anything, it indicates that the trans-Atlantic debate on these issues will not go away. Sheer numbers reinforce that conclusion. It seems painfully plain that with a resumption of reasonable economic growth, and hence growth in energy demand, in Western Europe, Europeans will continue to face the choice of more Persian Gulf oil or more Soviet gas, or some combination. That makes future "pipeline" disputes altogether too predictable.

DIFFERENT PLACES, DIFFERENT PERSPECTIVES

The humanitarian contacts between East and West Europe are other stakes held by Western Europeans, especially Germans, and not shared by the United States. The 300 000 ethnic Germans who have been allowed to emigrate from Eastern Europe and the Soviet Union since the early 1970s are evidence of that stake; the three million ethnic Germans that remain are reminders of how much the state of East–West relations matters. For the Federal Republic, East–West relations become a family affair in ties to East Germany. Chancellor Schmidt said during the 1980 crisis over the American hostages in Iran that he sympathized with the plight of those fifty odd people because he had to worry about the twenty million East Germans hostage to the Soviet empire.

To be sure, there are differences among the Europeans as well. Those are frequently significant, but they are also muted by common

European membership in the Common Market, by common awareness of sharing a divided continent, and by common interests in
keeping the Federal Republic firmly embedded in European arrangements. British governments are torn between their European vocation
and their desire to play on what remains of the "special relationship"
with United States, and they, especially under Prime Minister
Thatcher, often have been more tempted than other Europeans to
follow a hard American line toward the Soviet Union. Yet London
defied the call for an embargo on pipe in 1962, and it reacted as sharply
as Bonn or Paris to the American effort two decades later to prevent
European subsidiaries of American firms from participating in the
Soviet pipeline project. Some of the specific British interests at play in
the latter episode were similar to those in Germany: particular
industries in the depressed North would have been hard hit by an
embargo.

The approaches of other European countries reflect differences in
interest, tradition and domestic politics surrounding foreign policy.
France, while still insisting on its independence, has moved back to a
position much more critical of the Soviet Union. That was notable
during the Polish crisis. It reflected a recognition by national leaders of
the changed superpower balance of power and a sharp sensitivity to the
more assertive German role in pursuit of East-West detente. It also
derived from the change of leadership in France and the particulars of
coalition government under Socialist leadership: with the pro-Soviet
French Communists participating in government, a tough anti-Soviet
policy was a constant humiliation to them, and a constant reminder of
their marginal status in the coalition.

A variant of that domestic political dynamic has been at play in Italy.
There, the urge of the Italian Communists (PCI) to look respectable
and fit to govern served to moderate their approach to foreign policy.
During the debate over intermediate nuclear forces (INF) they
acquiesced to Italian deployments of cruise missiles with only token
opposition. That stance was driven almost entirely by domestic
politics; had the PCI calculated that strong opposition would have
served its domestic electoral interests, the stance would have changed.

In the northern NATO members, policy toward the Soviet Union is
cast against deep-rooted pacifist traditions that spread across the
political spectrum. That merges with the psychological counterpart to
free riding: as small nations, the northern Europeans know there is
little they can do to affect their own security, and virtually nothing they
can do to affect Soviet behavior, but they also know they will feel

keenly the effects of superpower tension. That means they sometimes seem to worry more about American policies than Soviet ones, and that their politics reflect a vocabulary of detente and arms control which is often at odds with the American preoccupation with Soviet global power.

The specific, concrete stakes that are different between Europe and America contribute to, and merge into a different perspective, one that derives as well from the fact that we are here and they are there. Europe is more stable than it was a decade or two ago. That is true despite Poland and despite concern over the continuing Soviet military build-up in Europe. The tangible fruits of detente in the form of the web of negotiated agreements – between West Germany and the states of Eastern Europe, and the Quadripartite Agreement of 1971 over Berlin – are no small part of the reason for that stability. The agreements over Berlin have all but eliminated that city as a barometer of East–West relations. Yet it serves as a reminder of the Western stake in a continuation of that stability. For Germans the reminder has an ironic twist: that greater stability has been purchased by postponing yet more any possible resolution of Germany's division.

Soviet military might is greater now but seems to Europeans less likely to be used, at least in the direct ways that were the fear two decades ago. Public opinion data in the Federal Republic, for example, provide some confirmation for both propositions. In a 1982 poll more than half the respondents saw the Warsaw Pact as militarily superior to NATO, while only a tenth held the opposite view, and about a third saw the two alliances as roughly equal.[14] At the same time, only about a third of respondents in a 1981 poll considered the Warsaw Pact a military threat to West Germany, while two-thirds did not; by contrast in 1952 more than 80% considered the Soviet Union a threat, and more than half did so in the late 1960s. There is, however, some evidence that the perception of threat increased in the early 1980s. All these results need to be treated with considerable skepticism because of the effects of asking questions different ways over time.

Certainly that stability in Europe is an interest that Europeans and Americans share. Yet Western Europeans are bound to feel that interest especially keenly; it is, after all, their neighborhood. In part that reflects the essentially regional preoccupations of the Europeans by contrast to the more global vocation of the United States. That difference in perspective comprises both interests and capabilities. In, for example, a global effort to counter Soviet power, the United States may be prepared to see the temperature in Europe rise somewhat – for instance, by curtailing trade or other exchanges. Europeans, however, will feel the effects of that increase in temperature more directly than will the United States. It will range from the tangible – lost sales that are likely to be more important to them than to Americans – to the psychological – increasing fears of confrontation that feed economic jitters and make it harder to manage particular issues, like the deployments of new American missiles.

At the same time, given their more limited capabilities, the Europeans will feel that their actions matter little in the global effort to contain Soviet power. So they may feel thrice affected: having little to contribute to global policies and thus little say in their construction, but bearing a heavy share of the regional consequences of those policies. Temptations toward free riding will be strong: actions by individual European nations will be perceived as making little difference, and from a narrow regional perspective, the "benefits" of those global policies may look more like costs. Hence the cries that "the West should not be the one to transport tension into Europe, or to increase the tension there."

This difference in perspective will pervade a wide range of issues. For Europe, especially Germany, a nuclear issue like INF is pre-eminently political; for the United States it is technical. That assertion is customary wisdom, seldom examined. In part, it reflects no more than the American propensity to isolate issues and believe in technical solutions. It also reflects the disparity in power between the United States and the Federal Republic: American security with regard to the Soviet Union can be affected by American technical decisions in a way that no comparable German decisions can affect German security.

Yet it also means that individual issues will be seen against a broader political backdrop in the Federal Republic much more than is the case in the United States. An issue like INF is seen not first in light of abstract military requirements but as a constituent element of a broader political relationship. For the Federal Republic to accept the American missiles beginning in 1983 was not just to complicate relations with East Germany and with the Soviet Union; it was to reinforce, once more, the division of Germany and of Europe. That was a powerful shaper just beneath the surface of the public debate. Or consider arms control. Americans ask that it enhance security in light of technical military analysis. That analysis, to be sure, includes assessments of the other side's intentions. But those considerations are paramount for Germans and other Europeans. They are likely to ask first what the face of negotiations signals about the other side's intentions, about the political climate.[15]

WHO LEADS AND WHO FOLLOWS?

There are so many ritual phrases in European-American relations, but none more so than "leadership." The layers of crust on that word are so thick that it is hard even to make out the essential issues. The reality has been changing. Some of the numbers speak for themselves. The change is structural. But what it implies for the future of trans-Atlantic relations: on that there is no agreement. On that score much of the analysis is tailored to suit the analyst's purposes. If the purpose is to berate Europeans for not doing more or, conversely, to justify a European initiative that cuts across the American bow, the refrain is "America can no longer lead." But that refrain becomes "still, no one else can lead" if the purpose is to exhort the United States or justify European inaction.

The change in relative economic power of the United States and Western Europe is clear. Europe is now as rich as the United States, and several European countries are richer. Again, some of the West's current problems derive from past successes, and thus are to be envied, not decried. In 1950, the war-ravaged Western European economies accounted for 17.3% of global GNP, while the United States made up 33.9%. By 1980 Europe's share had risen to 28.6%, while the United States had fallen to 23.3.[16]

That change in relative economic standing has been paralleled by a shift in the relative political weight in the trans-Atlantic relationship. The change is hard to quantify, and the United States remains the predominant partner. To be sure, Europeans have not automatically acquiesced to American preferences in the past. The Franco-British Suez invasion of 1956 is the most obvious example; the lukewarm European support for the war in Vietnam, despite much American arm-twisting, is another; and the leaden European response to Henry Kissinger's Year of Europe initiative in 1973 a third. But as US political weight declines, Europeans are now even more prepared to articulate and act on interests that differ from those of the United States, even if they still see – and sometimes hide behind – the limits on their own ability to "lead."

The Federal Republic illustrates both the extent of the change and the limits that remain. Nothing German Chancellor Schmidt might say to Soviet President Brezhnev in Moscow in the summer of 1980 could put the SALT treaty back on the rails or begin to engineer a political solution to the Afghan crisis. Yet Schmidt did do nuclear business quite directly with Brezhnev, something unthinkable a decade earlier. He at least put pressure on the Soviet Union – and thereby the United

States – to make progress. In November 1981 he went even further, in effect establishing a parallel line to Washington's INF negotiating approach to Moscow.

The Federal Republic is also more able to insulate its interests from superpower tension. After Afghanistan, Schmidt spoke glowingly in both public and private about the importance to both halves of Europe of protecting their detente from the new tension between the superpowers. The conservative government of Chancellor Helmut Kohl, that took office in September 1982 and was confirmed by a wide margin in the elections of March 1983, made clear again and again that there would be little change in German foreign policy. In the early 1970s the Christian Democrats (CDU) and their sister party, the Christian Social Union (CSU) had criticized the *Ostpolitik* of Willy Brandt; by the 1980s they had made it their own.[17]

The limits of the Federal Republic's room for maneuver are even clearer with regard to East Germany than elsewhere in its foreign policy,[18] but even there Bonn has been able to protect its interests in sustaining relations. Chancellor Schmidt's spring 1980 meeting with East German leader Honecker had to be cancelled in the wake of Afghanistan, but the two orchestrated the cancellation to put the best possible face on it. Inner German relations did turn frosty in the autumn of 1980 with the East German decision to raise travel costs for visitors from the Federal Republic, a turn that probably resulted more from the nervousness of the East German regime than from Soviet pressure. The Kohl government, however, quickly demonstrated its readiness to match its good words about inner German relations with cash. In 1983 it made a loan of over a billion *Deutschemarks* to East Germany, a loan negotiated by the arch anti-communist and *bête noir* of the Germany left, CSU party boss Franz-Josef Strauss. When, after the beginning of the US missile deployments, the Soviet Union reacted by announcing that new nuclear missiles of its own would be deployed in East Germany and Czechoslovakia, the East German regime was visibly dismayed. It made little secret of its desire to cooperate with Bonn in sustaining inner German relations despite the deployments.

By the mid-1980s there were signs of change – in West German attitudes toward both the East and the United States – beneath the continuity of official policy. Yet whether those represented real change or merely the latest turn in the cycle of changing German attitudes toward American leadership in the alliance: answers were, in the nature of things, hard to come by. Trying to sort out trends in public attitudes in Europe and the United States is the subject of the next two sections.

The political mood in Germany was tinged with anti-Americanism, with neutralism, and, above all, with a nationalism, this time on the left, that did seem a real departure from the last two decades. Out of power, for example, the German SPD broke with the consensus that had characterized the previous decade of German foreign policy. It voted overwhelmingly at its special party congress in Cologne in November 1983 to reject the December 1979 decisions, decisions that had been taken by an SPD government. Perhaps this was only the natural tendency of parties out of power to gravitate toward their ideological stalwarts; perhaps the SPD would confront the choice of moving back toward the center on security issues or risk being cast into the political wilderness for a long time, the fate that befell it from 1949 to 1960. Similarly, the "Greens" – an eclectic mix of anti-establishment, anti-nuclear and environmentalist activists, voted into the Bundestag for the first time in 1983, began to splinter almost as soon as they arrived. Yet perhaps the views they represented would seep into the political consciousness of Germans beyond those who voted Green, especially young Germans.

If these puzzles cannot be answered, at least they can be put in context. Germany has always been what geography dictated: the land in the middle, between East and West. Somehow playing the two off has been the task of German statecraft for a hundred years, even if the forms have differed greatly – from the *Schaukelpolitik* (see-saw policy) of Bismarck, to the Rapallo treaty with the Soviet Union of the Weimar period. The several decades after World War II represented the most "western" German policy since the Holy Roman Empire, thanks to the forced loss of East Germany. In the longer view of history, that period and the degree on the dependence on the United States are likely to seem unusual. It was thus little surprise that *Ostpolitik* balanced the ties to the West with new links eastward. Nor should it necessarily surprise if dependence on the United States becomes still more rankling and temptations in German politics to make a new adjustment in the balance of East and West persist.

Second, nationalism in the Federal Republic, either on the left or right, will not necessarily equate with a demand for reunification. German history has not produced the identification of state and nation common to most societies. During the German *Bund* (confederation) of the 19th century, many states existed within the German nation. Thus, Germans of 1980, like those of 1880, can be nationalists without being unifiers (or reunifiers).[19]

Finally, as the nuclear discussion of chapter two suggested, dramatic changes in German policy will be inhibited by the lack of alternatives on the horizon. If the people of the Federal Republic were offered reunification on terms that did not seem tantamount to Soviet tutelage, they would accept it. But the Soviet Union is not about to make such an offer. Over time, as dependence chafes and the Soviet Union looks less and less menacing, German conditions may change. But the time for the radical reordering of the European status quo that would make reunification possible is still a long way off.[20]

CURRENTS IN EUROPEAN POLITICS

Beneath specific national interests and changing patterns of leadership in trans-Atlantic relations lie longer-term changes in political attitudes, in both Europe and America. Those clearly bear on the alliance and how it frames policy toward the Soviet Union. Yet the changes are gradual, and so their effect is hard to discern in particular episodes. Thus it is easy either to exaggerate or to dismiss them. The evidence that can be mustered to support arguments about the changes and their effects is hardly compelling – impressions and anecdotes buttressed by public opinion polls, their results notoriously variable depending on how questions are asked.

Most common American stereotypes of political developments in Europe of recent years have been, for example, wild exaggerations. Europe is not about to be swept by a tidal wave of neutralism, pacifism or anti-Americanism.[21] The trends are not simple. On the surface, public opinion polls record considerable stability in basic views on the alliance and the United States. Yet there are hints of changing attitudes among young people, even in the case – the Federal Republic – where surface continuity is also the most striking. If most Germans, even young Germans on the left, remain attached to the NATO alliance, it seems equally clear that the alliance to which they are attached is different than the one to which Americans have been accustomed.

Recent polling data is suggestive on both propositions. An Allensbach poll in 1981 found that 56% of Germans answering "liked" Americans and only 18% did not. (Certainly, the implications of such findings are especially ambiguous; no doubt polls in 1935 would have found that Germans and Britons also esteemed each other highly). More to the point, 80% expressed support for staying in NATO, only 6% for withdrawing – the same results as in 1969. At the same time, 30% thought the Federal Republic should always support American foreign policy while 56% were prepared to go it alone in some cases.[22] It is striking that as many as 30% of Germans still would have their country support the United States more or less unreservedly.

The poll results are similar in other European NATO countries and have not changed much over time. Large majorities in all of them save France, thought in a March 1981 USICA poll that NATO was "still essential" for their nations's security: 70 to 15% in Britain, 59–28 in Italy, 66–21 in Norway, and 62–15 in the Netherlands. In countries where trend data are available, there has been no change over a decade. Similarly, when asked to choose between continued alliance in NATO and getting out of NATO to become a neutral country, large majorities opted for the former, again except in France, which divided almost evenly (45–40 in favor of alliance). However, about a fifth of the respondents in both Germany and the Netherlands was undecided on this question. If anything, the poll results over time suggest that support for neutralism has diminished. In 1973, for example, Germans divided almost evenly (42–41) over whether remaining "militarily allied to the United States" was preferable to an "attempt to be neutral." A decade later there was much less support for the neutralist option.

Not surprisingly, the poll results support other evidence about the controversial aspects of trans-Atlantic relations. It hardly comes as a shock to see that Western Europeans are deeply preoccupied about nuclear weapons. In a 1980 poll, a 64–19 majority in the Federal Republic said that the country should use "military weapons" to defend itself against attack, and a 53–31 majority was prepared to do so "even if the war is fought primarily on the soil of the Federal Republic," but only 15% favored defense "if nuclear weapons have to be used on the soil of the Federal Republic." The German evidence that is available does suggest that the unwillingness to use nuclear weapons has increased over the last two decades. Asked to choose between avoiding war at all cost, even if it meant living under a communist government, and defending democracy, even if it led to a nuclear war, Germans in 1955 chose the former by 36% to 33, with 31% undecided. By 1981, the result was 48 to 27, with 25% undecided. As two analysts concluded, "if these findings to not represent a feeling of 'better red than dead,' they do suggest a feeling of 'better red than incinerated.'"[23]

In those circumstances it is no surprise that the effect of having American nuclear missiles stationed in Europe was a matter for disagreement. In 1982 Germans came closest to Americans in believing that those weapons would provide greater protection, rather than increase the chances of an attack: the results were 41–27% for Germany, and 55–14% for the United States. The results for other countries were 25–24 for Belgium, 31–24 for France and interestingly, 29–42 for Britain, the only country in this poll where the missiles were perceived as more provacative than protective.

In most Western European countries, the attitudes of young people, especially better-educated young people, seem significantly different from those of their elders. Those differences are especially pronounced in West Germany and Italy. From what evidence is available, difference in attitude between generations is less pronounced in the United States.[24] In Europe, the younger better-educated people are more tempted by neutralism than their elders, less impressed by the United States and less prepared to defend their countries by military means. For example, of those university-educated people over fifty sampled in a 1981 poll, only small percentages favored neutrality over NATO: 5 per cent in Britain, 18 in France, 5 in Germany, 14 in Italy, 5 in the Netherlands, and 7 in Norway. But those percentages rose considerably among the 18–34 year old university-educated: to 27% in Britain, 33 in France, 28 in Germany, 39 in Italy, 30 in Netherlands, and 36 in Norway.[25]

Exactly what those results mean is hard to know. Do they suggest different attitudes that will remain as those who hold them come to lead their societies, especially since the differences are most pronounced for the better-educated young people most likely to become leaders? Or are the findings just the result of youth, with young Europeans likely to move toward more orthodox views as they grow older? Confident predictions would be suspect. And notice that even among the youngest university cohort, there is still majority support for NATO in all European NATO countries. At the same time, especially in Germany and Italy the differences in attitudes among different age groups does appear to be much sharper than in the past.

Explanations why that might be so can only be speculation. Certainly the formative experiences of older Germans and Italians went especially deep – both the trauma of war and defeat, and the postwar reconstruction with the aid and on the model of munificent America. Lacking both experiences, it is not surprising that younger Germans and Italians differ from their elders in attitudes toward both war and the United States. By contrast, older French people were less prone to idealize the United States early in the postwar period, so differences between them and the younger generations are less notable. For their part, the experiences of Britons have been more continious than those of their continental counterparts – neither the trauma of defeat nor the experiences or reconstruction, and continuity in both relative affinity for the United States and in postwar economic decline.

In predicting the effects of changing attitudes on future policy, a middle-ground bet is safest: Europeans will remain committed to the link with the United States, but they will view that tie more critically than in the past. In the German case, for example, the poll results hardly suggest that the Federal Republic is about to leave NATO and turn neutral. Rather they suggest a more assertive German role *within* the NATO framework, one in which Bonn's pursuit of parallel lines to Moscow on INF will seem a natural expression of national interest, one in which real decision-making will be more fully shared and thus in which unilateral American actions, such as over the neutron bomb, will be deeply rankling. Europeans will be more tempted by "equidistance" between the superpowers even as they remain American allies. For Americans, needless to say, that will seem a double standard and will be irritating.

AMERICAN UNILATERALISM?

In asking how manageable the politics of the European-American relationship will be in the future, changing political currents in the United States will be at least as important as those in Europe. And predictions about their implications are just as hard to make. Those changes will come on top of the features of American politics that make it hard to manage a tolerably coherent foreign policy and to give political weight to an understanding of European politics as they bear on US choices: the number of individuals, groups and parts of the American government with interests in Western Europe, the extent to which particular, narrow interests can have their own way, especially by acting through the structure of Congress, and so on. In sum, the changes in American politics on the horizon point in the direction of further fragmentation in the making of foreign policy.

"Coherence" ranks with "leadership" in the rhetoric about American foreign policy and relations with allies. And it is about as helpful as an abstraction. Certainly, it is logical for Europeans to want coherence from the United States (and vice versa): who, after all, prefers "incoherence"? As partners still dependent on American action, even if less so than in the past, some predictability from the

United States makes it easier for the Europeans to adjust accordingly. That urging for consistency no doubt is increased by the deep-seated conservatism of European societies and their governing establishments.

Yet the kind of coherence Europeans would prefer in American foreign policy simply is not in the cards. Indeed, it is not only unlikely; it may also be undesirable, at least by the light of American politics. Foreign policy is bound to be – and to some extent should be – a reflection of the pluralism of American society. Different interest groups will easily get into the game, and sometimes they will prevail. Strictly "national" interests, in security for example, are strong in European-American relations, and may generally override narrower interests, for instance economic ones. That will occur more frequently in American relations with Europe than is the case with regard to other regions of the world where security interests are less pressing. But it will not always occur even when such central "national" interests as containing the Soviet Union are at play: witness the spectacle of a deeply conservative President lifting the grain embargo against the Soviet Union in 1981.

Interpreting the political changes now afoot is perilous business. In the United States as in Europe, surface support for NATO and for its military commitments has remained strong, even strengthened. In a 1982 poll, 66% of the American public and 86% of the "leaders" wanted to maintain or expand the US commitment to NATO: in 1974 the comparable figure among the public at large was 53%. Sixty-five per cent of the public and 92% of the leaders were prepared to send US troops if the Soviet Union invaded Western Europe, figures which also had grown over the preceding decade.[26] Some of what appears to be changes may in fact be just the latest turn in familiar cycles of American politics, thus simple interpretations mislead. That was the case with the "conservative tide" of the 1980 elections. In other changes there may be less than meets the eye. Consider the shift in political demographics away from the East toward the Sun Belt, which Americans cite and Europeans fear as a source of profound change in America's foreign relations. That migration actually has been going on since World War II – Ronald Reagan was the region's fourth postwar president – and it is not easy to show how it has altered American foreign policy.

Still, the demographic shifts away from those parts of the United States traditionally most associated with Europe will have some effect. Moreover, the growing Latinization of the United States is bound to matter once the Latin populations, like blacks before them, become voters.[27] These changes are not ones for today or tomorrow; their effects will be gradual, perhaps almost imperceptible. Past immigrant groups have not always been special pleaders for the countries they left, sometimes quite the contrary. And the new "Latin American" immigrants come overwhelmingly from Mexico and a few countries in the Caribbean. Still, the direction of the changes, if not their speed or precise effects, seems clear: they point to an American politics that gives less pride of place to Europe and its interests, that is more insular than in the past, with such attentions to matters foreign as it can muster going less to Europe than in the past.

Distaste for involvement in foreign affairs is a fine old American tradition. There are signs that it has increased slightly in the post-war period, though that conclusion needs to be treated with caution. In 1982, 35% of the American public in one poll – but only one per cent of the leaders – thought it better for the United States if it stayed out of world affairs. That figure for the public at large represented an increase from 25, 25, and 29%, respectively, in 1947, 1956, and 1978.[28] In the late 1970s and early 1980s the political manifestation of these sentiments just beneath the surface was less isolationism than un-ilateralism – reflected in frustration and impatience with allies, and a feeling that if the United States must act in the world, it should do so on its own, unencumbered by the reservations of its allies. Signs of those feelings were apparent during the Iranian hostage crisis in 1980, in the aftermath of the Soviet invasion of Afghanistan the same year, and in reactions to the events in Poland in the early 1980s.

Even if age cleavages in public attitudes seem less obvious in the United States than in some Western European countries, on both sides of the Atlantic the generation that created postwar alliance structures has passed from the scene. For those younger Americans who support NATO, as for their counterparts in Europe, the alliance is less an object of sentiment than of practicality. To the extent it promotes real American interests – and only to that extent – it merits support.[29] There is an element of defensiveness in that support; it is only that the status quo looks better than embarking on the uncertain path toward any alternative. Certainly younger Americans harbor few of the grand hopes – for European unification or for trans-Atlantic partnership – that characterized the early postwar period.

Other strands of "elite" opinion seem apparent alongside this mainstream view. One would describe itself as "Atlanticist" but would express deep disappointment at the state of the alliance and, in particular, of European support for American initiatives in foreign policy. Another view would share the mainstream assumption that the alliance should be supported to the extent it safeguards real American interests. To this group, however, that is no longer the case; at a minimum, the United States can no longer afford to give such priority to Europe when vital American (and Western) interests are threatened in Southwest Asia (and Central America). Yet a third view, a small minority even among the minority, might properly be described as isolationist.

The danger is not that either Europeans or Americans will decisively turn their backs on the alliance. Pro-alliance and pro-NATO sentiments will continue to predominate. Rather the danger is that the common denominator of attitudes, elite and public, on the two sides of the Atlantic will more and more diverge. Both European and American support for the alliance will be more conditional than it has been in the past, and the conditions will be more opposed. For their part, Europeans will support the alliance but on the conditions that they participate more fully in making decisions and that their interests are recognized even when those interests do not coincide with those of the United States.

American support, too, will be conditional. But Americans will want to be looking for just what Europe is least likely to provide: decisive actions in crises, unambiguous support for US initiatives, inside and outside Europe, and strong rhetorical backing. Thus there is the risk that attitudes will grow further apart even as both Europeans and Americans say – and mean – they support the alliance. Americans could easily feel more and more isolated in the world, hence frustrated and more tempted to go it alone. At the same time, Europeans would see themselves as bullied and their interests as neglected, thus want to condition support for the alliance still more.

DIFFERING POLICIES: ACCEPTABLE OR NOT?

On the evidence of this chapter, the United States and its allies in Western Europe will disagree more often in the future than in past even over this central issue of policy toward the Soviet Union in Europe. They will disagree for reasons rooted in their "national" interests as given form in their domestic politics. And the disagreements will be more apparent because the United States is no longer able to impose its policy choices on its allies to the extent it could in the past: witness the distance between the pipeline disputes of 1962 and

1982. Given attitudes on the two sides of the Atlantic, the disagreements will produce frustration in the United States and resentment in Europe.

On its face this summary sounds like a recipe for the end of the alliance, the stuff of which editorial page commentary is made. But the conclusion needs to be cast both backward and forward: backward to see how different the present state of affairs actually is from what has obtained in the past, and forward to assess how much trans-Atlantic differences will matter. The history of the alliance at least provides a caution against the presumption that unanimity over policy with regard to the Soviet Union is vital.

The allies have disagreed often even over this central issue. Until 1959 the Social Democratic opposition party in the Federal Republic was prepared to accept neither NATO nor West German participation in it. The pipeline dispute of 1962 differed from its successor two decades later mostly in that the Federal Republic acquiesced to the United States in the former but opposed it in the latter. De Gaulle quickly and strongly sided with the United States in crisis – especially the Cuban missile crisis – but at other times he sought a "mediating" role between the superpowers even as he remained the ally of one of them. His conception of a new order in Europe went far beyond what the authors of German *Ostpolitik* had in mind; de Gaulle sought a new status quo, while the Germans were prepared to recognize the existing one in the interest of making the East-West divide more tolerable.[30] De Gaulle's withdrawal of France from NATO's integrated military command in 1966 looked at the time like a major blow to the Alliance in Europe, though in the end the other allies turned out to be able to cope with it.

Identical European and American policies have not been a notable feature of the alliance's history. That raises the question: how much agreement on action within the alliance is necessary in the future? How much is politically possible? Interests do differ across the Atlantic; so do the constraints of domestic politics. The costs and benefits of different policies toward the Soviet Union are different for Europeans and Americans. It is, for example, relatively easy for Washington to reach for the instrument of economic sanctions against Moscow because, apart from grain, those sanctions cost the United States relatively little. Past American actions mean that there is little left to embargo.[31] (In purely economic terms, foregoing the future benefits of expanded Soviet-American trade does impose costs on the United States, but that cost is less visible politically.)

By contrast, economic sanctions are more costly to Western

European countries – economically and, especially, politically. That is now a fact even if European policies during the heyday of detente were important in producing it. (And the pipeline episode of 1962 is a reminder that European interests in trade with the East, on a scale different from American, predated the 1970s.) The Federal Republic, for example, did apply economic sanctions for political purposes against East Germany during the 1950s and 1960s. That, however, was generally regarded as a failure, though Bonn has on several occasions since the 1960s sought modest political moves from East Germany as a condition for *new* credits – the carrot instead of the stick. In contrast to the 50s and 60s, the detente of the 1970s and 1980s, for all its fits and starts, seemed to most Germans of whatever political hue to have resulted in a degree of human contact across the inner German border that was worth protecting. Thus Germans in particular – but Europeans in general – will pause and pause again before contemplating economic sanctions against the Soviet bloc, even in response to serious Soviet transgressions. The same is not the case for the United States.

The roots of that trans-Atlantic difference suggest that somewhat different European and American policies may not only be necessary given the interests and politics of the allies. They may be no bad thing. In the final analysis, we do not know what will produce the kind of change in the Soviet Union and Eastern Europe we all seek. On how to deal with the Soviet Union in Europe as on how to respond to security issues outside Europe, there is no monopoly of wisdom on either side of the Atlantic. In those circumstances, relatively tough American policies coupled with European readiness to sustain ties to the East could amount to a sensible hedging of Western bets.

Eastern Europe illustrates the dilemma for Western policy. Europeans and Americans share a fervent hope for a lessening of the Soviet grip on Eastern Europe. Given geography and history, Western Europeans are all the more keenly aware of the consequences of a divided continent. But the events of Poland in 1979 and the early 1980s showed just how uncertain both Europeans and Americans were in responding to change in Eastern Europe. The European, especially the German instinct was not to rock the boat, to accept even the imposition of martial law in December 1981 as preferable to overt Soviet intervention. Yet European actions of the detente period – growing humanitarian contacts with Poland and, more important, the readiness to extend large credits – no doubt were among the reasons why the *Solidarity* union arose in the first place.

By contrast, the United States was tempted to apply sanctions in an effort to impose costs. But on whom? The worst case for which Western foreign offices had planned did not occur; Soviet troops did not pour into Poland. Should the West then apply sanctions against the Soviet Union? Or against Poland? In the end the United States had no clear answers. It focused its rhetoric on the Soviet Union, arguing that martial law was tantamount to Soviet invasion, and it applied sanctions against both Poland and the Soviet Union, while at the same time permitting some forms of food and other aid to help mitigate the worst consequences of the Polish chaos.

That result among the Western allies was messy – and it played some part in producing the ensuing debacle over the gas pipeline – but it was not necessarily bad in substance. It could be seen as reflecting a sensible hedging of bets: the tougher American line directed toward the Soviet Union served as a deterrent against Moscow taking the next step and invading; while a more concilliatory line from the Europeans directed at Poland may have given Polish leaders arguments with Moscow for retaining some margin for maneuver in Warsaw. More generally, for the United States to concentrate on signalling firmness to the Soviet Union, while the Western Europeans pay relatively more attention to doing what they can to mitigate the worst consequences for Eastern Europeans of the divided continent may not only reflect differing perspectives and capabilities. It may make sense in substance as a rough division of labor.

The dilemma is that we simply do not know what will produce the change in Eastern Europe we seek; the chain of cause and effect is too scrambled. Nor is the situation much clearer with regard to the Soviet Union. The most that can be said is that the two extreme – but widely held – positions of recent years are wrong. One is the "European" view that increased economic contacts across the East-West divide will moderate Soviet behavior. The weak form of that argument underpinned the American conception of detente in the early 1970s: enmeshing the Soviet Union in a web of relationships would provide incentives for moderation. In that form the argument is accepted across the political spectrum in Europe.[32] Sadly, however, there is little to prove it is true. At least it is hard to point to concrete evidence that detente has moderated Soviet external behavior; nor does history provide much support for the general proposition in other cases.[33]

By the same token, simple arithmetic makes clear that Western military spending cannot "race" the Soviet Union into collapse, at least not soon, even leaving aside effects on the Western nations. Suppose, for example, Soviet defense spending currently is 20% of Soviet GNP –

at the high end of current Western estimates. Suppose also that Soviet GNP grew at only two per cent per year while Soviet defense expenditures kept pace with (increased) American by growing at 5%, an estimate well above what the Soviets seem to have managed in recent years. Then, ten years from now Soviet defense expenditures would consume a little less than 27% of GNP. That is a very high figure but not one that self-evidently would lead to the collapse of a system whose citizens, sadly, are no strangers to deprivation.

Much the same argument holds for efforts to limit Soviet economic growth by constraining most forms of Western economic dealings with the Soviet Union. A concerted effort to limit both technology transfer and Western credits to the Soviet Union would have a long-term effect in limiting Soviet economic growth.[34] That would make it harder for the Soviet Union to sustain its military build-up. Such a policy would be hard to implement, both because it would smack of "economic warfare," hence be resisted by Western Europeans, and because it would be hard to control leaks of technology through neutral and other non-participants in the effort.

More important, however, even if the policy were successful, its effects on Soviet *behavior* would still remain uncertain. The pace of the Soviet military build-up might not slacken even if that pace were harder to sustain; consumers might merely be compelled to tighten their belts further. A Soviet Union under economic pressure might become more restrained abroad. But, under seige or worried that time was running against them, Soviet leaders might become more truculent. Deepened economic straits in the Soviet Union surely would mean still harder times for Eastern Europe, thus raising the probability of turmoil in that region. And as suggested earlier, it is far from clear *that* is in the West's interest. Finally, even if the effects on the Soviet Union were deemed desirable, they would have to be weighed against the costs – economic and political – of the policies for the Western nations themselves.

The point is simply that in some areas of policy toward the Soviet Union, especially economics, the effects of Western actions are unclear, or debatable. For example, the middle-ground conclusion about both the US grain and pipeline sanctions is that neither hurt the Soviet Union much; both may have cost the US as much as they cost the Soviet Union.[35] That suggests, first, that a considerable degree of difference among the policies of the allies carries little cost; since we do not know what will produce the effects we seek, for the allies to try somewhat different lines probably does little harm, analytically at least. Second, and more important, the uncertainty about effects should make for caution by all the allies in asserting that their policy is right, and that the disagreement of others is crass, or high-handed, or cowardly. Agreement on issues like economic sanctions seldom is worth a major row in the alliance; that game is not worth the candle. Whether leaders on either side of the Atlantic will be able, in particular instances, to act from that understanding is another question. But at least the understanding should be a starting point for decision-making, something high on the checklist for leaders confronted with calls for action.

Yet the harder question is whether such an implicit division of labor, analytically defensible, would be politically sustainable. There would be the risk of a backlash on both sides of the Atlantic, especially the American. Americans, in Congress and elsewhere, already show familiar signs of frustration with what they see as European weakness, a feeling that America does the hard things while Europe does the nice ones. Those attitudes could become much more widespread, threatening basic alliance arrangements, such as the stationing of American military forces in Europe. Several times during the Polish crisis, for example, American senators threatened to introduce new Mansfield-style amendments requiring the US to withdraw troops from Europe if the Europeans went ahead with the Soviet gas pipeline.

The risks of political backlash are greater still because in many areas of policy toward the Soviet Union the actions of US allies in Western Europe will be even more important than in the past to American purposes in foreign policy. That is clearest in East–West economic relations. However Americans regard the growing economic and other links between Western Europe and the Soviet Union, the fact remains that much of what the "West" has in the way of both carrots and sticks in dealing with Moscow resides in the hands of the Western European nations. American sanctions on specific commodities, grain or high technology, may inflict some costs on the Soviet Union, but even those American actions can be undercut to some degree if the Europeans do not act in concert. The bulk of economic relations are Western European, not American. The United States can try to use the residual instruments of predominance – special American leverage in international banking or the long reach of American law, as in the pipeline instance – to coerce Europeans. But those surely are counterproductive; they only erode any European willingness to cooperate.

Thus the chances of recriminations across the Atlantic, and especially of deepened American frustration, are all the greater the next time Soviet actions are at issue in an Eastern European crisis or a Third World conflict. In those circumstances American leaders will be under pressure to take an action that is less than war but more than nothing. They will be tempted by economic sanctions of some sort, despite all the cautions. Equally predictably, Europeans will be deeply reluctant to go along. Particular strain will descend on the role of the Federal Republic. American secretaries of state will march to Capitol Hill to be interrogated about what the allies are doing to help. They will be able to point to military measures outside Europe by Britain and France (and even Italy). But in those circumstances recitations of German economic aid to Turkey will be less than impressive.

CAN THE ALLIANCE POLITICS BE MANAGED?

Can the allies cope with these tensions arising from these politics of policy toward the Soviet Union? The elements of a "yes" answer for particular episodes can be found, although that is no guarantee that the allies will summon the requisite adroitness in any given case. As a backdrop to particular episodes, moreover, several factors will mitigate the European-American tension.

In particular instances, the first requirement for American policy is that it be selective in making demands of the European allies. Many demands are not worth pressing given the uncertain effects on the Soviet Union of the demanded actions plus the certain strain on domestic politics in Western Europe arising from the demands. Surely the demands are not worth pressing to the point of making their fulfillment a test of alliance cohesion. To do so is only to divert the world's attention from the Soviet action that provoked the response to the disarray in the West over how to respond. That was the case in the aftermath of the Soviet invasion of Afghanistan. Arguments among the allies over sanctions came to overshadow the near-universal condemnation of the Soviet Union, even by Third World states not normally counted among the West's backers.

Selectivity may consist in reducing demands to claims on allies that are self-limiting in character. If the intent is sending a signal to the Soviet Union, economic measures that are limited in duration are preferable to open-ended ones. Europeans will be more likely to go along, and alliance leaders on both sides of the Atlantic will run less risk of setting in motion public expectations that cannot be fulfilled. Sanctions alone were never likely to force the Soviet Union out of

Afghanistan, but the open-ended character of the American sanctions announced after the invasion elevated that goal into the public's test of the policy, thus assuring failure.

By the same token, in January 1982 the NATO allies announced three objectives of their sanctions against Poland and the Soviet Union: an end to martial law, release of political prisoners and a resumption of dialogue between the government, the Catholic Church and the *Solidarity* union. Those objectives, set in the heat of the aftermath of martial law, were wildly incommensurate with the effect of the sanctions. Thus, the sanctions were bound to look a "failure" in the public's eye, and the allies were equally bound to argue over when they should be lifted. Sanctions limited in time, whose termination was in public perception less conditional on Soviet actions that leaders did not expect, would have reduced that image of failure. Similarly, political measures, such as the boycott of the Moscow Olympics, by nature have the required self-limiting character, even if they are often hard enough to implement in their own terms.

In the heat of crisis American leaders will not find it easy to be selective in making demands on their allies. Arguments that they will be better served by selectivity in the long run will bounce off the political pressures of the moment. Yet recent cases suggest that those immediate pressures need not be over-riding. The 1982 US decision to extend the pipeline embargo was not, for example, taken under the pressure of domestic politics. It was not an issue like so many in international economics where domestic interests were sharply constraining. On the contrary, American domestic economic interests opposed both the original ban and its extension. Nor was there grass-roots pressure to extend the embargo; indeed, only specialists understood what the extension meant. The Administration had ample room to pose and deal with the question in pure foreign policy terms, and to incorporate sensitivity to the concerns of alike. It was in precisely those terms that the decision was taken, regrettably.

Or consider the US response to the shooting down by the Soviet Union of a South Korean civilian airplane in September 1983. It let international opinion and the airline pilots carry the burden of responding, rather than getting out in front. The sanctions were limited and mostly symbolic: short bans by most major airlines on flights to Moscow, the closure of all remaining Aeroflot offices in the United States, and the like. To be sure, the Administration took some heat from the right; public opinion polls soon after the event showed that as many as half the Americans polled thought the Administration's response too soft. Yet that sentiment was relatively short-lived. The Administration was well-advised to suffer it rather than embark on a more ambitious response which probably would not have succeeded in making the Soviet Union contrite but probably would have turned international attention away from the Soviet action to the divisions within the Western alliance.

A second requirement for American policy is echoed in the discussion to follow of security issues outside Europe: in those instances when European cooperation is important to American purposes, Europeans will have to be more deeply involved in American policy-making than in the past. That is unavoidable given that many of the levers of policy toward the Soviet Union, particularly in economics, are in the hands of the Europeans. If American purposes require actions that make large claims on European politics, the Europeans will have to be involved in decisions. That change of practice will not only be a frustration for American policy-makers. It will also mean that resulting decisions often will be distinctly second-best in the eyes of Americans. But the alternative to frustration and second-best is likely to even worse: American demands followed by European refusals, to no substantive purpose and with open feuding in the alliance.

For Europeans, there are counterpart requirements to American selectivity and readiness to share decision-making. In episodes of particular East-West tension, Europeans will need answers to the question: if you are not prepared to impose sanctions, what more are you doing?[36] Those answers will need to be fairly concrete, and that will mean painful choices – over increasing conventional defense efforts in Europe, for example. But it will not do to respond, in effect, that "we see the problem, but there is no area in which we can do more." By the same token, if Americans are prepared to share decision-making when real cooperation with Europeans is necessary, the Europeans will have to be prepared to engage in the process. They will not be able to remain aloof as in the past, their role limited to a faintly condescending critique of American choices after the fact; they will need to be prepared to make proposals of their own for action. Old habits will have to change on both sides of the Atlantic.

Strain between Europe and America is predictable in particular instances. Even if they are manageable, those instances will not always be managed; on that score the history of the alliance is painfully plain. Yet the cumulative effect of these strains will be less than popular prophesies would have it. Several factors will mitigate the strain.

The first is the consensus at the center of the alliance on the continuing need for military insurance against the military power of the Soviet Union in Europe. Americans and Europeans will disagree over how much insurance and in what form and provided in what measure by whom. But the need for insurance in the form of military forces will be agreed by all but fringe groups on both sides of the ocean. Not only will there be continuing agreement on the need for insurance, but NATO in something like its current form as the primary instrument of that insurance will also command broad support. NATO will be more controversial than the need for insurance: there will be recurring enthusiasm in Europe for non-nuclear, territorial defense or for independent European arrangements and in America, for dramatic innovations in NATO strategy or for sharp changes in the global pattern of American military deployments.

Yet none of those changes will come to pass, certainly not soon. The recurring enthusiasms will, however, be drained more by failings in their objects than by any powerful emotions in support of existing NATO arrangements. Europeans and Americans will continue to view their Alliance in somewhat different ways, and those differences will grow sharper. They will concur mostly in that NATO is a necessity, not that it calls forth popular enthusiasm in their nations. That pragmatic support is, however, no bad thing. On the contrary, democrats in the industrial nations no doubt would find it cause for alarm if military alliance aroused public fervor. With *that* danger we are all too familiar.

As a guide to policy, the relative consensus at the center of the alliance suggests the merit in emphasizing continuity and minimizing the "newness" of any particular measure, especially in the military realm. For example, any adjustment in NATO military doctrine and practice – toward more interdiction of second and third echelon Soviet forces, with greater use of precision-guided munitions – is bound to be small. To advertise that shift as *the* solution to NATO's defense problems, as enthusiasts often do, is both bad policy and bad politics. It raises expectations that cannot be fulfilled, and it arouses political controversy over the measures. Both the dashed expectations and much of the controversy are needless.

By the same token, it is unwise to tie particular steps to a detailed assessment of the Soviet threat that is agreed among the allies. They simply will not come to such an agreement; they will, however, concur that the threat is real and needs to be countered. They will not, for example, agree that the Soviet Union now evidences more interest in nuclear war-fighting than in the past. Thus, that argument for additional NATO nuclear deployments, like the cruise and Pershing missiles, will be unpersuasive. Instead, it makes much more sense to keep arguments for any new measures on grounds over which broad agreement is possible: that Soviet conventional and nuclear capabilities in Europe continue to grow, even if that does not necessarily signal that those forces are more likely to be used; that weapon-for-weapon balance is not necessary but that too pronounced a disparity risks the credibility of NATO's strategy; and thus that adjustments in nuclear deployments will from time to time be necessary.

A second factor mitigating trans-Atlantic strain is the degree of American acquiescence in the proposition that stability, hence security, in Europe should be insulated from broader currents in East–West relations. In fact though not in rhetoric, a succession of American administrations has accepted that detente can be divided. The extent of that acceptance was most notable by the administration for which it would have seemed least likely – the Reagan Administration. Within six months of taking office, that Adminisration moved forward with the Geneva negotiations over intermediate nuclear forces (INF), notwithstanding the Administration's emphasis on building up American defenses, its hard rhetoric toward the Soviet Union and its deep skepticism over arms control in general.

Two years later when the Soviet Union shot down a civilian South Korean airliner, Reagan Administration condemnations of the act were followed immediately by the pledge not to let even that incident interfere with the INF talks. That same month, September 1983, the Administration retreated from its human rights demands in the Madrid review of the Conference on Security and Cooperation in Europe (CSCE); at the same time it agreed to a follow-up conference on European security in Stockholm, an idea both it and its predecessor administration had viewed with deep misgivings. In all cases the motive was to accomodate the interests of the West Europeans; the effect was to extend the "divisibility" of detente.

Public opinion polls also suggest a willingness to accommodate European views even when those do not coincide with American. On that score, the American people often may be more compromising than their government. In 1982, for example, when asked how the United States should respond to the Soviet–West European gas pipeline deal, the most popular response (37%) was to "let our allies pursue policies they think best." Twenty-seven per cent favored putting diplomatic pressure on the Europeans, and only 15% thought the United States should impose economic sanctions if other methods

did not work.[37] If the fact that "we are here and they are there" means
that Americans and Europeans see issues through different perspectives, it also makes for some tolerance of those differences. To a
considerable degree Americans are willing to let Europeans "over
there" decide what is best for them even if their decisions do not match
American preferences.

A final factor mitigating the strains is the simple fact that they
become familiar. Trans-Atlantic differences that lead to sharp disputes
the first time are less striking the next time they are played out. Strains
cumulate but so do techniques for containing them. The two sides may
not understand each other better the second time, or be much more
willing to retreat from their positions, but at least the differences are
less surprising. There is less temptation to label the other's position as
treachery, a fatal break in the cohesion of the alliance.

4 Defense Beyond Europe

It is easy to cover many aspects of post-war relations between the United States and its allies in Western Europe with a rosy glow of nostalgia. That is particularly the case for dealings over issues beyond Europe. It is also particicularly misleading. The history of the alliance has been more one of disagreement than of agreement over what to do about issues outside Europe: Indochina in the 1950s, above all Suez in 1956, and Indochina again in the 1960s, this time with European and American positions reversed. Now, it is Washington that entreats its European allies to pay more attention to security issues beyond Europe; two decades ago it was the reverse, Europeans urging and American leaders resisting. History seems to testify to the proposition that in trans-Atlantic relations there are only a few positions, and so the alliance partners keep exchanging those positions.

The American entreaties of the late 1970s and 1980s to increase allied cooperation outside Europe, especially in the Persian Gulf and Southwest Asia, raise questions parallel to those that ran through the previous chapter: how common are American and European interests beyond Europe, and how compatible are their politics? How alike should their policies be? These questions are both easier and harder for issues outside Europe than for those inside it: easier because the questions are less covered by rhetoric of past unity; harder because the history may be forgotten or romanticized, and because recent events may suggest that security issues are now so pressing that history is only dimly relevant. Moreover, "national" interests, domestic politics, perceptions of capabilities and views of the nature of the threat are intermingled in a way that muddies discussion of these issues.

My conclusions about this set of questions run parallel to those of the previous chapter. Differences of interest across the Atlantic (and among the European nations), always present, are sharper now; those differences may, however, be less deeply embedded in domestic politics on both sides of the ocean than are differences over how to deal with the Soviet Union in Europe. Again, both history and logic provide grounds for thinking that the allies could tolerate considerable divergence in their approaches to issues beyond Europe. Yet the risk that differences will arouse a political backlash is high, perhaps even higher than is the case for issues inside Europe: it is tempting for Americans to see the interests at stake in the Persian Gulf as more important to Europeans than to Americans. Since the Persian Gulf is distant from both Europe and America, there is little reason to concede Europeans a claim to special expertise in dealing with it. Thus it is imperative that Europeans share – and are seen to share – risks as well as burdens in dealing with issues outside Europe.

THE SHADOW OF HISTORY

The shadow of alliance history is particularly long with respect to this set of issues. European memories are noticeably more durable than American, and, after all, for most of the post-war period it was the Europeans that sought to engage the United States in issues beyond Europe and the United States that held back. The geographical limitation in the North Atlantic Treaty to areas north of the Tropic of Cancer[1] was included not at European insistence but at American. The United States feared being drawn into European colonial conflicts. To be sure, the United States attitude toward the colonial powers and their former colonies was somewhat ambivalent: on the one hand, the colonial powers were acknowledged as important allies at a time when NATO was abuilding; on the other, the United States had put pressure on them to divest themselves of their colonies and continued to do so. Joined by Britain, Washington put enormous pressure on the Netherlands to grant independence to the anti-communist nationalists in Indonesia. To pre-empt Congressional action, the US temporarily suspended Marshall Plan aid to the Netherlands, which capitulated in August 1949, granting unconditional independence to Indonesia.[2]

The shaping of the Treaty reflected these varying European and American interests. France, for example, pushed for the inclusion of Italy, at the time problematic, because the French wanted to extend the Alliance into the Mediterranean, thus strengthening the argument for the inclusion of then-French Algeria. There was also the notion of an alliance with three categories of members: a core group, plus associate members linked by strictly military relations (Portugal) or given one-way aid in return for limited cooperation (Sweden), plus a more peripheral category of, for example, former colonies. The idea appealed to some Europeans and also to some Americans, though to the latter for different reasons: it would have provided for a differentiated link to, especially, Portugal, an ideological outcast from which the allies only wanted real estate in any case. American Undersecretary of State Robert Lovett derided the idea as "resident members, non-resident members and summer privileges,"[3] and it never was a starter. Leaders at the time recognized that it would have institutionalized temptations toward free-riding, by permitting countries to have most of the benefits of full membership at less cost and responsibility. Still, it is intriguing to speculate about how the issue of security threats beyond Europe would look now if NATO had developed in such an expanded form.

It continued to be clear that the United States could not foresee circumstances in which it would need European support beyond Europe, and, lacking that foresight, calculated that an expanded relationship with the Europeans would only constrain American flexibility. As early as 1952 the French cabinet adopted a resolution arguing that France "deserved to receive support without fail" in Indochina from their allies.[4] Two years later the French sought, without success, American help for their beleaguered garrison at Dien Bien Phu.

In 1956 German Chancellor Konrad Adenauer was confiding to his diary his own misgivings about the limited character of NATO. Without a common political approach, the common military policy of the Alliance could not be effective. When he raised these ideas with American Secretary of State John Foster Dulles, the latter was favorable but also made explicit the argument that the United States, unlike the Europeans, had global interests and thus needed freedom of action to protect them.[5] The next year, after Sputnik, Adenauer wrote a memorandum criticizing the United States for neglecting the political aspects of NATO because American leaders wanted to keep their options open in the Middle East and Asia. What Adenauer seems to have had in mind was a common foreign policy, a notion very much akin to what American administrations sought in the aftermath of the Iran and Afghanistan crises more than two decades later.

The most celebrated effort to change the character of the NATO Alliance was General de Gaulle's September 1958 Memorandum to the British and American governments proposing a directorate of those two plus France. That was generally perceived by the Anglo-Saxons as a ploy to increase France's – and de Gaulle's – power. It appeared to demand the unthinkable – a French veto on the use of

American nuclear weapons, *anywhere*.[6] The proposal never was seriously considered, and de Gaulle probably did not expect that it would be – for example, he passed it to the NATO Secretary General the day before sending it to Washington and London, and the Secretary General, a Belgian, predictably objected vehemently on behalf of the small NATO members. Eisenhower offered a number of objections, among them that the proposal would give the smaller allies the impression that "basic decisions affecting their own vital interests are being made without their participation" and that it was an effort "to amend the North Atlantic Treaty so as to extend its coverage beyond the areas presently covered."[7] The latter was yet another indication that the United States was content with a geographically limited Alliance.

De Gaulle made still more explicit suggestions during the Kennedy Administration for broadening the scope of the Alliance, and was similarly rebuffed. In September 1960, before the American election, he made a broad proposal for an expanded Alliance, noting that much had changed in the ten years since the North Atlantic Treaty had been signed, when the immediate problem was confined to Europe. His language again smacked of *directoire*, but it also evokes American commentaries twenty years later: "We think that, at least among the world powers of the West (France, Britain and the United States), something must be organized, as far as the Alliance is concerned, with regard to the political and occasionally strategic conduct of the Alliance outside Europe, particularly in the Middle East and Africa where those three powers are constantly involved . . . If there is no agreement among the principal members of the Atlantic Alliance on matters other than Europe, how can the Alliance be indefinitely maintained in Europe? This must be remedied."[8]

President Kennedy, apparently unsure what to make of the idea, did not reply. Eventually, he appropriated some of the idea in his "Declaration of Interdependence" speech in 1962. However, at that point, as two years earlier, the central issue was the nuclear question; to talk of "sharing decisions" meant sharing nuclear decisions, something neither Kennedy nor presidents before and after him had any intention of doing, and the most Kennedy did was nod rhetorically in the direction of de Gaulle's suggestion.

The instances of Suez and Vietnam neatly illustrate the symmetry – and frustration – of the trans-Atlantic debate over issues outside Europe. It is hard to overstate how much the British and French feel betrayed by the Americans over Suez, even now, a generation later.

Here was their major ally, not just failing to support them but explicitly opposing them in connivance with the principal adversary, the Soviet Union. American anger over the lack of European support in Vietnam is weaker – at least the Europeans were bullied into keeping their opposition relatively quiet – but that anger was one of the strands in the move to reduce the American garrison in Europe in the late 1960s and early 1970s. And Vietnam still contributes, at least on the American right, to the feeling that Europe is too pusillanimous ever to take firm stands over issues outside Europe.

The frustration of this trans-Atlantic griping is that its effects continue despite the rights and wrongs as history now would assess them. The United States probably was right over Suez, and most Americans would agree that the Europeans were right about Vietnam: it was not a strategic objective worth the price, and to boot, it dangerously diverted American attentions from more important issues elsewhere, and not just in Europe. But that is not the point. If the Americans were wrong about Vietnam, they may also be wrong about Afghanistan. The two sides of the Atlantic may switch position again. (And it is worth remembering that since Vietnam the French have actually used force outside Europe more often than the United States.) The minimum lesson of postwar history is that neither Europeans nor Americans will automatically accept the other's view of issues beyond Europe. And of course the Europeans themselves will often be divided.

INTERESTS AND CAPABILITIES

What ought to be clear, but too seldom is in discussion of the alliance, is that European-American differences are rooted in real interests that diverge. What is less clear is whether those differences – and the difficulties thus posed for policy-making – are markedly greater than in the past. Certainly some past sources of difference have no present parallels. The colonial period is now past, and the residual issues over which the United States and its European allies might have reason to differ seem much more manageable: the Falklands episode was hardly in a class with Suez, and differences occasioned by France's quasi-colonial relations with its former African colonies pale by comparison to Indochina or Algeria.

Yet other differences seem greater now, or at least more salient. Oil is the most obvious case in point. The bare figures do not tell the entire story but they are suggestive. The United States and its major

European allies all depend on oil for about half their total energy requirements. But in 1979 oil imports accounted for 45.7% of total oil consumption for the United States but 100% for the Federal Republc, 80.7% for France (and 45.5% for Britain, a number that was declining as North Sea oil came on stream).[9] Of those imports, only 38.7% came from the Middle East (including Libya) for the United States, but 72.2% for France (and 41.9% for Germany). Thirty per cent American oil imports came from the Gulf, as against 62% of European imports.

These relative patterns are not likely to change soon. Conservation and other sources (primarily coal, gas and nuclear) could reduce everyone's dependence on oil imports, but the United States will remain in a relatively happier position than its major allies, save Britain. The US retains enormous coal and gas reserves which the Europeans generally do not. Of all the trans-Atlantic nations only France has been able to dent its imports with nuclear power, and even it may confront the same domestic pressures as elsewhere, making that effort hard to sustain.

Whatever the numbers mean, they surely mean two things: particular European countries have somewhat different interests in imported oil, but generally imported oil, and imported oil from the Middle East and Gulf, are more important to them than to the United States. To be sure, the differences are often overstated: to say, as Americans sometimes do, that the United States economy could survive a complete cut-off of Gulf oil while Europe could not may be true in technical terms. But, politically, it amounts to saying that the United States would be prepared to sit by and watch the destruction of the entire structure of postwar Atlantic relations, to say nothing of the European economies themselves. Thus, the real extent of difference is less than sometimes supposed. But it is significant and will continue to be.

On its face, it is not clear what that difference of interest should imply for European policies. Americans are tempted to argue that it should make Europeans even more attentive than Americans to threats to the supply of Gulf oil, hence more prepared to take action to address those threats; after all the oil is, in an important sense, more crucial to them than to the United States. Yet since the oil is essential for them in the short run, that becomes a constraint; for the Europeans, the short run imperative is likely to dominate longer-term interests. By contrast, the United States, less immediately dependent, has more freedom for the maneuver. Hence policies like those pursued

TABLE 4.1:   *Oil imports from the Middle East and Gulf, 1960–80*

	Oil imports as % of total energy consumption			1980–% of Oil Imports from OAPEC Countries
	1960	*1970*	*1980*	
United States	5.2	8.1	15.9	17.9
France	45.3	80.0	90.8	65.8
Federal Republic	9.4	51.0	59.1	45.5
Italy	73.4	95.6	90.4	65.0
Britain	23.9	49.5	4.3	63.0

SOURCES: UNCTAD, *Statistics Yearbook 1984*; US Central Intelligence Agency, *Handbook of Economic Statistics*, (Washington, 1981)

by France after 1973 – a staunchly pro-Arab stance, coupled with efforts to make bilateral oil deals with Arab producers and with firm opposition to any grouping of consumers that might be construed as hostile to producers – were frustrating for American leaders, but they were not necessarily irrational from France's perspective.[10] They may have been short-sighted, but they were not irrational.

Differences of interest mix with, and are compounded by differences in national capabilities. Even if the Europeans were, for example, as worried as the Americans about the Soviet military presence adjacent to the oil-producing regions of the Gulf, their own efforts could do little about it, at least directly. France intervened with military force more often outside Europe than the United States in the late 1970s and 1980s – twice in Zaire's Shaba province, in the Central Africa Republic (formerly Empire), and several times in Chad's civil wars. Those instances, however, were both distant from the Soviet Union geographically and relatively distant from direct Soviet involvement.

Of the European allies, only France and Britain retain forces in or for possible deployment to the southwest Asian region. Those capabilities could play a role in minor contingencies, but if larger forces were required, particularly to deter the Soviet Union, they would be marginal by comparison to American efforts. France's 3000 plus troops at Djibouti, however, still are the largest Western force in the region.[11] Before the Soviet and American naval build-ups in the Indian Ocean in the late 1970s, France frequently was the largest naval presence there, with between a dozen and twenty ships.

In 1980 France announced the creation of a new French Legion brigade with light armor and a parachute capability. In the several years after that, defense decisions by the government of François Mitterrand moved toward increasing the mobility of French conventional forces; however, with nuclear forces consuming larger shares of austere military budgets, the price of that was pressure to draw down the French conventional presence in Germany. In addition to the Djibouti garrison, in 1984 France had significant forces in the Central African Republic (1000), Gabon (450), Ivory Coast (900), and Senegal (1200), as well as several thousand-odd peacekeeping troops in Lebanon.

For its part, Britain had an intermittent naval presence in or near the Persian Gulf (3–4 ships) after the beginning of the Iran–Iraq war in September 1980. Yet notwithstanding the 1982 Falklands operation, Britain's ability to move men and equipment is likely to be more and more limited as naval forces are drawn down and improvements in airlift deferred. Within the Persian Gulf region, the British presence is unobtrusive but worth noting. In the early 1980s Britain had several thousand military and civilians providing training and other defense services in Saudi Arabia, Kuwait and Oman, and other countries of the region. Oman's forces, which patrol the Straits of Hormuz, still depended on seconded British officers.

The other allies, such as Holland, on occasion have participated in naval deployments outside the European area. But those allies have no significant military capabilities beyond Europe. For the Federal Republic the lack of capability is reinforced by the earmarking of all forces for NATO; that in turn is reflected in a deep reluctance in domestic politics to become involved with military force outside Europe. Given Germany's policy of not exporting arms to "areas of tension," there was sharp controversy in 1984 over selling tanks to Saudi Arabia. Economics made the deal attractive; domestic politics made it difficult.

Thus, for Europeans, dependence on Gulf oil makes for policies of expedience in the short run, while lack of capabilities may make for a sense that they can do little about some important threats to their interests even over the long run. The latter is free riding of a sort, since from the perspective of most of the European nations, building military forces for possible deployment well outside Europe would be extremely expensive for small (private) gain. It is no surprise that the two European states, Britain and France, that retain military capabilities beyond Europe do so for reasons which have to do as much with particular benefits as with collective defense: residual colonial responsibilities mixed, especially in the French case, with continuing economic and cultural links.

THREATS ABROAD, POLITICS AT HOME

So far the discussion has treated trans-Atlantic differences over issues beyond Europe as largely independent of arguments on the merits of any particular case. It has asked how the different interests, or capabilities, of the United States and Europe might indicate different approaches, in the Gulf for example. Some of those different approaches look to Americans like a form of free riding on the part of the Europeans: Europeans have a freedom and a reason to take particular actions precisely because they know the United States will not or cannot follow suit. Yet that analysis hardly is meant to deny the possibility that official Washington and its European partners may simply hold different views of a particular issue outside Europe. Europeans may take a position and wish the United States did, too; their perceptions of the nature of the threat may simply be different.

   The problem is that policies on both sides of the Atlantic reflect a mix of perceptions of interests, national politics, capabilities and perspectives of the threat. That mix is not easy to sort out. Consider the aftermath of the Soviet invasion of Afghanistan in 1979. German officials, for example, constantly echoed the view that the Soviet invasion was a grave matter, and the West had to react strongly. Yet another view of the threat, seldom explicit, broke through the surface of the debate.[12] In that view, Afghanistan mattered but did not change the basic East–West balance. Soviet weaknesses remained. Besides, the invasion owed something to Western policy: to signals of disinterest in the fate of Afghanistan after the April 1978 coup and to America's inability to provide much by way of positive incentives for Soviet restraint in Soviet–American detente, for instance by getting SALT II ratified. This view also stressed the interest in protecting European detente even in a time of superpower tension, an obvious reflection of the different stakes discussed in the previous chapter. The West should not be the first to import tension into Europe from outside it. Finally, the different capabilities of the allies were also at play in the debate. If the catch phrase of the time, "division of labor," sometimes seemed to Germans to mean that the Federal Republic did the "nice" things – like providing aid to Turkey – while the United States took responsibility for building military power outside Europe, that also reflected in part Germany's perceived inability to do much in the military realm outside Europe.

Similar differences in perception of the threat ran, and continue to run through trans-Atlantic discussions of the Gulf and Middle East, again mixed with differing perspectives of stakes and capabilities. Much of that debate has become tiresomely stylized. The arguments barely meet. For example, Europeans surely are right to say that unless the United States presses for serious movement on the Palestinian problem, its military efforts to shore up the West's position in the Gulf will be hollow. Yet that argument often is overstated to sound as though the Palestinian issue is the only key to stability in the region. It is made in good season and bad; changed circumstances, like the expulsion of the Palestine Liberation Organization (PLO) fighters from Lebanon in 1982, barely dent the argument at all. In that form it glances off the American debate, dismissed as a debater's point and an excuse for European inaction. It smacks of free riding in the ways I have alluded to earlier.

If American leaders sometimes sound as though the Palestinians are no part of the problems of the Middle East and Gulf, Europeans often talk as though they are the entire problem. If recent history has taught anything, it is that the Middle East tangle defies black-and-white characterizations: there are plenty of tensions there that have nothing to do with the Palestinians; even in concept, there is neither a single, clear Palestinian "problem" nor a definitive "solution"; and the Arab states themselves are at least as nervous about the Palestinian question as anyone else.

Yet even if the argument in substance seldom is joined, there are distinct views of the threat and how to respond to it, just as there are alternative views of interests at play beyond Europe. One main alternative view of the threat is often labelled the "European" view, as I do, but not just Europeans hold it. In this view, the primary threat to stability in the Gulf, and thus to Western interests, is not Soviet military power but rather internal unrest in the Gulf states themselves. That unrest might be fomented and abetted by the Soviet Union, but often, as in revolutionary Iran, Moscow may have little or nothing to do with it. This view does not reject the argument that the West needs more military weight in the region, but it does raise hard questions about the purpose of that military force. Again, those criticisms often are overstated and stylized. Critics try to have it both ways: nothing the Western nations conceivably could do would be enough to meet serious Soviet threats, such as Iran; smaller efforts, however, would look to states in the region like preparation to take control of oil fields, and not necessarily at the request of local rulers.[13] These arguments again verge on debater's points, but surely it is fair to ask what exactly is the point of more military force in the region.

There is weight to the concern that Western military force is at best tangential to the real problems of stability in the region. Worse, there is the possibility that the effort to build that force could become a factor for instability, not stability, by identifying friendly Arab states too closely with the West in general and the United States in particular, thus providing targets for internal dissidents. Planning for the American Rapid Deployment Force (RDF), including arrangements for American use of facilities in Egypt, Oman, Somalia, and Kenya, raised that concern, no matter how carefully successive US administrations tried to deal with it. The bigger the RDF became in an attempt to deter Soviet military power, the greater the need for facilities in the region and the greater the risk that those could become focal points for internal opposition.

In this context, the lack of movement on the Palestinian issue is dangerous in two senses. Palestinian populations in the Gulf could become more radical and constitute threats to existing regimes; evidence on that score is so far inconclusive, and the threat, if real, seems distant. Yet it is no accident that Kuwait, the Gulf state with the largest Palestinian population, has been the most rhetorically supportive of Palestinian rights and the most aloof from cooperation with the United States. More straightforward is the concern that so long as the United States looks like it is in Israel's pocket on the Palestinian question, Arab propaganda will make even moderate states in the region reluctant to cooperate with the US. That reluctance would only be increased if the United States talked of a "strategic consensus" with Israel, as it did early in the Reagan presidency, or began to implement closer military-to-military cooperation, as it did several years later. In this view a more forthcoming American attitude at least would make the United States less of a target for Arab rhetoric and could begin to put the Palestinian monkey on the Arabs' back, making more visible the deep divisions in the Arab world over what exactly to do about the Palestinians.

In part, these "European" arguments surely are correct. Western military might is, at best, a minor part of strategies designed to deal with the instability in the Gulf that is the primary threat to Western interests. The American preoccupation with military measures and with the Soviet threat — with only nods to the importance of more political elements in a strategy – looks to Europeans mistaken and possibly dangerous. Europeans will continue to have little capability to contribute much in military terms but reason to be concerned that those military efforts may affect their interests.

Yet the stylized form in which the arguments are often made obscures the real issues, and makes the problem of managing the alliance harder, not easier. When there are few ideas for the political and economic elements of strategy to deal with instability, "European" arguments that the United States is over-emphasizing the military dimension sound to Americans self-serving. When Germans talk – as they did during the early 1980s – about the need for economic assistance and more forthcoming North–South strategies as ways to approach instability in the Third World, those arguments, fair enough, sound to Americans like a cop-out, an excuse for not helping or a desire to protect cozy arrangements in Europe from the intrusion of nasty realities elsewhere.

These differences among the allies – in interests, capabilities and perspectives of the threat – are embedded in varying degrees in the domestic politics of the allies. For most of the smaller European NATO members, the primary constraint on actions beyond Europe probably is money – the politics of budgeting. Polls taken of the EEC countries in 1979 and 1981 underscored both the strong priority for welfare over defense spending and, perhaps more surprisingly, the fact that the priority scarcely declined between 1979 and 1981 despite the increase in East–West tension during that period.[14] To some extent, these domestic politics in the smaller European countries can be seen as reflecting temptations toward free-riding since those countries know that whatever they spend in meeting security threats outside Europe will add virtually nothing to the efforts of the larger countries. That temptation presumably affects military spending and economic assistance alike. However, the effect on military spending may be more pronounced: defense efforts beyond Europe may look to many citizens dubious as well as wasteful and as a diversion from defense at home; by contrast, economic aid may command broader support, from those who see it as a humanitarian act as well as those who focus on its possible security dimension.

There are also some special inhibitions on actions beyond Europe built into the domestic politics of particular European countries. One, mentioned earlier, is the restriction of the Federal Republic's military forces to the NATO area; partly imposed and partly self-imposed, it now runs deep into the political context of foreign policy. Another is the anti-colonial and anti-interventionist traditions of the Nordic countries. Similar sentiments among political groups in other countries – for instance, the socialists and social democrats – mean that using military force outside Europe is immediately controversial in a way that is not the case for the United States. Even in the larger European countries that have sent forces outside Europe – Britain, France, perhaps Italy – the political support for those actions frequently is thin and thus the sensitivity to casualties correspondingly high. That was clear in 1983–84 as the contingents of the multinational forces in Lebanon, especially the American and French contingents, began taking casualties.

For the United States the political constraints are of a different kind, primarily political. Most plainly, the United States will remain deeply constrained in framing venturesome political approaches to the Middle East. More forthcoming postures on the Palestinian question, or an effort to co-opt the PLO by dealing directly with it simply may not be in the cards. How much the domestic cast of the Middle East issues might change is a question beyond the scope of this book. Some change seems afoot, halting and frequently reversed; at least the Camp David agreements between Israel and Egypt, and the subsequent poundings of which the PLO was subjected have scrambled the common public stereotypes of the region.

Only several comments about future domestic politics can be made with any confidence. One is that American administrations will continue to have more leeway in policy toward the Middle East early in their tenures but will be more constrained closer to elections. The quadriennial contest among Democratic presidential aspirants to outbid each other in support for Israel is familiar. Yet since Republicans now aspire to Jewish votes and support as well – nearly half of American Jewish votes went for Mr Reagan in 1980 – that contest in bidding for votes extends into the Republican Party as well.

A second is that much will depend, as in the past, on whether Americans and the American Jewish community perceive that a particular political initiative does not threaten Israel's security, and might enhance it. On one analysis, Israel has a historic, but relatively small, window of opportunity, since it now has a degree of military superiority over any realistic coalition of Arab opponents that it cannot hope to retain. On this analysis, now is the time to make concessions, from a position of strength, in pursuit of a more durable political framework in the Middle East, and it would be tragedy if Israel did not grasp that opportunity. The history of the Middle East offers, sadly, little evidence that Israel's own politics will produce a major move on its part absent considerable prodding from the United States. So American pressure will be necessary if the opportunity is not to be lost.

That is close to my own view. But it may be that continuing fragmentation in the Arab world will mean that Israeli military superiority nearly as overwhelming as at present can be maintained for some time. That is not to gainsay the danger that the political climate will deteriorate, not improve, each time a negotiating opportunity is passed and each time the weakness of an Israeli opponent, like the PLO, becomes the opportunity for military victory, not for negotiation. But the danger of losing time may not loom large in American domestic perceptions of the Middle East; hence American administrations may continue to find it difficult to build a basis of politcal support for pressing Israel to make significant concessions, for instance on the West Bank, in the interest of the peace process.

Clearly, one reason the United States is prone to emphasize military approaches to the problems of the Gulf and the Middle East is that those are easier in domestic politics than, for example, an attempt to move forward on the Palestinian issue. More broadly, the United States knows how to build military power; its record at trying to build stability in less developed countries through political and economic measures is mixed to say the least. That reinforces the American tendency, visible from time to time and likely to recur, to be almost nostalgic for the clarity of the Cold War, when the good guys were easy to distinguish from the bad and when building military power to contain the latter seemed the obvious thing to do.

The crisis over the American hostages in Iran and the aftermath of the Soviet invasion of Afghanistan in 1979 illustrate how much domestic politics – and passions – of the moment color perceptions of threats. The conjunction of the two was unfortunate, a source of confusion. Analysts on both sides of the Atlantic agreed that the hostages were a side-show, however tragic, to the more serious security issues posed by Afghanistan. That, however, was not an assessment the Carter Administration could easily make its own, and it was driven, by reasons that are understandable but regrettable, to invest too many chips in the hostage crisis.

In those circumstances, European arguments that sanctions against Iran were the wrong policy for the wrong place at the wrong time – more likely to stiffen the forces of intransigence within Iran or to drive the country toward the Soviet Union than to secure the release of the hostages – were on the mark. But they could scarcely be made. Europeans thus felt themselves compelled to support bad American policies lest they be faced with worse ones – military action. In the event they got both. Yet, paradoxically, the failed American rescue mission of April 1980, had few of the consequences in the Gulf which had led Secretary of State Cyrus Vance to oppose it, in large measure perhaps because it failed. And it did have the effect of draining away the growing pressure in American politics for tough action, thus laying the basis for a return to negotiation which ultimately succeeded. (Indeed, since a *failed* raid looked in restrospect like the best way to balance internal with foreign policy requirements, more than one European insinuated to me at the time that perhaps the American government had planned to fail. I could only smile and say that the government I knew was hard-pressed enough to plan to succeed).

POINTS OF STRAIN

For the foreseeable future, the Middle East and Gulf will continue to be the focus of European-American differences. The imperative of oil and the differing vulnerabilities of Europe and America give a sharpness to differences of interest there that have no counterparts for other regions. It is possible to imagine that a decade hence the situation in South Africa might contain similar elements: different degrees of economic or raw material vulnerabilities among the allies reinforced by political currents moving in sharply different directions – for instance, American blacks, a better organized political force more interested in foreign policy than now, lobbying Washington hard for real pressure on white South Africa. Yet even there the economic interests will not match those of oil, and the domestic politics, on both sides of the Atlantic, of southern Africa's human tragedy will be mixed: in the United States, anti-communism and images of massacre will compete with black self-determination.

Trans-Atlantic differences over other regions are likely to be less severe but more political in character. Central America is the prime example. It will continue to be a trauma for the United States, and Europeans will continue to be critical of American policy. However, concrete European stakes in Central America barely exist; the European discussion of the region is one of political symbols. Those symbols frequently will collide with those that dominate the American debate. Yet because European stakes in the region are so small by comparison with their interests in the trans-Atlantic tie, government leaders will have an incentive not necessarily to defer to the United States, but at least to minimize tension over the issue. They will not be able to control symbols thrown up by their own domestic political debate, but they can mute the issue in government-to-government dealings. Central America will be an irritant in the European-American relationship, in itself probably manageable but contributing to the weight of strains that creates the risk of a serious break, a point addressed later.

This is not the place for a detailed discussion of issues in Central America. Suffice to say that trans-Atlantic dealings are complicated not just by the symbolic character of the European discussion, but also by the confusion of the American debate. Public opinion polls suggest the degree of confusion. For example, in a 1982 poll, concern among Americans over "Latin America" increased sharply (though from a small base), to rank ahead of concern over relations with allies in Western Europe, for example. Yet the same poll found virtually no support for direct military intervention in El Salvador even if the leftist guerrillas were about to win (80% of the public and 90% of the "leaders" opposed intervention).[15] The polls provide some confirmation for what seemed apparent in the mood of the early 1980s: Americans were concerned about Central America but uncertain about what to do, and they saw no threat that justified spilling American blood.

In my view, the United States does have a specific, and narrow, interest in restricting Cuban and Soviet military power in the region. And it does have stakes in political developments as they might bear on political stability in Venezuela and especially Mexico. But the United States' concrete interest in whether the government of Honduras is Marxist, right-wing authoritarian or somewhere in between is weak.

Yet the American debate of the early 1980s did not reflect that or any other clear strategic conception. For example, the report of the Kissinger Commission on Central America, delivered to President Reagan in January 1984, wandered all over the map in defining the threat to US interests in Central America. At one point it said that "indigenous reform, even indigenous revolution, is not a security threat to the United States." Yet in other places is suggested that revolution could not be purely indigenous. At others it focused on the threat of Soviet forces and bases, while at still others it emphasized American credibility, implying that the US could not tolerate radical regimes in Central America even if they did not pose a specific security threat.[16]

Public attitudes in the United States reflected a volatile combination of ignorance, paternalism and notions of "backyard" which long have characterized American public opinion toward the region. That meant that the America public could become roused over the prospect of communism in the region, then when it sensed that the Reagan Administration was becoming too involved in El Salvador, it could swing quickly back to images of Vietnam, of open-ended commitments to places where the "good" guys were difficult to separate from the "bad" and which did not in the end seem to matter all that much in any case.

On both sides of the Atlantic, much of the discussion of Central America has been at the level of symbols rooted in domestic politics. Yet at the core what happens in Central America matters to Americans, even if they are not quite sure why, in a way it does not for Europeans. The issue may be largely symbolic, but it is not entirely so. For much of the European left, especially in France, criticism of American policy is a natural, all the more so because so little other than principle is at stake. In August 1981, the Mitterrand government in France signed a joint declaration with Mexico urging recognition of the Salvadorean guerrillas as a "legitimate political force," and later the same year France sold the Sandinista government of Nicaragua $15.8 million in arms. The military emphasis in the Central American policies of both the later Carter and the Reagan Administrations accorded nicely with the European left's stereotypes of the US as adventurous and of the two superpowers as not all that different in their external behavior. Central America, and the American invasion of Grenada in 1983, became arguments for European "equidistance" between the superpowers.

For the Federal Republic the situation was similar, though compounded by the Central American activities of the German party foundations – especially the two big ones, those of the Social Democratic and Christian Democratic parties. The activities of those foundations, in supporting political parties and trade unions, date back to the 1960s.[17] To the Germans those activities looked like natural expressions of solidarity with fraternal groups; so did the wider activities of the Socialist International and the Christian Democratic World Union. (By 1984, however, the Socialist International had broken with the Sandinista regime in Nicaragua over the latter's drift toward authoriarianism.) Americans, however, neither knew the history of those Europeans activities in Central America nor shared the perspective from whence they came. The activities thus looked, at best, like meddlings, at worst, as treacherous if they ran against the grain of American policy.

Central America was at least a complication in alliance relations. When, for example, the Reagan Administration early in its tenure made a hard sell to its allies of evidence that the Cubans and the Soviets had been involved in providing military aid to the rebels in El Salvador, Europeans were puzzled about what they were buying even if they found the evidence strong. Why was an American administration making such an issue with them of El Salvador? What lay behind the immediate pitch? When it ensued that some of the evidence was not genuine, that was even more disconcerting, and it damaged American credibility on other issues.

Trans-Atlantic strains over Central America and other regional issues besides southwest Asia will continue, mostly at the level of political symbols, even if the effects of these strains are not severe. In some cases the strains will reflect the global preoccupations of the United States in contrast to the more limited concrete interests of the Europeans. The cast of American politics will make for attentiveness to Soviet influence and threats of communism; from time to time that lens will predominate. By contrast, the influence of European unions, party foundations and multinational political organizations like the Socialist International will reinforce European tendencies to view regional issues, beyond Europe as well as within it, in terms of indigenous social change. It is all too predictable that from time to time those different political casts will sharpen and collide. As in the aftermath of the hostage crisis in Iran and the Soviet invasion of Afghanistan, American public opinion, angry and frustrated, will be looking for Soviet goblins behind regional turmoil. In those circumstances, European arguments will sound to Americans weak and self-serving, and their activities in the region may, as in El Salvador, be regarded as meddlesome.

HOW MUCH UNITY?

It has now become ritual on both sides of the Atlantic to assert that the gravest threats to Western security lie outside Europe, not within it. Yet that assertion papers over, rather than resolves, the differences of stakes, capabilities and perceptions of threat discussed in this chapter. It is much easier to agree on the ritual assertion than on what it implies for the actions of the United States and its allies, and for relations among them. In particular, agreement to the general proposition does not settle the question how much unity among the allies is necessary and how much is possible.

Answers to those questions are not easy to find. Yet several observations, parallel to those of the previous chapter, emerge from the foregoing. In some areas, less-than-complete unity between the United States and its allies does not seem bad, and may even be desirable. In analytic terms, given the political constraints on American action in the Middle East, it may have made sense for, say, France to have maintained links to Iraq that the United States could not. Even if the motivation for those links was the search for private benefits – Iraq agreed to increase oil deliveries to France in the late 1970s –[18] the ties may be in the collective interest by providing Iraq an alternative to complete dependence on the Soviet Union.

Even with regard to the Palestinian question, a different line of European policy may carry some advantages. At least it may maintain lines to the PLO that the United States does not have; it may to some extent diminish the Arabs vision of "Western" intransigence on the issue. And it may serve as a goad to the United States to re-think its own posture. For example, despite Washington's initial worries, the eventual form of the European Community's Venice Declaration of 1979 probably was helpful by linking justice for all (read Palestinians) to security for all (read Israelis). To be sure there are sharp limits on the utility of a different line of European action. Since the Europeans long since were dismissed by the Israelis as sold to the Arabs and since the Arabs recognize that only the United States can deliver Israel, that means that different European policies amount to putting pressure on the United States to put pressure on Israel. That is uncomfortable at best and puts the focus of strain from different approaches directly on European relations with the United States.

In many cases, however, American policies depend for their effect on some degree of cooperation by the Europeans. Even the freezing of Iranian assets in the United States during the hostage crisis, in form a unilateral action, depended on considerable (unadmitted) support from British and French banking systems if it were not to be circumvented. Similarly, American economic sanctions, whatever their political effect, would have had little economic bite without parallel European actions. In 1977 Iran received only 17.1% of its total imports from the United States but depended on the EEC for 43.3%.[19] If the United States pressed for economic sanctions against the Soviet Union in response to Soviet actions beyond Europe – as, for instance, after the invasion of Afghanistan – the situation described in the previous chapter would obtain: in gross economic terms the Europeans hold most of the cards, even if theirs are also declining; grain is the exception to that, but it is too hard in domestic politics; the United States has some means of extending its reach unilaterally, through European dependence on licensing agreements with American firms or through interlocking arrangements among banks, but that exercise of "extraterritoriality" is sure to be particularly resented by Europeans.

Even in the military sphere some degree of cooperation is necessary. Europeans generally share the feeling that the West needs to increase its military strength for contingencies beyond Europe. They have understood that they will be called upon to do more in the realm of defense, mostly inside Europe and mostly by meeting existing commitments. They, Germans included, took the point that American efforts in the Persian Gulf and Indian Ocean will mean some reduction in what the US can do in Europe, and they indicated a readiness to "fill the gap." The Federal Republic's willingness in the early 1980s to expand contingency plans for German naval operations in the Baltic was one evidence of that commitment.

Europeans can also contribute by allowing the United States more flexibility in the use of its forces stationed in Europe to meet threats beyond Europe. More sharing of such facilities as the Europeans have beyond Europe would also be helpful; American use of British-owned Diego Garcia is an example. British use during the Falklands crisis of the American base at Ascension Island, which is leased from Britain, was a twist which demonstrated that cooperation need not be only one way, Europeans aiding larger American efforts. American airlift in support of French and Belgian troops in Zaire during the second Shaba crisis in May 1978 was another such example.

The coordinated naval presence of the US, France, Britain and others during the early stages of the Iran-Iraq war in 1980–81 suggested the virtues of cooperation. It was only loosely coordinated; the French rejected any multilateral discussion, insisting that all consultations about their participation be only between them and the Americans, "great" powers consulting as equals. Yet the presence of more navies than that of the United States still reinforced the intention to deter any expansion of the war. Perhaps more important, the multinational character served to diminish concerns of local states that would have been aroused by a US-only force – for instance, that it was merely camouflage for an attack on Iran.

The multi-national force sent to Lebanon in 1982 initially had some of the same virtues, though changing circumstances made it a disaster in the end. In the summer of 1982 US, French and Italian units deployed to Lebanon as a peacekeeping force to oversee the withdrawal of PLO soldiers. At that point the multi-national character of the force muted any image of American predominance, and it gave the European participants some claim to participate in decision-making. When the force was returned in September and October, however, this time with a small British participation, fighting among the Lebanese factions soon resumed. In the circumstances the peacekeepers became identified as protectors of the government of Amin Gemayel, thus as partisans in the factional conflict. In October 241 Americans and 58 French were killed in simultaneous suicide bomb attacks. By February, public support in the United States for keeping the US troops there – then some 1500 – had completely eroded, and the Reagan Administration announced they would be withdrawn, apparently with little or no advance consultation with the allies.

On many issues American policies will depend on European assistance; that means Europeans can frustrate American initiatives even if they cannot implement their own. On other issues, European participation can raise the chances of success or diminish the risks and side-effects of American policies. Answers to the question "how much unity is necessary" slide from calculations about the substance of particular issues to the political costs of pursuing divergent policies. For example, an argument in substance in support of the European initiatives with regard to the Middle East of the late 1970s and early 1980s was outlined above, but there was also a substantive case against those initiatives: whatever European doubts about the Camp David peace process or about America's commitment to the Palestinian cause, those initiatives, undertaken in frustration, put little pressure on Israel while threatening to undercut Arab moderates by taking more extreme positions on the PLO than those moderates themselves.

As important, at some point those trans-Atlantic differences in approach, perhaps acceptable in substance, become unsustainable in alliance politics. Henry Kissinger said of the Middle East: "It is not helpful that there exists an American policy in the Middle East and a European policy for the Middle East. Unless they are coordinated, which they are not now, they run the risk of undercutting each other."[20] His comment is not necessarily correct about the substance of policy; in that sense both American and Europeans might be right. But he is almost certainly correct in assessing the political implications of divergences. Strains across the Atlantic set off by issues beyond

Europe are not likely to result in a major alliance crisis, though the Arab-Israeli tangle of issues should make for caution about too-sweeping assertions of that kind. What is more probable is that over time strains over issues beyond Europe could eat away at the basic trans-Atlantic relationship.

Mansfield-amendment style pressures from the American Congress to withdraw American troops from Europe have been quiet but not absent in recent years. In the 1960s and 1970s those pressures tended to come from the left of the American political spectrum, from those who simply thought the United States had too many commitments in too many places or who thought, like Mansfield, that improving East-West relations rendered the presence an anachronism.[21] (Interestingly,these liberals who fretted about too many and too fixed commitments had inherited that position from conservatives of a generation earlier, like Senator Robert Taft.[22]) Yet even in the 1960s and 1970s one of the currents in the move to withdraw forces had been frustration from the political right over the Europeans' failure to make common front with the United States over Vietnam. When pressures re-emerged in the 1980s, the came from the right: from neoconservatives, like Irving Kristol and Norman Podhoretz, who were tempted to condition the American troops presence in Europe on a tougher European position toward the Soviet Union, or from strategists and members of Congress, like Senator Ted Stevens, who thought that Europe should be able to defend itself or who would cut back forces in Europe to build up capabilities for use in the Persian Gulf.[23]

Those pressures, just beneath the surface of the political debate, could be awakened, perhaps dramatically, by a perception that Europeans were not doing their share to meet the real threats to security, threats outside Europe. Just as "division of labor" – the new label now in fashion – cannot mean that in Europe the Europeans pursue detente while Americans concentrate on defense, it cannot mean that beyond Europe the Europeans do the easy or nice things – providing economic assistance to Pakistan – while the grubbier, military tasks fall to the United States. Europeans must share risks as well as labors.

Isolationism, that proudest of traditions in American foreign policy, is dead, but its kin, unilateralism, has been a constant thread in postwar relations between the United States and its allies. It has been on the rise in recent years, partly reflecting nostalgia for past American strength, never mind how true the image, but also reflecting impatience with friends and allies. Europeans share some of that impatience, though for different reasons. It is part resentment at pre-emptory American tactics, for instance with regard to sanctions against Iran; part fear at where American actions are leading; and part awareness that the United States cannot or will not protect European interests outside Europe coupled with the knowledge that Europeans cannot do much on their own to compensate. The combination of those impatiences on both sides of the Atlantic is a recipe for serious strain in basic alliance structures.

THE SHAPE OF A BARGAIN

Issues beyond Europe give rise to a paradox which, like those that inhere in the nuclear issue or defense and detente in Europe, cannot be made to go away: European and American interests are somewhat different, and will remain so, a difference compounded by differing capabilities and perceptions of the threat. At the same time, the United States is, and will remain, dependent to some degree on European actions. Interests may diverge but dependence continues. No grand bargain or formula can make interests identical, but dependence provides incentive to try to manage those differences. The guidelines for managing this set of issues run parallel to those for defense and detente in Europe: a recognition that interests differ, and a "division of labor" based on that recognition; plus shared risks and shared decisions commensurate with stakes and contributions.

Most of those differences of interest are of long standing: witness the global responsibilities of the United States by comparison to more limited European stakes. Some are sharper now, due to the West's increased interest in the Middle East and Gulf, Europe's greater dependence on Gulf oil or, more generally, to the changed balance of power between the United States and Europe which has made Europeans less reluctant to articulate differing interests. Those differences of interests are natural enough in an alliance of sovereign nations. They are hardly pernicious, even if to talk of them is uncomfortable. Yet to pretend there are no differences runs far greater risks over the long term. It would misconstrue the problem of coping with issues beyond Europe in the alliance, thus increasing the chance that the nations on both sides of the Atlantic will see actions by others as capricious, or weak, or disloyal. What is necessary instead is the recognition over time, by both leaders and publics, that different interests may lead to different approaches and that, within limits, those differing approaches are acceptable. There is still an argument to be had over where the limits lie. But that should be the form of the argument, not mutual accusations of short-sightedness or treachery.

Similarly, the history of the postwar period should drive home the lesson that neither Europe nor America has a monopoly of wisdom. That seems particularly the case with regard to issues beyond Europe. It is of course the hardest lesson to remember, much less to institutionalize in interallied dealings. But it should make for more modesty, on both sides of the Atlantic, in pressing views on the other. At least it should make for more reluctance to take the failure to agree as a sign of weakness or insensitivity.

What is true of interests is also true of capabilities. Several European states will have some military potential beyond Europe, but that will be modest. There is no escaping that fact. To press hard for them to do more outside Europe would be expensive for little gain; it makes sense for them to concentrate whatever more they can do on defense in Europe, not outside it. Similarly, the political constraints on American policy with regard to the Middle East are a fact of life. To say that is not to justify the lack of effort to relax them, just as recognizing European limitations in defense is not to excuse the failure to do more. But plainly the United States will find it difficult to frame venturesome policies toward the PLO, even if the American president were inclined to do so.

That suggests the rough shape of a "division of labor," though the term is unhelpful. It conjures up a degree of formal negotiation that is not, in fact, likely to be the case and would, as an objective, only lead to disappointment. The bargain will have to be rough and mostly implicit. Of course, to the extent that parts of the bargain could be explicitly negotiated, the analytics suggest that could be desirable, reducing temptations to free riding by assuring all the countries that if they do more their partners will do likewise, and by a given amount. Yet the obstacles are formidable. The "bargain" would be one across apples and oranges, virtually impossible to make commensurate. All the nations would have every incentive to argue that all the things they planned to do anyway would fulfill their part of the bargain. That would hardly diminish free riding, and it would produce more acrimony among the allies than the results would be likely to justify.

For all those reasons the bargain should be more political than formal, more implicit than negotiated. The United States will continue to have a comparative advantage in building military forces for contingencies beyond Europe, and it is logical that it bear the brunt of doing so. In the military realm, France and Britain have some existing capabilities which are worth maintaining: the French presence in the Gulf and Africa, residual British responsibilities in the Gulf, plus Britain's limited capacity to move forces. For the other European states, any military activity beyond Europe will be occasional and largely symbolic, though important for the reasons mentioned below.

Inevitably, most of what Europeans can contribute will be financial and political: economic assistance from Germany and others to Turkey, Pakistan and other important countries (Germany, France and Britain provided $325 million in economic aid to Turkey in 1981, and $240 million to Pakistan);[24] similar French activities in Africa and elsewhere; British military training and economic assistance and so on. The problem of course is that these actions will look to Americans easy or commercial by comparison to American military efforts. European political approaches will be even more liable to generate misunderstandings. It will remain easier for Americans to accept in principle that French relations with Iraq are in the collective interest than to deal with the specifics of European policies that seem to cut across American efforts. It goes without saying that those difficulties will be all the greater for sensitive questions, ones more deeply enmeshed in American politics, like the Palestinian issue.

There is no easy way around those difficulties. What is important is that Europeans share, and are seen to share risks as well as tasks. That makes it crucial, for example, that Europeans participate in Western military efforts beyond Europe, even if that participation is as much symbolic as real: American use of European-owned bases outside Europe, participation in naval maneuvers beyond Europe, clear flexibility for the United States in using European facilities and European-based forces for non-European contingencies, and the like. That symbolism will be crucial to managing the politics of the issues beyond Europe. Without it the Americans, in Congress and elsewhere, could come to see Europeans as prepared to spend billions insuring against military contingencies in Europe that are, admittedly, the worst but also the least likely, while unwilling to do much about more probable military contingencies outside Europe. If there is anomaly in a Europe unable to defend itself without America, so, too, is it anomalous that thirty-five years after the war the United States is still the pre-eminent military protector of Western interests outside Europe, interests that are easily as important to Europe as to America. Those perceptions, already present, could grow to constitute a threat to basic trans-Atlantic links.

Clear European participation will also be necessary if European governments are to have claim to a voice in American deliberations. For the United States the obverse is also true, as underscored in the previous chapter: if Americans expect Europeans to participate in ways that are helpful, they will have to be prepared to concede a measure of influence to Europeans that has not been customary in trans-Atlantic relations. If the United States wants – and needs – a broader pattern of cooperation, it will have to be prepared to concede some of what Adenauer and de Gaulle sought a decade ago, and what Eisenhower and his successors resisted: serious European participation in decision-making. As elsewhere in the relationship, that is hard; it runs against ingrained habits on both sides of the Atlantic. It requires real sharing on the part of Americans and real responsibility on the part of Europeans. But, from a narrow US perspective, it will be the only way to limit European temptations to free riding, and to call forth the degree of European participation on which many American efforts will depend for their success.

STAKES AND CONSULTATIONS

It is not easy to imagine that this rough bargain could be managed over the long run. Certainly, no deft innovations in process will make it easy to manage; no new committees or forms of summit meetings between the American president and his colleagues will suffice. It is more a matter of habits of thought than of organization. Certainly the first necessity, for this set of issues as for others, is for Americans and Europeans to be frank in discussing their differences. For their part, Americans are prone to deal with their European allies almost in psychological terms. They presume that Europeans surely will follow an American lead if just the form of consultation is right. Process becomes a substitute for substance. Worse, Europeans abet that tendency. A parade of European leaders to the Oval Office during the Iranian hostage crisis told President Carter that Europeans agreed with his analysis of the situation and view of the threat; differences were only over tactics. Plainly that was not true. There were different analyses in Europe, different interpretations of threat, stakes and vulnerabilities.

There was a certain logic to that degree of European deference a generation ago. So long as the central European preoccupation was deterrence in Europe, their interests ran to reassurance. In that sense their interests were much like they still are on the nuclear question. The substance of American policy was less important than the fact that

Americans were confident in it. Now, however, neither European deference nor American preoccupation with process makes sense. The former does not reflect European interests, and the latter will not suffice to call forth European cooperation.

Serious trans-Atlantic discussion of stakes and perceptions should not be allowed to bog down in marginal issues of process or organization. One of those is the geographical scope of NATO. The United States and its allies need to talk frankly and cooperate better. Whether that takes place inside or outside NATO is a secondary matter, at least in the short-run; NATO has a role to play, but the allies do not find it impossible to cooperate if the will is there, and institutional issues should not be allowed to hang up the debate. Expanding NATO into a fully global Alliance is attractive but improbable, less because of the limits of the North Atlantic Treaty or of France's strict constructionist attitude toward it than because of the differences in perspectives and stakes separating the United States from its European allies, especially the smaller ones. It is not worth spending much effort, or many political chips discussing that question. Over time, interests beyond Europe should make for broader NATO consultations. Recent NATO ministerial meetings went much further than before in explicitly recognizing the need to meet threats beyond Europe and the implications for NATO of efforts to do so.[25]

Yet it is intolerable that how Europe and America consult about a major matter of foreign policy beyond Europe often is itself a political issue. Witness the unhappy minuet that ensued when the United States sought to arrange a summit of the major Western foreign ministers in the early aftermath of the Soviet invasion of Afghanistan. In February 1980 France said it would not participate in a US – proposed meeting of allied foreign ministers to discuss the crisis. French Prime Minister Barre said that "France does not wish to contribute to any reawakening of the Cold War by adopting an extreme attitude."[26] Europeans fear that consultations mean only opportunities for American arm-twisting. The United States sees a cacophony of European voices or, if the Europeans insist on concerting themselves in advance in EEC political cooperation, becomes impatient with the delay or the comprised results that emerge.

NATO at least has the virtue of providing a routine place to talk about political and military issues inside Europe. By most accounts, for example, NATO's contingency planning during the recent Polish crisis was tolerably good. Problems arose after the imposition of martial law in December 1981 because the allies could not agree on what the contingency was: Washington saw it as tantamount to a Soviet invasion, while the Europeans tended to view it as bad but far from the worst outcome.

The allies lack equivalent means for dealing with issues outside Europe. What is needed is a mechanism for beginning to prepare now for the next Afghanistan or the next Iran. That sort of contingency planning is hard for governments to do on their own, harder still when cooperation with other governments increases the risk of leaks that could produce the results that planning aims to avoid. New mechanisms should be more restricted in participants rather than less – even given the natural resentment of the smaller NATO members – and less rather than more formal. The loose grouping of the seven countries that take part in the Western "economic" summits is about right, although there will remain the familiar problem of how those deliberations feed into other insititutions with an interest, NATO and the EEC in particular.[27]

Inevitably, dealing with issues beyond Europe will involve considerable *ad hoc*-ery. Discussions will center on specific questions and involve those allies with interests or with something to contribute. The analytics suggest the possible virtues of somewhat more formal coordination, particularly among the Europeans. That should bring aggregate capabilities more into line with interests, and thus reduce the chance of what looks to Americans like free riding in European dealings with the United States. To some extent political consultation in the EEC does seem to produce that effect – EEC declarations on the Middle East, for example, have been more "moderate" than those of individual European nations, like France. Yet that may ensue more because compromise among ten very different nations results in a lowest common deonominator than because collective procedures produce more sense of "responsibility," at least by American lights. For most issues, however, the EEC is too big and cumbersome, with too many participants with little (or idiosyncratic) stakes, unlikely to take quick or decisive action (though sanctions against Iran are an example to the contrary).

There is no shortage of mechanisms if the will to cooperate exists: bilateral consultations of various sorts; *ad hoc* discussions among more than two allies; the four power group – the US, France. Britain, and the Federal Republic – justified by Berlin but in fact dealing with a range of issues in and beyond Europe; the seven summit powers; EEC political cooperation; and NATO itself. The only justification for creating any additional machinery, for instance as the outgrowth of the

Western summits suggested earlier, would be to diminish the risk that the US and its allies would have to start afresh in each new crisis, having learned nothing from the previous ones, or that how to consult would itself be the first issue of contention. Form should not drive substance; what we say matters more than how or where we say it.

There also seems little alternative to more summitry in dealings with regard to both Europe and beyond. The reasons grow directly out of the changes in the structure of trans-Atlantic relations: European acquiescence can no longer be taken for granted; issues are more imbedded in domestic politics on both sides of the Atlantic, and heads of state will be reluctant to delegate to subordinates much lattitude on questions which more and more affect political survival; and alliance relations involves more and more intersections among issues of different sorts, with only heads of state in a position to decide those trade-offs. For instance, Chancellor Schmidt frequently asserted to semi-private meetings that he, President Carter and their colleagues had fixed the outlines of what became the December 1979 NATO decisions on intermediate-range missiles at the Guadaloupe summit in January 1979. That meeting clearly involved bargaining across a range of issues from missiles in Europe, to SALT, to issues beyond Europe, to the dollar.[28]

The advantages of summits and the lack of alternatives are clear. But so are the risks. The more private they are, the greater the likelihood that conversations will be frank and serious business will be done. But greater also will be the chances that the memories of summiteers will be different, that they will not clearly de-brief their subordinates, or that bargains will be forgotten. For example, President Eisenhower surely understood that he and British Prime Minister Macmillan had done a deal in March 1960: the United States would support the British nuclear deterrent by letting Britain buy a new American missile, Skybolt; in return, Britain would let the United States use the submarine base at Holy Loch, Scotland. But it suited the interests of neither man to make that link explicit, and so the respective agreements made no mention of it. The link was hardly forgotten by Macmillan and his colleagues, but it was lost in the American transition to the Kennedy Administration. It was eventually rediscovered but not before a serious row in Anglo-American relations; Washington at first assumed it was Britain's responsibility to devise an alternative when Washington cancelled the Skybolt missile on cost-effectiveness grounds.[29]

Summits also, by their nature, depend critically on the personal chemistry of the heads of government. If that is bad, direct contacts between leaders can become unhelpful or worse. For example, during the early stages of the Federal German election campaign in the spring of 1980, Chancellor Schmidt several times used language in speeches that seemed to call for some sort of moratorium on deployments of intermediate-range missiles in Europe, though he did not use the word "moratorium." That sounded, to Washington, like precisely the "negotiate-before-deciding-to-deploy" strategy NATO had explicitly rejected in December 1979. If Schmidt did not mean a freeze on both sides, then he was suggesting only that the Soviet Union freeze its systems while NATO proceeded ahead with preparations for its own deployments, an unlikely possibility. Each time, the language touched off a minor row with Washington, and in June President Carter sent the Chancellor a letter that even the State Department characterized as "rather brusque." In the end, the Germans insisted, not very convincingly, that Schmidt had been misunderstood.[30]

What is striking, however, is that by that time relations between Schmidt and Carter, and between their machines, were so bad that no one could pick up the telephone and ask frankly what was afoot. If, as is likely, Schmidt's language was primarily for domestic political consumption, that would still have worried Washington because of its possible effect on the Netherlands or Belgium which had not yet agreed to accept the missiles they were scheduled to receive. But it would have changed the form of the concern.

Another example, discussed in the previous chapter, is the row over President Reagan's decision, hard on the heels of the Western Summit in June 1982, to extend the ban on exports related to the Soviet gas pipeline being built by the Western Europeans to European subsidiaries or licensees of American companies. European leaders felt not only angry in substance but deceived: all the signals before and during the Summit had indicated that while the United States opposed the pipeline, it was prepared to treat it as a *fait accompli*, with only direct American participation ruled out. But all accounts, Mr. Reagan had not taken the final decision at the time of the summit; it was to be in some measure contingent on what the Europeans were willing to do in reducing Western credits to the Soviet Union, and it was finally taken in some pique when the United States got much less than it wanted on the credit issue.

That sequence all too graphically illustrates the problem: European surprise suggests that the ceremony of the summit pushed aside any serious discussion of how entrenched the positions of the two sides were and how summit outcomes might bear on related decisions. Having become routine, the summits were occasions only for reassurance or ritual agreement, not for serious business. That has become the case with the seven-nation Western summits;[31] it is even more of a problem for NATO summits, which are twice as large and briefer. Yet if summits cannot prevent public rows over issues they discuss immediately beforehand, it fair to ask what they can do.

Here as elsewhere in coping with the European-American relations, there are no panaceas, certainly not in process. There is no alternative to recognizing that differences across the Atlantic exist, that some are real but not all are intolerable, and discussing those differences frankly. One implication of that discussion is likely to be to make clear that NATO is a limited regional alliance that must be buttressed by other arrangements beyond Europe. NATO's claim on American money and attention would be correspondingly reduced. That is hardly an appealing outcome. But it is better than what might ensue from an accumulation of trans-Atlantic misunderstandings papered over by appeals to solidarity. The real danger for NATO is not that it will be seen as ineffective, only irrelevant. In the early days of NATO, there was a neat one-to-one correspondence between the nature of the perceived threat to Western security and the scope of the institution designed to deal with that threat. That is no longer true. NATO, even if effective, will seem, particularly to Americans, relevant to only a narrower and narrower slice of the security threat Europe and America confront.

5 The Impact of Economics

In his ill-fated "Year of Europe" speech in 1973 Kissinger asserted that "political, military and economic issues in Atlantic relations are linked by reality, not by our choice nor for the tactical purpose of trading one off against the other."[1] At that time, however, Europeans feared that the Administration's purposes were precisely tactical – to use its military pre-eminence in the alliance to extract economic concessions from its allies. In January the dollar had been devalued, for the second time in two years. In June, amid deep concern over steep inflation, President Nixon announced a package of economic measures, including a request for authority to control agricultural exports. Controls on soybeans were put in place by July, to the dismay of Europeans. At the same time, the United States was pressuring its allies to offset the "additional" cost occasioned by the stationing of US military forces in Europe, rather than in the United States; this action by the American Executive occurred under the shadow of Congressional threats, led by Senator Mike Mansfield, to withdraw some American forces from Europe. And in the autumn the Arab oil embargo turned the Year of Europe into a year of European–American bickering.

Kissinger's comments appeared ominous because they seemed to cut against postwar practice among the allies. Typically, economic and security issues had been kept apart, with policy-making proceeding down separate "tracks" dominated by distinct groups of experts. Separate tracking seemed to many to reflect a hierarchy of values in the alliance, with security as a collective good paramount, "high politics." The allies also shared an interest in an open international economic order, but that was secondary. In particular, keeping quarrels over specific economic questions, "low politics," separate minimized the chances, in this logic, that those wrangles would damage the pre-eminent security interests of the allies.

Yet this distinction between "high" politics and "low" can mislead.

123

Economic issues might have been "low" politics by comparison to the force of appeals to shared security interests, but they were sometimes "high" domestic politics within the allies. Decisions were directly connected to jobs and domestic prosperity, hence to the political prospects of national leaders. Of that, national leaders had no doubt. The force of those issues in domestic politics increased over time, especially for the United States, the subject of this chapter's next section. That political dimension, once arisen, often acquired a life of its own.[2]

Within economics, trade and international monetary affairs also were generally handled along separate tracks, despite the clear connection between them: if the currency of any ally increased in value relative to those of its trading partners, its exports became more expensive and its imports from others cheaper. International money was, day-to-day the preserve of technical specialists, bankers and central bankers. Critical decisions, tightly held, went straight to the top of government. For example, the decision to devalue the American dollar in 1973 was worked out in a week of discussion between Treasury Undersecretary for Monetary Affairs Paul Volcker and European and Japanese counterparts. Only a handful of senior officials in Washington, plus a few others at Treasury and the Federal Reserve, even knew what was afoot.[3]

In the years around the Kissinger speech, there were reasons to believe separate tracking was coming to an end. Security and economic agendas among the allies seemed likely to cross more frequently in the future, whether by conscious tactical choice of national leaders or, as Kissinger implied, through the force of changing circumstances as reflected in the demands of domestic politics. The place of both security and economics in the alliance seemed to be changing.[4] With a relaxation of East–West tensions, at least in Europe, the preeminence of security objectives was less certain.

At the same time, as the allies coped with recession and inflation after 1973, economic interests became more salient. That was particularly so for the principal ally, the United States. There had been a tolerable domestic consensus in the United States in favor of "benevolent" policies toward Europe – exporting dollars through keeping large number of American forces in Europe, for example, or letting the Germans systematically undervalue the Deutschemark in an effort to spur exports – so long as the costs of those policies were negligible or barely visible.

Yet as the costs of "benevolence" became more apparent, the

United States was bound to be tempted to "behave like one of the rest." As efforts to maintain the value of the dollar ran against goals of domestic economic management or undercut the competitiveness of American exports, pressure built to change the parity of the dollar. As American industries began losing exports to European (or Japanese) competition, they began to demand national action on their behalf. All these pressures argued not merely for changed or more aggressive economic policies *vis-à-vis* American allies; they also seemed to suggest that the primacy of security over economics would be less sacrosanct.

Yet the predicted end of separate tracking has come true only in part. It does seem evident that citizens on both sides of the Atlantic now notice connections among economic issues more than in the past. That is my first conclusion in this chapter. And the "atmospheric" connection between economics and security alluded to by Kissinger has become somewhat stronger: there is more risk that cumulating disputes over one set of issues will make it harder for the allies to cooperate in pursuit of shared interests in the other – a second conclusion. Yet specific linkages between security questions and economic issues have continued to be rare, my third conclusion.

The managing of economic and of security issues in the alliance are bound up with each other, but in ways that are most often vague, elusive of specific description. Several connections between economics and the nuclear issue were touched on in earlier chapters. One is the special sensitivity of the nuclear question, hence its role as a kind of barometer of the trans-Atlantic relationship. When there are strains between Europe and America for other reasons, including economics, the nuclear issue emerges as a symbol of Europeans' lack of confidence in the United States.

The second connection is the domestic counterpart of the first. It was striking the extent to which anti-nuclear sentiments of the early 1980s reflected generalized insecurity, borne of economics as well as fears of nuclear war. "Not only is the world a more dangerous place, but I can't find a job either," the protesters seemed to be saying, sometimes almost that directly.[5] Difficulty in managing national economies made it more difficult for governments to manage the nuclear issue. The failing was domestic, but to the extent people recognized the international aspects of their economic straits, it was also an inter-allied link between economics and security, albeit an indirect one.

Most of the connections across the economic and security agendas are of this atmospheric type, whose effects are hard to calibrate. Wrangles over, say, macroeconomic policy no doubt feed frustrations on both sides of the Atlantic: European feelings that the United States is not reliable and American urgings toward unilateralism, a longing to go it alone. Both sides find it harder to infuse their deliberations with sensitivity to the other's politics. Parochial concerns gain ascendency, and cooperation across all issues becomes more difficult.

POSING THE ISSUES

To judge by recent writings, if the Atlantic alliance does not break apart over policy toward the Soviet Union, it will divide irreparably over economic issues. Growing protectionism to the point of trade wars, increasingly divisive debates over national economic policies, and the collapse of international financial institutions: these are the stock-in-trade of popular commentaries.[6] Yet debates over economic issues run through the history of trans-Atlantic dealings. So the question again intrudes: what has changed? How different is the framework for managing the alliance now than in the past? Are current disputes sharper than past ones, and thus more likely to leave enduring bitterness in their wake?

A first approach to those questions is to recognize that, in concept, economic issues among the allies differ in several ways from security matters. In both there is an element of shared interest – collective good – but that collective good is less tangible in the case of economics. NATO's defense arrangements produce a collective good – security. That is not tangible, but the arrangements themselves are fairly concrete – troops, tanks and aircraft. The good may be valued differently by different members of the Alliance, and all may be tempted by free riding, since all would prefer that their partners provide the lion's share of the collective good. Yet they would all agree that the security arrangements have value for all.

Economics is different. The set of trade and financial arrangements of which the United States and Western Europe (and Japan) are the center – the international economic system – may usefully be conceived as a collective good, for all the reasons outlined in chapter one: all participating nations can be better off, or at least no worse off, because arrangements exist; one nation's enjoyment of the "good" does not necessarily diminish another's; and so on. But the arrangements that constitute the system – the rules, norms and practices – are both intangible and of little value in themselves. What nations value are the trade and investment opportunities made possible by the system, along with the happy consequences for their political relations of those rules.

Economics is different from security in another way as well. There is a much more explicit element of competition to collective arrangements in the former than in the latter. As Chapter 1 noted, the principle of comparative advantage says only that there can be gains through trade. It does not say anything about how those gains will be distributed. One trading partner could take all the gain, the other none. Thus, the allies have cooperative interests in sustaining economic arrangements that will permit them to realize gains from trade, but their stakes in how those gains will be distributed are competitive.

Moreover, in theory if I produce only grain and you produce only computers, we can trade to enjoy the benefits of comparative advantage without our products competing with each other directly. In practice, however, we will only discover – and be driven toward – our comparative advantage through competition. Thus, competition between firms in the United States and its allies is the point of the open economic order. It is not a sign that collective arrangements are breaking down, but rather that they are working well. That observation is trivial, but it is so often lost in dire prediction about the consequences of growing "economic competition" between America and Europe.

Competition across states enhances competition with states, hence the competition is inherently political, another important difference between security and economics. The interests of citizens of a particular NATO member may be seen as roughly similar: all would prefer as much security as possible, and all would prefer that their state pay as little for it as possible. Of course, the real world is not precisely like that. Security decisions divide citizens of a particular nation in the ways that appeared over and over in this book: those decisions involve how much risk to bear and how, who will bear it, where weapons will be located, whose economic oxen will be gored by restraining trade with would-be adversaries, and so on.

Yet economic issues are inherently adversary within countries as well as between them, in a way that is much more visible in economics than in security. Even if trade based on comparative advantage could make every nation richer than it would be without that trade, the same cannot be said of every citizen of every state. The process of adjustment to different economic acitivities can be painful, as we have seen again and again. Comparative advantages probably suggests that neither the United States nor its allies should be in the business of producing steel; rather they should be shifting to higher technology goods. But making such an adjustment would mean losing jobs for steel workers, depressing particular regions of countries – costs that are hardly shared equally across citizens of one society.

In open political systems the effects of that kind of need for adjustment become political issues. Groups hurt by the process of economic adjustment seek assistance or protection from their governments to soften the impact. Often they get it. Governments respond, compelled by the claims of domestic politics or motivated by arguments that other national interests outweigh purely economic calculations. Those forms of government assistance or protection then become issues between states, as well as within them; what looks necessary to one nation is perceived as unfair competition by its trading partners. Politics is inherent in the process of adjustment.

The central question surrounding Western economic relations are difficult to pose, let alone answer: are trans-Atlantic differences of interest in economic issues becoming much sharper? If so, to what effect? How do the continuing tensions in trade and economic dealings affect national attitudes toward other basic alliance arrangements, including those in the realim of security.

These questions, especially the last, are seldom addressed, even badly. Like the other issues in this book, they are difficult to answer, with messy reality seldom yielding definitive answers. It is not easy to dig into the critical details of how nations manage economic issues. Economic issues, arcane and technical, have attracted fewer case studies and less of the insider journalism than the "sexier" security topics in alliance relations.[7] These obstacles are reinforced by the separate tracking of economic and security issues among the allies. Thus the number of people, in or out of government, trained to deal with the intersection of economics and security is small. Moreover, most analysts who try come from traditions of political science or political economy. Their interests run to structure, to how the international economy is changing, not to the issues of alliance management in the context of domestic politics that are my concern.[8]

As a result, serious assessment of the implications of economics for alliance relations is even rarer than for other issues. As for other issues, it seems that things are worse now than in the past, but saying exactly why is even more difficult. By the same token, memories may mislead; past episodes are past, thus are bound to look pale by comparison to problems that lie ahead. Yet the US and Western

Europe have been arguing over EEC Common Agricultural Policy (CAP) since the beginning of the Common Market: witness the "chicken war" of the 1950s. In the 1960s and early 1970s American balance-of-payments problems were explicitly at issue across the Atlantic and became implicitly linked, through the Mansfield Amendments, to the maintenance of the existing level of American military forces in Western Europe. The issue has receded, but remains beneath the surface, a point repeated in earlier chapters.

The allies disagreed sharply in the wake of the 1973 energy crisis. And arguments over basic economic strategy, reflected in disputes over interests rates or currency values, had become almost habit by the early 1980s. During the 1970s Europeans worried that the US was pursing too expansionary an economic strategy, thus pressuring them to do likewise. By the 1980s, European concerns had reversed: the tight American monetary policy driven by enormous budget deficits would send the West into a downward economic spiral. The concern had shifted but was no less sharp.

From a historical perspective, not much has changed despite all the disputes. The international trading system has not collapsed; quite the contrary, despite concern over rising protectionism on both sides of the Atlantic, the system probably is more open now than two decades ago. Americans have, for example, complained, justifiably in their view, for several decades about the discrimination inherent in EEC trade arrangements. Yet the total imports of EEC countries grew from 12 percent of their gross domestic product in 1953 to 24 percent in 1980, an increase that reflected not only a relative rise in trade within the community but also a relative rise in imports from outsiders.[9] Similarly, with imaginative management the international financial system has coped, successively, with the dollar devaluations of 1971 and 1973, with the multiplying of world oil prices in 1973 and again in 1979, and with the need to bail out Brazil, Mexico and other industrializing countries in the early 1980s. To be sure, many of the more recent "successes" are yet fragile. There was bitter controversy in 1983 in the United States over replenishing the International Monetary Fund; international responsibilities bumped against the politics of financing national budgetary deficits.

WHAT HAS CHANGED?

So are there reasons to believe that economic dealings will be more divisive among the allies in the future than in the past? There are several. The first and most general is that more people, on both sides of the Atlantic, recognize the impact of economic dealings with the other. The salience of economic issues by comparison to security questions in public opinion has been mentioned in earlier chapters. Virtually every recent poll reports similar findings on that score. The lack of good time-series data makes it hard to support more detailed assertions, but other findings point in a similar direction. For example, a 1982 poll asked people in eight of the allies to choose from a list of ten sources of current international tensions. "U.S. interest rates and the dollar" was picked by 45% of the French (more than any other item, with "superpower activities in the Third World" next with 29%), 28% of Germans, and 19% of Italians.[10]

This attentiveness to economics has been due, in part, to recession. People everywhere have become more attentive to foreign "threats" posed to domestic jobs or income. Once alerted, they will remain attentive even during periods of economic growth. Throughout the postwar period, Europeans have been more dependent on trade than has the United States, and they remain so. Aggregate trade is, for example, about four times as important to the Federal Republic as to the United States; German exports amounted to 25.6% of German gross national product (GNP) for 1981, while American exports totalled only about 8% of American GNP.

Yet if trade remains more important economically to Europeans than Americans, it has none the less become dramatically more important to Americans than it was. In 1950 only 6.4% of US final merchandise sales was exports; that reached 9.0% in 1970 and leaped to 19.7% in 1980. As both Americans and Europeans face increased competition from newly industrializing countries in Asia and Latin America, they will have all the more reason to notice the effects of foreign competition, even from each other.

For the United States, some numbers help explain this increased attentiveness. In 1949 the United States had not only a strongly positive trade balance over-all, it also had a surplus in every industry category save petroleum, where the negative balance was small.[11] By 1960, however, that had changed. The US had negative trade balances for food, crude materials, fuels and basic manufactures, although with the exception of fuels, none of these deficits was large when compared to exports. The differential competitiveness of distinct categories of American industries was becoming clear: by 1960 older industries, such as footwear and textiles, were in trade deficit while industries with intermediate and advanced technologies still had trade surpluses. By 1970 these differences were more pronounced. Textiles, and iron and steel were in deficit even though they were protected by "voluntary" agreements negotiated during the 1960s. American imports of auto-mobiles significantly exceeded exports. Conclusions about these aggregate categories must, however, be treated as no more than suggestive, since some particular industries – cheese and toys, for example – were worried about foreign competition virtually from the start of the postwar period.

What seems clear is that "American" interests in the international economic order became more diverse. In the 1950s an open interna-tional economic order was relatively costless for most Americans: the United States had a trade surplus in the over-all merchandise account, and the international involvement of corporations was small, all the smaller for banks. By the 1960s, however, American labor had reason to oppose growing competition and to seek protection from it; competition meant lost jobs which, at best, meant painful transition for workers and losses in membership for some unions.[12]

The interests of industry were split. Those industries whose domestic operations were threatened by foreign competition became protectionist; those that depended on exports remained in favor of openness. The value of direct US investment abroad increased ten-fold between 1950 and 1975, further diversifying the interests of American business. In some cases industries escaped foreign competi-tion by moving abroad; in others, it was protectionism *abroad* that they sought to avoid by moving. After 1958 when European currencies became convertible, American banks also began moving overseas, enhancing their interest in open international arrangements. In 1960 the assets of foreign branches were a scant 1.3% of the total assets of American commercial banks; by 1973 they were 14.2%.

It is also hard to tot up the changes in the balance of political interests. The American labor movement has, on balance, probably been protectionist for most of the postwar period. In a recent poll, only 21% of labor leaders (but 81% of business leaders) opposed tariffs. What occurred in the course of the 1960s and 1970s is that several important labor organizations, like the United Auto Workers, former-ly free traders, switched sides. The gap in attitudes between "leaders" and the public at large always has been big, and it remains so. In the same 1982 poll cited above, "leaders" strongly (67%) favored eliminating tariffs – though support for that position slipped from 75% four years earlier. By contrast, 57% of the public thought tariffs were necessary.[13]

Similarly, the role of the American Congress also has been

ambiguous. In the late 1940s, the period current writings often see as
the beginning of a golden age of free trade, Congress would not
approve the proposed International Trade Organization, leaving the
General Agreement on Trade and Tariffs (GATT) as an enduring
stop-gap. In 1962 Congress passed the Trade Expansion Act enshrin-
ing liberal principles: reducing tariffs was the goal, and the Congress
was prepared to defer to the Executive in trade negotiations. The same
year, however, Congress created the White House Special Trade
Representative (STR), in large measure because it felt that the State
Department, then handling international trade negotiations, was not
sufficiently attentive to domestic interests. (The Reagan Administration's proposal two decades later to merge STR and Commerce in a
Department of Trade suggested that events had come full circle: yet
another "domestication" of negotiating structures seemed necessary
to insure that domestic interests would be represented.)

Or the 1974 Trade Act, while still liberal, was markedly less so than
the Trade Expansion Act of 1962. It reflected the first increase in
Congress' role in trade negotiations since 1934; as it extended
negotiating authority in to the new area of non-tariff barriers, rather
than merely giving Congress a veto power, it stipulated that negotiated
changes in those barriers had to be accepted by Congress within 60
days. Congress also instructed the President to take restrictive
measures against countries that maintained "unjustifiable or un-
reasonable" import restrictions against the United States.[14]

What seems clearer is that American attitudes in the early postwar
period owed partly to a conjunction of special circumstances. America's commitment to the role of alliance leader was reflected in the
enthusiasm for – and relative benevolence of – the Marshall Plan and
the willingness to overlook European deviations from economic
openness during the process of reconstruction. Long years of Democratic majority had left a few southerners at the head of the relevant
Congressional committees; they were in a position to exercise the
commitment of their region's agricultural exporters to oppose industrial tariffs and promote exports. They were joined by some disting-
uished free-traders who had survived from the pre-war period, and by
economists, professional advocates of open markets and non-
discrimination, who had been projected by the New Deal and World
War II into senior planning positions in Washington.[15]

This conjunction of circumstances could not last. America began to
behave like other nations. Its sense of special responsibility became
more and more tinged with the feeling that the United States was

specially vulnerable to the unfair practices of others. Given American pre-eminence, the early postwar international economic arrangements gave pride of place to the particularly American preferences for letting the market work and for limiting the role of government in economic transactions. Preferential arrangements within the EEC ran against those predilections from the start, a fact first accepted and then more and more resented.

Other changing circumstances of international economics also made those American preferences less tenable.[16] Japan's growing involvement in international commerce was based on a national economy structured very differently from the American assumptions. So, too, were those of most developing countries and of the socialist world. The enormous growth of multinational corporations put the lie to the presumption of disinterested sellers and buyers dealing with each other at arms' length. Those multinationals also seemed to decide where goods would be produced for reasons that sometimes had little to do with comparative advantage. That was even more obviously the case for state-owned enterprises, which seldom were allowed by their government patrons to rise and fall with changing terms of trade.

Finally, the growth of barter trade – direct exchanges of specified imports and exports – by Eastern countries, developing nations and others inherently discriminated against the exports of third countries. That trade also began occuring in forms that made prices arbitrary or non-existent. While barter trade has remained small, probably less than ten percent of world trade, it has served to undercut further the initial American presumptions on which the open international trading arrangements were constructed.

Paradoxically, the regime of floating exchange rates after 1971 also contributed to making citizens on both sides of the Atlantic more aware of the effects of actions taken by their partners. Under the earlier system of fixed rates, decisions about currency parities were in form political – national decision-makers could make deliberate choices within economic limits. Occasionally, those choices became issues in domestic politics. The pound sterling, for example, came to be a symbol of British prestige in the 1960s. Successive London governments feared for their survival if they had to devalue it, and the domestic austerity measures necessary to keep it overvalued called forth support across the political spectrum. Yet since rates changed seldom, there was little public awareness of the economic effects of changes in currency values. In the United States, international money was seldom an issue in domestic politics. Congress was involved only in the initial postwar discussion of the monetary order in 1945–47 and, to a lesser extent, in the creation of Special Drawing Rights in 1965.

On the face, the move to floating rates should have made the issue less political. Market forces were to determine currency parities, not explicit decisions. In theory, government interventions in the market were merely to smooth fluctuations. (In practice, they have been more than that.) Yet, paradoxically, currency parities have become symbols in a new way; links between economic issues have become clearer, not less so. Public attention has turned from one set of policy measures – exchange rates – to another, more political still. When the dollar rises, not only do American exporters know their competitiveness is declining, but attentive publics in Europe see the constraints on their own economic management.

For instance, in the years after 1978 American interest rates were extremely high in an effort to contain domestic inflation. Yet with open capital markets those interest rates also attracted capital movements to the United States, driving up the dollar to a degree not reflective of underlying competitive conditions. Between 1978 and 1981, for example, currency movements made American exports 50% more expensive by comparison to the Japanese yen, while American inflation rates were 20% *higher*. For the US, that encouraged foreign imports, thus fuelling protectionist pressures. It also meant that Europeans (and Japanese) had to sustain higher interest rates than they would have liked lest their currencies depreciate further. Those high interest rates in turn impeded their economic recovery. When, as in 1977–78, US interest rates were low and the dollar weak, the consequences for Europeans were the obverse.

In both cases, Europeans saw themselves as the victims of American economic decisions driven entirely by domestic US priorities. Under the system of fixed rates, sustaining particular parities sometimes required, as in the case of Britain, much higher interest rates that leaders or publics desired. But with flexible rates the effects are more visible; there is no hiding behind particular parities as God-given, immutable. As one recent European analysis put it: "The United States is no longer strong enough always to have its own way, but neither is it so weak that it must take account of the wishes of its partners."[17]

If there are reasons why both Americans and Europeans are more sensitive to international economics, they are also at least as able as in the past to exert influence in national processes of governance to protect their interests. The classic study of American trade policy demonstrated more than two decades ago what seemed intuitively logical (and also runs through many aspects of public policy): specific, narrow interests were more likely to become aroused – and to lobby effectively – than broad, diverse ones. Hence medium-sized companies dependent on sales of a few products were more likely to become concerned about foreign competition than large diversified companies; within large companies, sales departments worried about competition from foreign imports were more likely to become vocal than were purchasing departments whose interests were served, in general, by access to cheaper imports.[18] The coalition of free-traders, loose and with diffuse interests, never has become organized in a way comparable to specific sectors hurt by foreign imports.

In the United States, these groups with special interests have been more and more able to trigger the attention of Congress. Congress has not granted what the groups sought – specific quotas or relief for one sector. Instead it has responded in line with American presumptions about how international commerce ought to be conducted. It has established procedures, like the quasi-judicial International Trade Commission, to make judgments about whether particular forms of foreign competition are unfair by American lights and thus justify relief to particular domestic industries.[19]

In Europe, the forms of relief granted to particular groups are different, but the process of seeking it is similar. For example, European consumers pay for the EEC's Common Agricultural Policy (CAP); in fact, they pay twice, once through taxes to subsidize higher prices and then through the higher prices themselves. Yet consumer interest, diffuse and unorganized, has been no match for the strong and specific interests of farmers, organized to keep cheaper imports off grocery shelves and to keep up farm incomes.

THE RISK OF SHOCKS

The risk of shocks to the economic system is a final reason to believe economics may be more divisive among the allies in the future. Shocks have divided the allies in the past; there is every reason to believe they would be more so in the future. Predicting the inherently unpredictable is a fool's bargain, but two possibilities stand out: a new oil shock and a collapse in the international financial system. In both cases, divisiveness would be increased by mutual perceptions of asymmetrical advantages; each side of the Atlantic would see the other as having special advantages in coping with the crisis or special blame for having produced it.

In international finance, the sheer size and speed of interactions is terrifying, and seem in themselves to imply the risk of a crisis. With open capital markets, any Deutschemark can be converted into dollar assets almost instantly, thus capital washes back and forth across the ocean. In 1981, the total debt of developing countries was $520 biliion, up from $71 billion ten years earlier. On the other hand, the imaginative recycling of petrodollars – finding safe and profitable investments for the surpluses of oil-exporting nations – has exceeded almost all expectations. In a system as complex as international finance, the risks of a serious crisis are themselves complex.[20] Yet for this analysis it suffices to observe that the chances of a major crisis are not zero. The possibility of a shock is there.

In thinking about a possible crisis, the weight of the United States in the system and the particular connections between domestic US and international financial markets are central. Overall, between 1974 and 1979, by illustration, there was no outflow of dollars from the United States through current accounts transactions; the years of large deficits were offset by years of large surplus. Yet during the same period outflows of capital from private agents, banks and official institutions amounted to $80 billion. Those eventually returned via purchases of US Treasury bills by European and OPEC central banks, and, to a much smaller extent, private agents. The outflows promoted international liquidity, but the inflows complicated the US task of managing its domestic money supply.

If a crisis were to occur, America's pre-eminence in the international economic system would mean Europeans would lay most of the blame on the United States. That would clearly be so if an American action seemed to touch off the crisis, as happened with the dollar devaluation of 1971. One future such instance could be an American effort, taken in frustration at a failure to control the money supply, to exercise some control over Eurodollars – assets held abroad, mostly in Europe, but denominated in dollars, totalling $1400 billion in 1981. Or, more extreme still, the United States might try to cut off dollar outflows. Neither move is likely because of the technical difficulty of doing so and because of the risk to US banks. But improbable American actions, taken in frustration, are hardly absent from the postwar history of economic affairs. Yet even if the crisis were not so closely connected to American action, Europeans would feel that the sheer weight of the US in the system meant that it could force, as in 1971, the burden of adjusting to the crisis on the Europeans.

The other candidate shock is oil. Notwithstanding the glut of the early 1980s, it is probable that some set of events will seriously disrupt the supply of oil within the next decade or so. Candidate scenarios abound: even more disastrous outcomes of war between Iran and Iraq; threats leading to the effective closure of the Straits of Hormuz; internal collapse in Saudi Arabia or another important oil-producing state; civil war leading to destruction of fields or ports; or a dozen others. None is likely. But that one will occur is probable. And it bears remembering that, depending on how tight the oil market is at the time of an interruption, even interruptions that involve fairly small total amounts of oil can multiply prices and set off a scramble among the allies. The price shocks of 1973 and 1979 were touched off by interruptions that initially took only small percentages of the world's oil supplies off the market. As prices rose, oil companies and others sought to build up inventories as a hedge against further price rises; this scramble then drove prices up further.

Such a shock could provoke the whole range of inter-allied strains evident in 1973. (A prolonged period of oil glut could also lead to strains, but those should be relatively manageable.) As in 1979, the oil-sharing arrangements of the International Energy Agency (IEA) might not be triggered. If they were, the chances are that they would not work well and would make people on both sides of the Atlantic resentful to boot. As with financial shocks, the two sides are likely to see the other as having advantages in dealing with the crisis. Europeans would see the US as in a privileged position due to its own domestic production and the proximity of "safer" producers like Mexico. (There would be similar perceptions within Europe of Britain and Norway, and considerable tension over their policies.) Both Europeans and Americans would want the other to begin releasing government oil reserves first; both would feel let down when neither acted.

Moreover, the American attitudes toward government planning and business-government relations mentioned earlier bear directly on energy. By tradition and practice, the United States is different from most of the European countries and quite different from some. By tradition it is standoffish in business-government relations, hence finds it unpalatable and difficult to plan to, say, mobilize private oil reserves. For the same reasons government stockpiles are hard to fill, prone to disappear and politically difficult to use. The US oil industry remains dominated by the large multinationals, not flexible enough to make the kinds of creative arrangements with oil producing states that will be required.

In sum, Raymond Vernon's conclusion about American perceptions of Japanese advantages during an oil crisis would hold true, in varying degrees, of how Americans would view Europeans: ". . . the United States is likely to see itself cast in the role of the country bumpkin – unheeding before the fact, unprepared after it, and unable to learn from its experience. Where the interests of the two countries clash, the fact that the Japanese have their plans and policies under better control will be felt by some Americans as being vaguely unfair."[21]

ECONOMICS AND SECURITY

People in both Europe and America now pay more attention to the place of economic issues in their relations. Yet despite that fact, specific linkages between economics and security have continued to be the exception, not the rule, contrary to predictions of a decade ago. It is hard to point to an example of a specific, tactical linkage in European–American relations comparable to the Okinawa-textiles deal struck by President Nixon and Japanese Prime Minister Sato in 1969.[22] Economics and security intertwined in the disputes over Soviet gas pipelines, in both 1962 and 1982. But in those cases the allies disagreed along both dimensions: the United States Administrations saw pipelines as dangerous dependence on the Soviet Union for modest gain to domestic economies. In contrast, the European governments calculated their domestic economic gains as significant and regarded a small increase in energy dependence on the Soviet Union as preferable to the alternatives.

In the instance of Okinawa and textiles, talks over the reversion of Okinawa to Japanese sovereignty were proceeding, but efforts to reach agreement on quotas for Japanese textile exports to the United States continued to founder on Japanese internal politics. The two leaders at the summit apparently struck a deal: reversion of Okinawa on Japanese terms – that is, no exception to Japan's normal policies on nuclear weapons for US bases on Okinawa – in exchange for a textile quota. In that instance the linkage was a disaster all around: when the deal leaked, Sato was roundly criticized at home, all the more because linking Japanese sovereignty to mere economics looked tawdry in

Japanese eyes. When Sato was unable to deliver, Nixon and Henry Kissinger felt betrayed, a fact which played some role in their subsequent offhand treatment of Japanese political interests.

The most specific linkages in trans-Atlnatic relations have centered on the presence of American troops in Europe. But those have been less tactical than driven by the interaction of the American Executive and Congress. No Executive has wanted to withdraw American forces from Europe, but many of them have confronted Congressional pressures to do so. Those Congressional entreaties have taken a variety of forms; they also have reflected a variety of motives, but economics has been prominent among them. In response, the Executive has used Congressional pressure as a tactic, arguing to Europeans in effect that, against its will, it must ask the European allies to do more for the United States lest Congress retaliate by drawing down American forces.

The link began in 1961. Faced with mounting balance-of-payments deficits, first the Eisenhower and then the Kennedy Administrations pressed the Germans to "offset" the foreign exchange costs of keeping US troops in the Federal Republic by buying American weapons.[23] Bonn agreed in 1961, and for the next few years the arrangement was relatively painless for Germany which was in any case committed to major new purchases of American aircraft.

As economics the deal made little sense: there was no reason to separate a bilateral account from the overall American balance of payments, less reason to isolate a so-called "military" sub-account, and still less to argue that the sub-account in turn should be balanced by German "military" purchases in the United States. It was in any case hard to make a compelling case that German purchases made under the arrangements were much larger than they would have been without any agreement. Economically, the "offset" arrangements were a side-show to the more serious American purpose – inducing the Germans and other Europeans to hold dollar reserves and not to exchange them for gold. But once the bilateral "offset" arrangement had been established, domestic American politics made it difficult to abandon.

The arrangement came to crisis in 1966, with a recession and a weak government in the Federal Republic. American pressures on "offset" played some role in bringing down the German government of Ludwig Erhard in the autumn of 1966. After difficult negotiations, both within Washington and with the new German administration, Bonn and Washington agreed in May 1967 to a new package. The US would withdraw up to 35 000 soldiers from Germany, and the Germans would both make new offset payments and make public their undertaking not to exchange dollars for gold – in effect agreeing to finance American balance-of-payments deficits to the full extent of German surpluses.

The link was reinforced by Congressional pressure. In September 1966, January 1967, and at intervals thereafter, Senator Mansfield introduced sense-of-the-Senate resolutions calling for substantial reductions in American forces in Europe. Money was no part of his argument – he believed that the US had too many commitments in too many places and that the warming East-West climate made existing levels of American forces unnecessary. His Senate supporters brought varied motives – some agreed with him, some were angry at Europe's tepid support for the United States in Vietnam – but they included those whose focus was economics. In any event offset was useful to the Executive in disarming Congress: if offset could be used, by whatever tortured logic, to suggest that it cost no additional foreign exchange to keep troops in Europe, then pressures to draw down the garrison could be undercut.

After 1971 the regime of floating exchange rates drained away whatever economic logic the offset arrangements ever had. There was little economic reason to "offset" any balance-of-payments "deficit"; under floating, overall deficits or surpluses would be taken care of by the market through changes in currency parities. However, Congressional attempts to force withdrawals of American forces from Europe continued, coming closest to succeeding in 1973. The form of the economic/security link changed, prefiguring the shape the issue took when it re-emerged a decade later: money concerns shifted from the balance of payments to the budget, and the Executive tried simultaneously to prod Europeans to do more and to convince Congress that they were – either in improving their own forces, especially through the activities of the Eurogroup (the European NATO members save France), or by compensating the US for the "additional" budgetary cost occasioned by stationing the troops in Europe rather than in the United States.

However, the force of the offset/troops link dissipated in the early 1970s. As the allies adjusted to floating exchange rates, American officials began to accept the German view that offset was economic nonsense. Against growing concern about Soviet capabilities and intentions, Congressional pressures against the stationing of troops in Europe subsided; there was, for example, no whisper of interest in a

Mansfield Amendment in 1975 or 1976. And in 1976 President Ford and German Chancellor Schmidt pronounced the traditional offset arrangement dead.[24]

However, some link between troops and money was not dead beyond resurrection. American pressures on Europeans, especially Germans, to do more on defense lest Congress force the United States to do less never entirely ended.[25] And the link re-emerged at the end of the decade, as previous chapters have outlined, reflecting growing American frustration and impatience, particularly in Congress, with the allies. If earlier congressional pressure had come more from the political left, among those who thought the United States was doing too much, this time it came from the right, among those who thought the Europeans were doing too little in the common effort to contain Soviet military power. The concerns expressed in the defense debate of October 1982 were typical.[26] The United States seemed to be doing too much, the Europeans too little. Lest the point be lost on Europeans, the Senate Appropriations Committee called for freezing US troops at their 1980 level, 331 700, thereby saving nearly fifty million dollars. The message to Europeans was clear and familiar: do more or we'll do less.

For the foreseeable future, these specific linkages will continue to be exceptional, rather than common practice among the allies. And if any ally is both tempted and in a position to forge such explicit linkages across economics and security, that will be the United States. The reason is straightforward: for the foreseeable future, the United States will remain more pre-eminent in the alliance in military terms than in economic. Hence the Executive may be tempted, or various interest groups may seek through Congress, to use the asymmetrical pre-eminence as leverage to extract economic concessions. Yet those linkages will be rare because they look crude, hence are resisted by the government's foreign policy managers, because they are hard to manage tactically, all the more so given what remains of "separate tracking," and because, as both crude and hard to manage, their consequences are unpredictable even to those who launch them.

At the same time, both the special American military role in the alliance and the presence of US forces in Europe as a symbol of that role will continue. No matter what the Executive does, there will be those in Congress, like Senator Stevens or Senator Mansfield before him, who will argue that the troop presence is large beyond need. As in the past, the arguments why will vary, but economics will sometimes be among them. Politicians may pick up the argument, as did Senator

Gary Hart during the Democratic presidential primaries in 1984. and so there will be pressures, usually implicit, sometimes pointed to by Executive Branch officials in sorrow as a fact, for Europeans to do more or pay more or concede more. That will amount to an intermediate link, between the general texture of the trans-Atlantic relationship and specific tit-for-tat deals between economics and security. At best it is a constant reminder to Europeans of their uncomfortable dependence; at worst it is a stick for beating Europeans, one members of Congress can use for their own purposes, economic or other.

It is intriguing that attempts to use the US military position to secure specific economic advantage never have touched the nuclear guarantee. American pre-eminence is much starker in that realm than in conventional forces. Moreover, conventional forces "only" cost American citizens money plus the threat to 300 000 American soldiers in Europe. By contrast, the nuclear guarantee compels Americans to run risks of nuclear war on Europe's behalf. Linkages to the nuclear umbrella have not been made primarily because the umbrella itself is intangible. Because it is not clear what it takes to extend the umbrella, neither is it obvious what would retract it, so threats to do so would not be very credible. No one, certainly not the French, thinks, for example, that France in unprotected by American nuclear weapons because it does not participate in NATO's military command. Nor would threats to reduce nuclear protection be commensurate with *any* economic demand, hence such threats would look dishonorable. Threatening to withdraw conventional forces "only" threatens the Europeans with having to do more themselves or accept more reliance on nuclear weapons to deter the Soviet Union.

For their part, Europeans will be unable to forge tactical linkages between economics and security simply because they lack the wherewithal to do so. The asymmetry of the relationship leaves them little scope to seek economic advantages through threats to security arrangements, or vice versa. The asymmetry is enhanced because "Europeans" do not act as one. All forms of bargains across issues will not, however, be precluded. European leaders, as in the past, may condition their acceptance of particular American initiatives on a forthcoming US attitude on other questions: the 1979 Guadeloupe summit, for example, apparently produced a rough bargain that ranged from interest rates and economic stimulus to cruise and Pershing missiles, and arms control.[27]

Similarly, European resistance to American initiatives in the realm of security sometimes reflects economic concerns, a negative sort of "bargain." European spending on military hardware in the United States is at least five times the flow in the other direction. Thus, Europeans resist American calls for new technology in conventional weaponry in part because they fear that the lion's share of that new technology will be made in America. That reluctance will be increased in the 1980s by deep European worries that their economies are falling behind the United States and Japan in advanced technology. So signing on to new technology as the central thrust in improving conventional defenses in Europe is doubly bad: buying more in the United States and financing further American leads in advanced technology in the process.

The baseline for thinking about how security and economics will interact in future trans-Atlantic relations is a projection of recent experience. That experience provides grounds for expecting the atmospheric connection to grow stronger, though not dramatically. Americans in particular, but Europeans as well, more and more will recognize that their well-being is affected by the actions of others, including allies. That sense of vulnerability, new in American experience, will color attitudes toward cooperation in general. If Europeans are perceived by Americans as narrow or selfish in economic terms, it will be more difficult to mobilize public and Congressional support for forthcoming attitudes on security questions. Similarly, if Europeans see the United States as arrogant and heavy-handed on economic issues, they will find it harder to support American initiatives on other issues. They will also be reluctant if those American initiatives seem notably tinged with economic self-interest.

Logically, this kind of atmospheric connection should be stronger during times of lesser preoccupation with the Soviet threat. In those circumstances, hitching economic grievances to security issues should seem less risky to contemplate, and leaders on both sides of the Atlantic should find it harder to argue that their publics should pay some economic price for Atlantic solidarity in the face of the Soviet threat. Suppose, for example that the deep recession of the late 1970s and 1980s had coincided with a period of East–West relaxation comparable to the early 1970s. Trans-Atlantic arguments over the sharing of burdens might have been much sharper, and the allies, especially the United States, more willing to threaten to do less in security if partners were not more forthcoming on economic issues.

Yet, with economic issues now more on the minds of both American and Europeans, even times of East–West tension might not suppress economic issues on national agendas. The poll data on European public opinion cited in Chapter 3 suggested precisely that: Europeans remained just as concerned about economic issues and just as committed to domestic social welfare spending after East–West relations turned cold in the lat 1970s. And if, as in that period, Europeans regard the United States as partly to blame for that tension, they will be even less likely to downplay concerns over economics.

American military pre-eminence in the alliance, and US conventional forces in Europe in particular, will continue to be both an atmospheric connection and a temptation to make specific linkages. Yet specific deals across agendas will continue to be rare. American leaders will be more tempted by them than will their European counterparts. In some cases, Executive Branch officials may seek to avoid making a link but may, as with offsets in the 1960s and 1970s, feel compelled to do so by Congress. Or, as with textiles and Okinawa, they may feel that linkage is the only way to solve their domestic political problems. For these reasons, specific linkages across economics and security, when they occur, are likely to be haphazard, sometimes confusing to their intended targets and usually counterproductive.

The haphazardness is more likely because specific linkages will arise, when they do, often out of personal contacts between heads of government. "Separate tracking" has meant that economics and security seldom cross, organizationally, short of that level of government, in either European machines or the American. Government officialdom everywhere hates summits because heads of government may not follow their scripts. The 1982 Versailles summit bespeaks the dangers. When President Reagan felt deceived by his European counterparts, especially French President Mitterrand, over the East–West trade issue, by all accounts he reacted in pique, retaliating by extending the ban on sales for the Soviet gas pipeline to also cover European subsidiaries of American companies. The result was a disaster all around: the United States was forced to back off but not before major feuding in the alliance. In other cases, when linkages arise out of the interplay of the Executive and Congress, resulting actions may be nearly as haphazard, and their effects nearly as unpredictable.

THE PATTERN OF POLICY–MAKING

Most of the time, then, the impact of economics on security dealings is indirect. Wrangling over economics gives rise to political issues that acquire a life of their own in the alliance, thus affecting the climate for cooperation on other questions. And in most of the instances when the damage has been the greatest, the pattern seems painfully plain: actions on economic issues were taken with too little regard for the interest in sustaining the alliance framework of cooperation. "Separate tracking" was too separate. Longer-term interests in the alliance never got injected into policy-making, were weak by comparison to other, more immediate "domestic" interests at play, or were dismissed as special pleading by the stripey-pants diplomats for "good relations" with foreign countries.

The pattern runs through a number of recent episodes. Several examples will underscore the point. The 1973 American decision to place export quotas on soybeans, for example, was perceived as an entirely domestic decision. The State Department was not involved at all in the initial decision, though it was called in to help pick up the pieces after the dismay of American allies and other trading partners became clear.[28] Similarly, Henry Kissinger, then Assistant to the President for National Security Affairs, was out of the game; he was represented only by a new junior staffer, whose role was limited to keeping abreast of what was afoot.

In restrospect, the whole affair looks unnecessary. Soybean exports were first embargoed on 27 June 1973, then placed under controls on 2 July, but all restrictions ended by 1 October. Yet in the process the United States incurred the costs of appearing an unpredictable trading partner and an unreliable ally. Warnings about the dire international consequences of imposing controls probably would not have carried the day against the idea, not with prices skyrocketing and farm prices in the lead. Yet it seems apparent that some of the worst international consequences could have been reduced had the process been different. At least a minumum of early warning to allies was compatible with the need to prevent advance notice of impending controls from leaking and setting off speculation on soybean markets. The risks of speculation were certainly no greater than for exchange rate changes, import controls or limitations on capital movements – all of which have been subjects of consultation among the allies in the past.

The package of economic measures taken two years earlier, in 1971, ran along a similar pattern. On 15 August 1971, President Nixon announced the "unthinkable," a package of economic measures that cut against everything his Administration had been saying for the previous months. All of those actions had some impact on American allies and trading partners, but for several measures the impact was immediate and direct: most important, the President in effect let the dollar float, by cutting it loose from the historic $35 an ounce of gold price, and the package also included a number of trade policy decisions, prominent among them a ten percent import surcharge.

Again, the economic context as it translated into domestic political pressures on the President drove the decision process.[29] Unemployment was higher than predicted, and inflationary pressure in the economy remained strong. Internationally, the US balance of payments was deteriorating sharply, and confidence in the dollar was eroding. There was a run on the dollar in early August; overall, the United States paid out approximately $3 billion (of a total holding of $14.5 billion) in reserve assets between January and September 1971, 40% of that in early August.

Organizationally, the central actors in the decisions were the President's senior economic advisors, the Troika so-called – Treasury Secretary John Connally, Chairman of Council of Economic Advisors (CEA) Paul McCracken, and Director of the Office of Management and Budget (OMB) George Shultz; with Federal Reserve Chairman Arthur Burns added, the Troika became the Quadriad. Of these, the dominant figure was Connally, newly arrived in the Cabinet (February 1971) but already in command of the process and with the President's ear. International events – the run on the dollar in early August – provided the stimulus to action, but those events then became the occasion for a momentous set of domestic and international economic measures – what Herbert Stein of the CEA called the "biggest weekend for economic policy since Roosevelt closed the banks."[30]

The President hastily convened his senior advisors at Camp David on 13 August. As with soybeans, none of the officials with responsibility for "foreign policy" was included. Secretary of State William Rogers was not invited, though he was consulted by telephone several times, Henry Kissinger was in Paris for peace talks with North Vietnam, and no one on either of their staffs attended the meetings. The circle of Washingtonians who were privy to what was going on widened on Sunday, 15 August, but not by much. Secretary of State Rogers informed the Japanese and Canadians (the two main US trading partners) only an hour before the speech, and the director of the International Monetary Fund received only a few minutes advance notice.

Predictably, the allies were aghast. While they generally were pleased with the announced wage and price freeze – since it meant the United States was getting serious about inflation – the rest of the package was dismaying: the end to dollar convertibility seemed high-handed, the import surcharge discriminatory, and the rest of the trade measures ominously protectionist. Connally proposed, and the President initially acquiesced in, tough tactics once the "gold window" had been closed, the US could afford to wait, and it would up to the Europeans (and Japanese) to propose new currency realignments (a devaluation of the dollar); meanwhile, the import surcharge would put pressure on them to be forthcoming on the currency and other trade issues.

Kissinger, deeply involved in secret peace talks with the Vietnamese and in preparations for both a Moscow summit and the breakthrough with China, first continued to remain aloof from discussions; apparently he was regarded as an interloper in international economics, and so he seems to have regarded himself. He became engaged only when he became convinced, and could persuade the President, that those issues threatened his business. The United States could ill afford to go to Moscow and Peking with the Western alliance in disarray. Thus, in December he temporarily wrested the negotiating mandate from Connally and worked out an agreement on currency parities with French President Pompidou at a summit meeting in the Azores, an agreement regarded by the Treasury as an excessive concession on the US part. (Kissinger's reticence to enter the economic arena paralleled that of his successor in the Carter Administration, Zbigniew Brzezinski. The latter was inactive during the European–American bickering over economic policy and the value of the dollar during 1977–78, becoming engaged only when he could convince himself that the division threatened "national security," his domain and expertise.)[31]

Also as with soybeans, my hunch is that better representation of general "foreign policy" interests in sustaining a framework of cooperation with allies would not have changed the decisions. The domestic context was overwhelming. The (few) men who participated in the decisions were fully aware of how momentous they were; that pushed all of them in the direction of assembling a broad package, not quibbling over details of its constituent parts. Even though the decision arena was limited, a fairly broad range of considerations seems to have been brought to bear. After the fact, even those who had opposed the import surcharge as unnecessary because currency parity changes would bring the US foreign exchange position into balance, and needlessly embittering to boot, probably agreed that it had been a useful bargaining lever with America's trading partners.

Yet those judgments need to be qualified in two respects. First, as with soybeans, the need for secrecy probably was compatible with more advance warning to allies. That was true even if Washingtonians deemed that real consultations – for instance through the IMF on the monetary issues – would not serve American purposes. Participation by "foreign policy" officials at Camp David and before would at least have impelled attention to allied reaction. It also might have reduced the frustration and sense of conspiracy which ran through many parts of the American bureaucracy in the wake of the Camp David meeting.

Second, while deliberations up through Camp David addressed a wide range of considerations, critical dimensions of the decisions were missing. Most obvious, there was little attention to what would happen after Camp David. What was the "right" price for the dollar? What were appropriate negotiating tactics? What kind of an agreement was sought? Some of these issues had been discussed within the government, but Camp David was launched with little serious attention to them. Nor was there any attention to related questions of how the economic decisions meshed with the broader international context. The decisions surely reflected a desire to "get tough" with the Europeans and Japanese over trade and the sharing of defense burdens. But how they fit with SALT, or with the upcoming Moscow and Peking summits, or with US interests in a European Community that was about to expand to include Britain, Ireland and Denmark: on these questions the deliberations were silent.

The steel dispute of 1982 also illustrates these perils of separate tracking, and suggests that the dangers hardly are limited to American policy. In January 1982 seven US steel producers filed petitions with the US Department of Commerce and the US International Trade Commission (ITC) alleging unfair subsidies on steel imports from 38 producers in eight countries, seven of them in Western Europe. On 10 June Commerce released a preliminary finding confirming unfair subsidies on exports from six of those countries, all in Western Europe. That finding came just before the Versailles summit and one week after the US and the European Community had begun discussion of an agreement to voluntarily limit EC steel shipments to the US. The preliminary finding was confirmed on 25 August. At that point the action shifted to the ITC, whose role it was to determine whether the unfair subsidies had done "material injury" to US producers.[32] Under the pressure of an October deadline for the ITC determination, in September the US and the EC reached an agreement to limit European steel exports to the US.

What is notable about the case on the American side is that, at least until June, the issue lay squarely within the domain of Commerce and ITC. Indeed the proceedings were quasi-judicial. Their purpose was to determine if domestic industry had been injured. There was little way – and from the perspective of those in charge of the issue, little incentive – to bring a broader set of concerns to bear. The State Department and even the Special Trade Representative (STR) had little access to the process, despite the obvious implications it had for their concerns. Both became active only after June, when a major trans-Atlantic row was already underway. Whether the timing and substance of the Commerce determinations served broader American interests, for instance in sustaining a climate of opinion in Europe conducive to the deployment of the Pershing and cruise nuclear missiles if need be, or whether there was another way to provide relief to American producers: these questions were hard even to pose before June.

Handling of the issue by European governments appears similarly narrow. One man's unfair subsidies are another's export promotion, but since the eventual Commerce determinations found subsidies ranging up to 26% of the value of the imports, the Europeans can hardly have been unaware of the potential problem. Yet is was equally hard for them to conjure creative approaches consistent with their broader interests, at least until very late. Domestic interests were pressing. Their steel industries were already in the process of painful contraction; in the circumstances no one was likely to suggest agreeing to still further limits on exports, at least not before US actions compelled such agreements.

MANAGING THE INTERSECTION

There are no obvious remedies for these perils of separate tracking. Day to day, separate tracking serves to insulate economics from security; it makes the allies less likely to condition specific actions on strict reciprocity from each other, especially across issues. Yet separate tracking also means that when those economic dealings come a cropper, relatively minor issues will become major irritants in trans-Atlantic relations.

As for other alliance issues discussed in this book, it would be useful for both policy-makers and commentators simply to recognize that there will be occasional disputes over economic issues and that those will strain alliance cooperation across the board. In some instances the United States and its allies ought to try to agree to disagree, to recognize that the best they can do is limit the damage. If my conclusion is correct – if economic disputes and their spill-over on other alliance arrangements will be greater in the future but not dramatically so – the damage should be manageable. At least that should be so absent the bad luck of a serious economic shock.

As so often in these pages, the guidance from past cases runs less to the process of alliance relations than to the substance of national policies. It would help if issues of international economic issues among the allies were better managed in their own terms. If so managed, they would less often give rise to issues in alliance politics whose effects then outlive the original disputes. Spelling out policy directions for international economics goes well beyond my purposes, but the example of American trade policy will serve to illustrate both the potential of and the obstacles to doing better.

The United States might, for example, seek specific bargains – over the behavior or state-owned enterprises or trade in services – with relatively small numbers of countries, instead of relying only on universal negotiations through GATT.[33] These bargains, unlike the restraints on trade negotiated with specific countries in the past, would be intended to contribute to opening markets, not to closing them in an orderly fashion.

Yet constructing such limited bargains goes against the grain of American practice in business-government relations, as discussed earlier. In the circumstances of the 1980s the United States would need to convince other countries that they had something to gain from entering into these bargains, as well as something to fear if they did not. That would mean equipping the American Executive with even more scope for imposing the results of negotiations on US industry than has been true in the past – Congress prepared to commit itself to the results in advance of negotiations and affected industries and their unions also visibly prepared to abide by the results. Such arrangements are not entirely unprecedented. Under the terms of the 1974 Trade Act, Congress agreed to consider, quickly and without amendment, any trading codes negotiated by the Executive under the terms of the Act. In return, particular members of Congress participated in the negotiations.

Yet the kind of arrangements comtemplated here would go well beyond that process under the 1974 Act. Even if they could be put together in American domestic politics, they would still raise uncomfortable implications for US allies and trading partners: an American Executive empowered to negotiate specific bargains designed to expand foreign trade and to make those bargains stick would also be powerfully equipped to restrict trade or to demand tit-for-tat reciprocity from partners.

If such limited bargains governing trade could be constructed, they would aim to pre-empt the resort to unilateral processes like those in American decision-making with regard to steel. The Commerce and ITC procedures for determing unfair subsidies were unilateral, reflecting national notions of fair play. They could be triggered by particular industries; once triggered, the quasi-judicial character of those procedures put them beyond the reach of foreign policy managers, even those at the top of the government. It would have been hard to lift the steel issue from its tracks in 1982 even had the dangers of the existing handling of the issue been more apparent than they were. In the instance of steel, separate tracking was too separate.

Early warning of economic issues or actions likely to cause trouble with allies is by nature hard to achieve.[34] Action on economic issues is spread across the government and beyond it, in agencies and institutions unfamiliar – and often impenetrable – to foreign policy managers. Even if those controlling an issue do not, as in steel, regard the intrusion of others as illegitimate, they will still resist it: witness the US Treasury in 1971. Or foreign policy managers, like Kissinger and Brzezinski, may be reluctant to become involved in economic issues, either because they are slow to recognize their importance or because they feel themselves interlopers on arcane and unfamiliar terrain.

Tinkering with government organizations will not produce the early warning, though it may help. What is needed is more a broadening of the task of alliance management, along with modest expectations – by all concerned, in and out of government – about how much early warning actually can be achieved. Certainly a State Department long on expertise and interest in economics, like that under Secretary George Shultz, helps. So does the presence of officials with broad international perspectives as key senior officials as Treasury, Commerce and the like. Similarly, a White House foreign policy operation, most likely in the National Security Council, strong but behind the scenes, could play an important role if it were stronger in economics than most have been. It would possess both the broad view essential to early warning and the legitimacy of Presidential authority needed to lift particular issues from their routine tracks. Counterpart officials and procedures, in and around the offices of prime ministers, are at least as necessary in Europe, where cabinet government often consigns particular issues more firmly to single departments than is the case in the United States.

An intriguing example of an enduring institutional link between economics and security is the alliance's (the NATO countries minus Iceland plus Japan) COCOM procedure for controlling the export of sensitive commodities to the Soviet Union and other Warsaw Pact countries. COCOM prohibits the export of technologies on three lists.

Of those, the most controversial among the allies is the third, that covering items with both civilian and military uses; moreover, some of those items are also available from non-COCOM members.

Drawing a balance sheet of COCOM's pluses and minuses is elusive. Participating nations sometimes simply have evaded restrictions. Flows of technology are notably hard to control, and sensitive technologies have leaked to the East from nations outside COCOM. There is no clear line between "civilian" goods and those with military potential. Computers help planned economies allocate resources as well as target missiles. Disagreements among the allies over the export of oil and gas extracting technology, recurrent in the last two decades, illustrate the problem of exports that might not contribute directly to Soviet military potential but that might do so indirectly by contributing to Soviet infrastructure, thus making military operations easier or more efficient.

Finally, technology moves abroad through exports of scientific know-how and production processes, not just products. At the prodding of the Reagan Administration, the allies moved to tighten COCOM restrictions and, in particular, to focus on know-how and key technologies, not commodities.[35] Predictably, however, it has been even harder to agree that a particular technology has military potential than to agree that a given product does.

Western exports of high technology may *both* aid the Soviet Union *and* confer economic benefit on the exporter. Measuring the security risks of particular exports, much less comparing those to the economic and political benefits (or costs) of the transfer is probably impossible. COCOM has never tried; it has never defined a systematic rationale for restricting particular commodities.[36] The other COCOM members reacted lukewarmly when the Reagan Administration proposed giving COCOM a small staff and attaching to it a committee of experts to advise on the military effects of particular transfers.

In the end, the main virtue of COCOM is probably that it exists. Its restrictions amount to a kind of lowest common demoninator on which the allies can find some consensus. Just as the allies do not agree on the nature of the Soviet threat in general, they are not likely to concur in assessments of the risks and benefits of particular exports of technology. Yet, just as the allies can agree that the Soviet threat is real and needs to be countered, so, too, can they agree that some commodities should not be exported to the Soviet Union. The task for alliance managers is to work, quietly, from the margins of that basic, if vague, consensus.

Whatever the conclusion about COCOM, the history of economics in trans-Atlantic relations underscores the risks of specific, tactical linkages between economic and security issues. Hence it counsels caution, particularly for the United States, in framing such links. They are hard to manage and to calibrate; as with offset, linkages begun for tactical purposes may gather other, more durable purposes and governmental proponents, and so become difficult to break once established. They may arise haphazardly out of relations between the Executive and Congress, and thus have unpredictable consequences for both their ostensible sponsors and their targets. As an instrument in managing alliances, they are to be resisted. The recent record has been tolerably good; but pressures to make tactical linkages will grow.

It will be harder to cope with the "intermediate" link – the temptation to attach other purposes or conditions to the stationing of American forces in Europe. However, either it serves *American* interests to have a credible American military presence in Europe or it does not. If it does, as I believe, then conditioning that presence on Europeans doing or paying more in some other realm is to make a threat that either is not credible or is risky, since carrying it out would only run counter to America's own interests. Nor is there any escape from the logic which suggests that it may be rational for Europeans, especially the smaller nations, to make less proportional effort than the United States, no matter how frustrating that may be for Americans.

Those who argue for reducing the US military commitment or threatening to do so if Europeans are not forthcoming need to recognize that they are arguing that the commitment is not in the American interest. They must have a clear notion of why it is not, of what alternative security arrangements in Europe would be preferable to the current state of affairs, for all its frayed edges, and of how we get there from here. In particular, arguments for threatening US troop withdrawals to goad Europeans to pull up their socks in their own defense are to be treated with particular suspicion. Why should they respond as Americans hope? If they did, would Americans – or Europeans – like the result? For example, with American ground forces withdrawn from Europe, the Federal Republic would be providing over 60 per cent of NATO's ground forces on the Central

Front, instead of the current 50%. And if the Europeans did still more, it is hard to see an alternative to most of that "more" being German. Perhaps Germany's partners in Europe would judge that acceptable, or at least preferable to the alternatives. I doubt it. But the questions – for both Americans and Europeans – are what will preserve stability in Europe and how much that is worth, not whether some imaginary future would be better than existing arrangements.

For those who manage American foreign policy, the objective, as much one of substance as of process, must be an awareness of the several audiences to which they must play. From that there is no escape. Exhorting the Europeans to spend more on defense tells the American Congress that Europeans are doing too little. Accusing the Europeans of being unreliable trading partners raises questions of why Americans are such reliable military allies. Exhortation and the accusations are from time to time necessary, but the costs need to be recognized. Separate tracking, reflective of separate bureaucratic machines, makes that recognition harder to achieve. Those who worry about trade, on both sides of the Atlantic, have their hands full resisting protectionist domestic interests on issues that are their full-time job; thinking about how their handling of trade issues will rebound on security questions is, in normal times, asking too much. This only increases the pressure on early warning and the need for trying to take a broad perspective at the center of government.

For Europeans, the counterpart lesson is the need to avoid actions that encourage American temptations to make linkages or make it harder to resist domestic urgings for them. For example, in the 1960s one part of the German government resisted offset while another part, central bankers and finance ministry officials, continually lectured the United States over its balance-of-payments sins. That could only encourage Washington to press for offset arrangements – one way to diminish the sin – even as other parts of the German government were resisting offset and the implicit link to troops it entailed. A similar anomaly was at play when Europeans lectured Americans over budget deficits in the early 1980s yet fretted about any reduction in American defense spending which might cut down the US commitment to Europe.

Again, such combinations of European views are not necessarily wrong. But an awareness of the costs is necessary. And the requisite awareness is not much easier for European governments to achieve than for their Washington counterpart. Governing machines in Europe are more centralized – or at least less fractious – than

Washington, but implementation often is more rigidly de-centralized in Europe, and cabinet form makes decisions once reached uncomfortable to re-open. But the danger to the alliance from economic issues is, external shocks aside, that minor strains and half linkages half recognized will accumulate.

6 Managing Alliance Politics

Whither the alliance? The question asks for a prediction. But the prediction depends both on trends in the structure of the alliance and on how it is managed. Some of the structural trends are ominous. Differences of interest across the Atlantic are sharper now than in the past and likely to grow more so. Those differences are more apparent because of the changing pattern of leadership in alliance relations. They are complicated by differences in national capabilities and perspectives; all those differences are compounded because they have become more and more embedded in domestic politics.

On the other hand, America and its European allies will retain powerful shared interests, epitomized by their stakes in defense arrangements to provide insurance against a range of security threats and in economic arrangements to make possible the benefits of relatively open economic intercourse. Indeed, in several areas – the economic dimension of policy toward the Soviet Union, for example – the allies are even more important to each others' purposes than in the past. That change is particularly striking for the United States, for which that kind of interdependence is unusual and uncomfortable, and especially difficult to handle in domestic politics.

More important, perhaps, the analysis in these chapters suggests lessons for how to manage the alliance to reduce the risk that differences will frustrate the pursuit of purposes that remain shared. Framing those lessons is the principal task of this chapter. First, the chapter lays out what I conclude in previous chapters about the framework of the alliance in the future: what has changed and what has not? To what implications? Then, it turns to the greater dependence of the allies on actions by their partners in some areas, and what that means for policy-making. The concluding section offers more specific guidelines for managing the alliance, especially but not exclusively for the United States.

156

THE FRAMEWORK OF ALLIANCE

The Nuclear Issue

Paradoxically, the nuclear issue will be relatively more manageable than others in alliance relations. Whether it *will* be successfully managed is another question. But it can be managed.

That conclusion seems a paradox when cast against the nuclear debate and anti-nuclear protest of the 1980s. The fundamental dilemma in NATO's nuclear arrangements outlined in chapter two cannot be made to go away. It is hardly new; it has been present from the beginning of the alliance. Yet it is sharper now, a state of affairs that will continue: nuclear parity will make Americans all the more attentive to the nuclear balance at all levels and to what would ensue if deterrence broke down. That attentiveness on the part of Americans will produce discomfort on the part of Europeans; the specific emphasis on war fighting will, in turn, look to Europeans like an interest in limited nuclear war, raising the fear that they are hostages not just to Soviet nuclear weapons but to American ones as well. All this will be played out in a climate in which public interest in nuclear issues will remain higher than over the decade and a half before 1980, in Europe and also in the United States.

Differences of interest in negotiations will also remain. Americans will continue to see arms control primarily in technical, military terms, asking what effect negotiated constraints will have on real military capabilities. Even beyond the Geneva intermediate nuclear force (INF) negotiations, Europeans will see negotiations primarily in political terms, especially given continued sensititity to nuclear issues among the public at large. They will ask what negotiations signal about the intentions of the two sides, and what they can contribute to broader political processes between East and West.

Yet despite these differences, the nuclear issues will be relatively manageable. Americans and Europeans share over-arching objectives – deterring any war in Europe and any use of nuclear weapons – even if they differ on precisely how to achieve them. As important, what has been the case throughout the postwar period will continue to be true: alternatives to existing arrangements are either unattainable or unpalatable, for all the reasons detailed in chapter two. Deterrence in Europe based pre-eminently on conventional weapons simply is not going to happen, given foreseeable economic and manpower constraints. Nor, given the understandable European preoccupation with deterring *any* war, nuclear or conventional, would Europeans like conventional deterrence even if they could have it. They will continue to find it hard not to believe that if the threshold for the use of nuclear weapons is raised very high, that for the use of conventional weapons must then be somewhat lower; conventional war must then be somewhat more thinkable.

There will continue to be periodic bursts of enthusiasm, most often American, for new weapons or new tactics to finally resolve the nuclear dilemma. But those will continue to founder on cost, on specific political shibboleths or if on neither of those, on the abiding unwillingness of Europeans to contemplate a major conventional war in Europe. For example, "assault breakers" and other precision-guided munitions for hitting deep into Soviet second and third echelon forces will be expensive nor is there much reason to believe that NATO could retain a permanent advantage in their technology. More important, moving very far in that direction would mean posturing NATO to be considerably more "offensive" than it now is, hence would be politically out of the question. That would be true even if NATO's purpose were only to enhance deterrence through the threat of conventional retaliation against Soviet forces in Eastern Europe.[1]

By a similar token, the opposite approach, moving toward territorial defense spread evenly across NATO and particularly West German territory might not be dramatically cheaper than existing defenses. And it would mean explicitly recognizing that NATO would trade West German territory for time in the event of war – also undiscussable.

At the opposite extreme, a truly independent European defense arrangement, with nuclear weapons to match, will continue to be a solution worse than the problem. It would have to mean, finally, clear German participation in decisions about firing. If, after all, Germans were not confident that the Unitd States would use some of its ten thousand nuclear warheads in their defense, they would have much less reason to believe the French or British would use some of their few hundred weapons to defend Germany. Moreover, both the French and British systems are explicitly national forces, by posture and doctrine, facts that will change slowly if at all.

Over the long run there is no way the question of German participation could be fudged. Some arrangement might be contrived in which French (or British) guarantees might supplement the American umbrella, but that would scarcely change NATO's nuclear dilemma. Yet for the foreseeable future a German finger on the nuclear trigger will be unacceptable to Europeans on both sides of the

East–West divide. And while a serious crisis in NATO nuclear arrangements, over INF or some other issue, would produce some increase in German interest in nuclear weapons of their own, a finger on the trigger will remain unwanted by the vast majority of Germans as well.

That means there is no alternative to something like Flexible Response, for all its frayed edges. "New approaches" will amount to tinkering at the margins, though experts will sometimes hint at, and publics will often hope for more. Those tinkerings are important; efforts to make NATO's nuclear posture more credible by withdrawing most short-range warheads and by doing what can be done to improve conventional defense are essential to managing the nuclear dilemma. But they must be seen for what they are: ways to manage a messy status quo, not once-for-all resolutions of the dilemma. Overselling new ideas will only raise expectations which cannot be met, and thus will in the end diminish public confidence, not enhance it.

The nuclear issue can be managed mostly because in the end the alternatives are so unattractive. But it can be managed also because governments have relatively greater control over the issue, over timing and tactics, than is the case for other issues in trans-Atlantic relations. For example, fewer lose words in public on nuclear issues from the Reagan Administration and demonstable movement on arms control of any sort would have done much to undercut anti-nuclear protest in the early 1980s, in Europe as well as in the United States. The evolution of the nuclear freeze movement in the United States is a case in point. What emerged from Congress in 1983 were freeze resolutions that merely exhorted the Executive to negotiate mutual and verifiable freezes with the Soviet Union. That was true despite the prospect of major new nuclear deployments in the United States and Europe, deep skepticism about the Administration's commitment to arms control, and occasional official talk of "superiority," "prolonged nuclear war," and "war winning." Better handling of the issue, especially in public, probably would have pre-empted even the watered-down freeze resolution that eventually ensued.

Even with better management, the temperature of the nuclear question will remain higher in the future than in the recent past. That is assured by nuclear parity, and the consequent debate among experts about what it takes to sustain deterrence and extend it to Europe in those circumstances.

Yet, more adroit handling of the issue would keep it off the boil. That conclusion is reinforced by deeper features in the public perception of nuclear issues. From the viewpoint of the early 1980s, public anxiety about nuclear weapons seemed a phenomenon that suddenly and mysteriously sprang up from the grass roots, or dropped full-blown from the sky. Certainly it was hard to know exactly why concern emerged when it did, rather than earlier or later. Even the combination of factors – stalled arms control, lack of confidence in the American Administration, imminent new nuclear deployments – does not add up to a satisfactory explanation. It may be simply that about once a generation nations have to come to grips anew with nuclear weapons, and that exactly what touches off a particular period of soul-searching is inherently unpredictable.

It is in one way a mistake to view the early 1980s as an aroused public opinion, preoccupied with the threat of nuclear war, forcing foreign policy elites to heed it. In fact, the process seems more nearly the other way around. What occurred is that the rough consensus on nuclear issues among experts or foreign policy elites broke down during the late 1970s. Leaders of the anti-nuclear movement became fully up to debating the intricacies of nuclear strategy or weaponry with the commander of the Strategic Air Command. And so, contending experts sought to mobilize public opinion. Or the fact of the debate increased concern among the public at large – "if there's a debate, perhaps I should be worried." Various public opinion surveys, granting all the caution with which they must be treated, suggest considerable stability in basic public views. As chapter 2 outlined, those basic views contained internal contradictions – the American commitment to both peace and strength, for example, or Europeans' attachment to NATO coupled with their allergy to nuclear weapons.[2] Basic views, including the contradictions, have changed little; the "face" that is politically apparent *has* varied over time.

That process is easier to understand in light of another aspect of public opinion: for most people the threat of war, and with it the salience of security issues, remained relatively low. When Germans, for example, were asked in the early 1980s what problem was most important to them, economic and domestic issues continued to receive over 80 per cent of the nominations.[3] Among "foreign policy" problems, "maintaining peace" consistently has been held to be most important, but over-all the percentage of Germans citing it declined during the 1970s. Fear of war did increase in the early 1980s but not by much.

The relatively low salience of security issues was also suggested, in an impressionistic way, by the German and British elections of 1983. Deciding what determined election results is fool's play, but let's play:

in both cases the opposition party sought to emphasize the nuclear issue, especially the impending deployments of INF. In both cases the emphasis seemed to hurt, rather than help. Both parties seemed to pay a price for attempting to shift the electorate's attention from the economic issues which were its primary concern. In fact, long before the cruise and Pershing missiles began arriving in Europe, in December 1983, their deployment was a foregone conclusion. The peace movement, frustrated, was also exhausted, and the attentions of the media and their public audiences had moved to other issues.

In that context the apparent paradox in public attitudes on security issues is more understandable. On one hand, as chapter 3 noted, large majorities in every NATO country save France continue to deem NATO "still essential" to their security. For example, a March 1981 poll produced the following majorities: 70–15 in Britain, 59–28 in Italy, 66–21 in Norway, and 62–15 in the Netherlands. Yet at the same time polls record considerable opposition to particular defense arrangements, especially nuclear deployments like INF. Given that security issues are not at the top of most people's concerns, what seems likely is that they react in a generally favorable way to the notion of buying some security insurance through participation in the NATO alliance. Yet when pressed further to contemplate unpleasant scenarios which they had not previously thought much about – like using nuclear weapons in their defense or having them stationed in their neighborhood – people retreat from the prospect. That paradox is less surprising on second thought.

These features of public perception carry both positive and negative implications for managing the nuclear issue. On the negative side, they suggest that efforts at public education on the nuclear issue are likely to fail. Most people will continue not to want to think about the issue and generally feel they do not need to. And so the public debate will ebb and flow; it will be frequently passionate but usually ill-informed, despite the efforts of the contending experts and elites.

More positively, there does seem space to manage the issue. The image of the "public" having reclaimed the nuclear issue from their leaders is wide of the mark. Some people have become more concerned, but most have resisted being drawn too far into the unpleasant details of the issue. They are less confident that the nuclear dilemma is being well managed. But the evidence hints that public attitudes provide room if national leaders are more sensitive in handling the issue.

In managing it, campaigns to "educate" the public at large, while worthy, will be less successful than attempts to re-establish a minimum consensus on nuclear issues among the experts and attentive public. if there is rough consensus there, the public mood will moderate, and rival elites and experts will be less able to mobilize public opinion.[4] The experience of the Scowcroft Commission established in 1982 by President Reagan to examine American strategic forces is instructive. Its report patched together a political compromise: several Democrats in and out of Congress agreed to support the MX missiles in exchange for a Presidential commitment to strategic arms control. In the process, the Commission ratified across a relatively broad spectrum of defense experts a set of propositions which had been disputed within that community, especially by the political right at the fringes of the Reagan Administration – that there is no "window of vulnerability," that strategic arms control should focus on stability rather than numbers, and that single-warhead missiles are preferable to those with multiple warheads.[5]

In fact, the compromise began to unravel almost as soon as it was stitched together. The climate for superpower arms control was inhospitable as the Soviet Union left the START talks at the end of 1983, and the Reagan administration's START position remained, at best, confused, leaving the Democratic authors of the compromise feeling they had been deceived in agreeing to support the MX. Yet, with better luck and a more sincere Administration commitment, the Commission might have succeeded in narrowing the agenda of the nuclear debate in the United States.

The Impact of Economics

As with the nuclear question, the allies should be able to cope with economic issues among them, and with the backwash of those questions on traditional security concerns. Like the nuclear issue, the temperature of economic disputes across the Atlantic will be higher, especially if periods of economic recession persist or recur. Tension is increased by the different attitudes toward relations between government and business on the two sides of the Atlantic. There is no question that disputes over economics make it harder for the allies to cooperate across the whole range of security issues. But that "atmospheric" connection between economics and security, even if it grows stronger in the future, still should be manageable. Witness Franco-American relations after the election of François Mitterrand in 1981: the French became much more direct and public in support of

American policies on basic security issues like INF than they had been during Giscard d'Estaing's tenure, even as the new Socialist government in France became much more critical of American economic policies than was its predecessor. At least the spillover of economics on security ought to be manageable in the absence of a major shock – a new oil crisis or a collapse of the financial order.

The reasons why economic disputes among the allies may be sharper in the future are not hard to find. More people on both sides of the Atlantic now are attentive to economic issues, no doubt reflecting the economic straits of the 1970s and 1980s by comparison to the 1960s and, especially in Europe, the diminished threat of war alluded to in the previous section. The primacy of economic issues in West Germany, for example, was mentioned earlier: when asked what are the most important problems facing their country, "foreign policy" ranks last for most respondents, being cited as very important by only 20 to 40% by comparison to over 70% who cite economic issues as "very important".[6]

Similar results hold for the United States. For three decades prior to 1973 a series of Gallup polls suggested that foreign policy dominated public concern. Since 1973, however, economic issues have been pre-eminent. In a 1982 poll, for example, 6% of the public listed "foreign policy" as a major issue (up from 4% in 1978), while 54 and 53%, respectively, cited general economic problems and unemployment as major problems. Similarly, when asked what was the most important foreign policy goal for the United States, "protecting jobs of American workers" ranked at the top of the public's list (cited as very important by 77%), though only 43% of the "leaders" thought it "very important."[7]

A preoccupation with economic issues is likely to persist. Even if the economic performance of the Western industrial economies is better in the 1980s than in the 1970s, the economic path will be bumpy, with uncertainty feeding public concern. Among the prospects, a return to the 1960s – with strong growth, low inflation and the expectation that both can be effortlessly continued year after year – seems nearly the least probable. More and more citizens on both sides of the Atlantic recognize both how economic issues connect with one another and how actions of their partners affect their own well-being. Europeans notice that high American interest rates compel them to follow suit, lest the value of their currencies fall sharply; that need then becomes a constraint on economic management – for good or ill. By the same token, American exporters understand that high interest rates also mean an expensive dollar, thus diminishing the competitiveness of their exports.

Equally, people on both sides of the Atlantic perceive that their own interest in international economics often diverge from those of their own countrymen. That perception has been discernible in the United States since about 1960, but it holds for the Europeans as well. Older, less competitive industries, like steel and automobiles, and their associated unions will seek protection from foreign imports; newer, more competitive sectors like high technology – and for the United States, agriculture – will want open competition; and banks with large international operations will want open financial arrangements coupled with some degree of insurance from their government against unhappy developments, such as the debt problems of Mexico, Brazil, and other industrializing countries in the early 1980s.

If both Europeans and Americans will identify their own economic interests, they will also be at least as able in the past to press their governments to safeguard those interests. They may have learned to harbor only modest expectations that governments can do much about general economic cycles, but they will still turn to governments to protect specific interests. That is most obvious in the trade area in the United States, through the ability of particular interests to make claims through Congress on the Executive Branch. In the 1980 reorganization of trade policy, for example, responsibility for administering anti-dumping and countervailing duties was moved from the Treasury to the Department of Commerce, in large part because Treasury was perceived by domestic industry as too reticent in invoking remedies available under the 1974 Trade Act. But similar pressures are at work in Europe; there, fragile coalition governments are often vulnerable to the entreaties of particular sectors, even relatively small ones like fishing.

These trans-Atlantic tensions, particularly in trade, are compounded by differing approaches to relations between domestic industry and government. For example, steel industries on both continents faced painful contractions in the 1970s. The United States responded consistent with the American tradition of stand-offishness between government and industry and of insistence of firm rules to govern international commerce. For steel that meant near-exclusive reliance on measures to regulate import competition at the border. In Europe, by contrast, where a much more active government role was the tradition and public intervention in steel already a fact, the response was more intervention through an industrial policy implemented by

both nations and the EEC. Intervention came in many forms –
government assistance to financial restructuring, regional aid for areas
hard hit by plant closures, import regulation followed by production
quotas, monitoring of investment to ensure that new money produced
restructuring, and so on.[8]

In the context of deep recession and pressure from steel industries
on both sides of the Atlantic, these differences in approach produced a
vicious cycle that could run through other trade issues as well.
Americans saw European industrial policies as unfair subsidies to
European exports, hence sought protection of their industry. Europeans both believed their industrial policies were sensible and were
upset by American economic policies which drove global interest rates
up. European policies thus continued to provide what Americans saw
as grounds for protection. Those differing approaches across the
Atlantic could easily lead to sharp disputes over other commodities,
automobiles for instance, and to outcomes which by limiting trade,
ultimately hurt the interests of both Americans and Europeans. The
likelihood of such disputes will depend in large measure on whether
the global economy is buoyant enough to drain the political heat from
particular disagreements. American policy toward industry may also
turn in a more "European" direction, albeit slowly, a course in vogue
with Democratic Party politicians and analysts.[9]

Still, for all the sources of increased trans-Atlantic tension over
economics, that tension still should be manageable absent a major
shock. Absent such a shock, it ought to be possible for both Europe
and America to achieve economic performance that, while pale by
comparison to the heady days of the early postwar period, still is
tolerably good. That performance, in turn, should enable the allies to
cope with economic disagreements and minimize the chances that
economic tensions would wash dramatically over existing security
arrangements.

If a serious shock did occur, bets could be off. For example, if
another oil shock came at a time of economic recovery when oil
markets were tight, it almost certainly would strain emergency
arrangements under the International Energy Agency (IEA) to the
breaking point. That break in cooperation among the allies would be
all the worse because both Europeans and Americans would see the
other as having advantages in the scramble for oil that would ensue.
All this could bear on security arrangements if, for example, (some)
allies decided to cut back dramatically on their military deployments to
save money or fuel, or if the allies began trying to cut whatever deal

with whomever they could to gain some oil supplies.

Even less dramatic circumstances would alter the relatively optimistic best guesses made here. If economic growth remained elusive and was accompanied by one or two pieces of bad luck – a minor oil shock, the collapse of several major international banks – protectionist pressures would be much harder to contain and trade could wind down, deepening the recession. In those circumstances, allies could begin to re-think their security commitments, the nuclear issue would be less tractable as nuclear fears became symbols of popular insecurity, and a general nastiness could pervade all trans-Atlantic dealings, economic and security.

More likely, however, economic wrangles among the allies will continue, and they will sometimes emerge as more general irritants in trans-Atlantic relations. But most of the time it should be possible to insulate basic security arrangements from these economic strains, because the tradition of separate tracking keeps security and economics apart or because leaders make special efforts to limit spill-overs. Direct linkages for tactical purposes have been and should continue to be rare. Given the asymmetry of trans-Atlantic relations – with the United States still pre-eminent in military terms but more and more like the rest economically – it will be American leaders that have some scope for making those linkages, hence may be tempted to do so. Yet the record suggests they mostly have refrained, for some combination of the perceived inappropriateness of these linkages against the history of separate tracking, the practical difficulty of making them in those circumstances and the unpredictability of their consequences, on the future actions of the US government no less than on the government of the intended target.

This will leave the "intermediate" link – efforts, more or less explicit, by Executive Branch officials or members of the American Congress to use the presence of American troops in Europe to press the Europeans to do more or pay more or concede more, in economics or security.[10] These pressures, too, have become nearly ritual in trans-Atlantic dealings, and so their force has diminished accordingly. But Europeans often will accede, albeit grudgingly. Since this link usually arises haphazardly out of relations between the American Executive and Congress, its consequences will also be unpredictable. But unless there is a nasty surprise or unless the handling of other issues, for instance security issues outside Europe, goes badly awry, the economic – "burden sharing" – dimension of this link should be manageable. Unilateral impulses in American politics may lead the

United States to withdraw forces from Europe. If that happens, perceptions that Europeans are pusillanimous in relations with the Soviet Union or in addressing security threats outside Europe no doubt will be much of the reason why. But feelings that the Europeans are being selfish on economic issues are likely to be much less central.

Defense and Detente in Europe

The other two sets of issues will be more difficult to handle, with greater risk of mishap or strains cumulating into serious ruptures in alliance arrangements. Changes in the framework of the alliance matter more with regard to these issues. The first is the heart of the alliance, policy toward the Soviet Union in Europe. Again, some differences between Americans and Europeans are of long standing; they are rooted in geography: we are here and they are there. Yet those differences of interest are more salient now, for reasons which frequently have been reiterated, in this book and elsewhere. East–West connections, economic and humanitarian, have built larger stakes for Western Europeans than for Americans. And with the decline in American pre-eminence in the alliance, Europeans are more prepared to articulate and defend interests of their own that may not coincide with those of the United States: witness the difference between West German actions in the pipeline disputes of the 1960s and the 1980s.

The differences seem to be supported by features of public opinion on both sides of the Atlantic. On the surface, support in both the United States and Europe for the basic alliance remains high. Polls, for all their defects, consistently record European support for NATO in the 60 to 80% range. And the willingness of American opinion to come to the aid of European allies if attacked by the Soviet Union reached an all-time high of 70% in 1980.[11] Similarly, in 1982, 58% of Americans in one poll wanted to keep the US commitment to NATO what it is, 9% were prepared to increase it, while only 11 and 4%, respectively, wanted to decrease the commitment or withdraw entirely. Among elites, so-called, support for NATO is even stronger. In the same poll the percentages were 79, 7, 12 and 1, respectively, for maintain, increase, decrease and withdraw.[12]

Yet beneath that surface there are more hints of change. In most of the countries of Western Europe, but especially in the Federal Republic and Italy, younger, better educated people – presumably just those most central to shaping future trans-Atlantic relations – differ noticeably in attitude from their elders. While still favorably disposed to both NATO and the US, they are more tempted by neutralism, less impressed by the United States and less prepared to defend their country by military means. These attitudes may be mere artifacts of age; today's European youth may resemble its elders once it ages. As Chapter 3 noted, the paucity of time-series data makes it hard to know for certain. But, on what slender evidence is available, these age cleavages do seem new in postwar European politics.[13]

These age differences are harder to see in American political opinion. Opinion clusters around the familiar poles – peace/strength, crusading internationalism of conservative or liberal stripe/desires to go it alone. The public holds apparently contradictory opinions at the same time, sometimes with equal strength. In the early 1980s it was possible to see a range of currents among political leaders. There were the traditional Atlanticists of the generation who built postwar arrangements. Another group, usually much younger, was Atlanticist by analysis more than sentiment or personal experience. For that group, the existing US commitment to Europe was a reflection of American interests.

Another strain, more tinged by unilateralist impulses, might be termed "disappointed Atlanticist." For it the alliance, once worthy, had become an affair in which the United States contributed far too much, the Europeans far too little, a view sometimes tinged with moral disapproval of Europe's softness. Finally, yet another group was more thorough goingly unilateralist. For it, the United States needed the flexibility to commit its resoures and forces where necessary to confront the Soviet Union; alliances were not necessarily bad, but they needed to be tested periodically to make sure they still fit American interests.[14]

The danger is that the common denominators of these attitudes on the two sides of the Atlantic will be more and more antagonistic. For their part, Europeans will cluster around a commitment to the alliance but to a rather different alliance than in the past. The commitment will be more conditional; Europeans will feel entitled to a more real share in decisions, will regard policies differing from those of the United States on occasion not as disloyal but rather as natural reflections of national interest, and will be rankled by American *faits accomplis*.

Yet the common denominator of American attitudes may be nearly the converse. Americans' commitment to the alliance also will be conditional; irritation and frustration with allies will be nearer the surface. And the American commitment will be conditional on

Europeans paying and doing more, bearing a greater share of the burden, and being prepared to take tough decisions and stick by them.

The chances of antagonism are increased because many American policies – especially economic relations with the Soviet Union – will depend on parallel action by the Europeans. They hold many "chips" in trade and technology transfer with the East. At least their actions can frustrate American policies. That will make it harder for the two sides of the Atlantic simply to agree to disagree. It seems clear, for example, that over the long term the Europeans have little practical alternative to importing. more Soviet natural gas; they will regard doing so as safer than dealing with Third World suppliers. That makes future "pipelines" predictable. What will seem to Europeans a prudent diversification of their energy future will all too easily look to Americans like Europeans sabotaging American efforts to put economic pressure on the Soviet Union.

However, three factors outlined in Chapter 3 will mitigate the trans-Atlantic antagonism, though none guarantees against serious strain. First, there will remain considerable stability at the center of the alliance. Even if Europeans and Americans differ on many aspects of policy toward the Soviet Union, they will concur in the need to buy some insurance against Soviet military power in Europe. They will agree on the need for NATO. That does not mean that they will agree on how much insurance, or in what forms or where, or paid for by whom. But the basic agreement will continue to provide an anchoring point for the alliance.

In managing the alliance, that suggests the desirability of minimizing the "newness" of innovations, especially in the military realm, and, to the extent possible, on not making particular policy adjustments contingent on a shared assessment of the Soviet threat. The allies will disagree on the precise nature of the threat; they will not disagree that it is real and present.[15] American leaders and analysts are tempted to advertise new technologies in conventional weapons, for example, as *the* solution to NATO's problem. Yet doing so is both untrue and unhelpful in managing the alliance. It is untrue because, as mentioned several times in this book, given costs and Soviet response, any innovation in technology will make only a marginal difference in NATO's defenses, though the margin can be significant. And it is unhelpful because it suggests a change in NATO doctrine that is bound to become the object of political controversy.

Second, many of the trans-Atlantic differences, new in the 1970s, are becoming familiar, hence almost ritual, by the 1980s. That may not make the arguments any less sharp in specific instances, but it does provide a certain pattern to the debate and to how it is contained. It begins to build, if not an understanding of positions on the other side, at least an awareness of them and their place in the other's politics. Ritual blunts shock and diminishes the chance of overreaction.

Finally, their rhetoric notwithstanding, a series of American administrations have acquiesced to a considerable degree in European desires that detente in Europe be insulated from East–West tension. They have accepted, in other words, the proposition that detente can be divisible. As Chapter 3 outlined, that acceptance was apparent in actions of the Reagan Administration: its embrace of INF arms control early in its tenure and its commitment to continue it through Soviet transgressions in Poland or in shooting down the Korean airliner, and its reluctant acceptance of the Stockholm conference on European security, a conference sought by its European allies as a means of keeping open some East–West dialogue in Europe.

Parallel to these official actions, public opinion data in the United States hint at a residual sympathy for European attitudes even when those differ from American. On that score the American public frequently may be more tolerant than the US government. In a 1982 sample of leaders, for example, 37% thought that the Europeans should be allowed "to pursue policies they think best" in the pipeline deal, while only 15% favored economic sanctions against them if other methods of persuasion did not work.[16]

Defense Beyond Europe

Many of the same strains are at play in dealings over security issues outside Europe. The allies do see their interests outside Europe – in the Persian Gulf for example – as somewhat different, and there are visible differences among the European nations as well. Those differences in interests are mixed up with differences in national capabilities and in perspectives of the threat, a mix that complicates trans-Atlantic discussion. Those differences are bound to result in different assessments of the costs and benefits of different strategies in, say, the Middle East. The principal risk is a backlash in the United States against a perception that the Europeans are doing little to protect interests that are more important to them than to the United States. A small case in point was the US invasion of Grenada in 1983: the unwillingness of even a conservative British government to participate, and the evident British unhappiness with an American invasion of a Commonwealth member, in turn produced a reaction in American public opinion.[17]

The history of the alliance testifies to how often the allies have disagreed over issues outside Europe: Indochina, Suez, Indochina again. Americans have denounced the Europeans as "parochial," except for narrow colonial issues, since the Korean War. Moreover, the allies have several times switched sides, with the Europeans sometimes pressing the United States to be more concerned about issues outside Europe, and sometimes vice versa. That at least suggests that some degree of difference among the allies with regard to issues beyond Europe may not be the end of the alliance. It is another testimony to the robustness of the alliance through changing circumstances. And it, in turn, *should* temper urges by any ally to assert that it has a monopoly of wisdom in any particular instance, though that kind of restraint has not been a prominent feature of the alliance.

Differences between Europeans and Americans (and among Europeans) are of several kinds, intermingled in debates over specific issues. One is differences of interest. Part of that difference is captured in the frequent assertion that the Europeans are regional powers, while American interests are global. Another part of it looks like free riding to Americans; from their perspective, Europeans can curry favor with Arab oil producers precisely because they know the US will safeguard other "Western" interests in the region – Israel's security or the presence of a military counterweight to Soviet power. There are strong incentives for Europeans to see events outside Europe through the prism of stability inside Europe, and to give precedence to short-run interests – access to oil, for example.

Yet the trans-Atlantic differences also run to capabilities. It may be that the Europeans are nearly as concerned about the military aspects of issues in the Persian Gulf but, with the limited exception of France and Britain, know there is little in the military realm they can do about it. Finally, some of the differences are straightforward differences in view. That is, they are not "free riding" even from the US perspective. Europeans act in one way not because they know that it would be irrational for the US to follow suit; rather they hold a view and wish the United States shared it. That no doubt was the case with the relatively more forthcoming European attitude toward the Palestine Liberation Organization (PLO) in the late 1970s and early 1980s.

The differences are, however, probably less embedded in domestic politics than are some of the differences over policy toward the Soviet

Union in Europe. European Jews, for instance, have had minimal effect on European policies, at least in countries other than Germany. Oil companies and their pro-Arab domestic allies may have somewhat more influence, but even that is not striking. At the same time, domestic politics do shape the differences in a less direct way. Even if they wanted, many European governments – and especially that in Bonn – would find it hard to mount significant military forces for contingencies outside Europe. For the United States the obverse is the case: building military forces is politically easier than framing venturesome political approaches to the Middle East.

For the foreseeable future the focus of trans-Atlantic differences over security issues outside Europe will be the Persian Gulf and Middle East. No other area combines the same degree of serious interests and threats with visible differences among the allies. Other issues beyond Europe will be irritants in the relationship, and they may add to the cumulative weight of strains. But they will not have the same potential risk of a break in basic alliance arrangements as the Persian Gulf.

For example, European objections to American policy in Central America in the early 1980s were rooted in political symbolism – images of U.S. intervention or militarism – backed by the tug of fellowship for comrades in the international organizations of socialist and Christian democratic parties. More tangible "national" interests hardly existed for Europeans. To be sure, those symbols were not trivial. But, for European leaders if not for their publics, they paled by comparison to the stake in relations with the United States. And so those leaders had, and will continue to have incentives to mute official criticism of American policy in Central America even if they cannot control their own domestic debates on that subject.

In minimizing the risk of a political backlash, principally in the United States, it is imperative that Europeans are seen to bear risks as well as burdens. Certainly, some rough and implicit allocation of responsibility according to comparative advantage makes sense: the Federal Republic can do little in the military sphere outside Europe, and some particular relationships (France and several African countries, Britain and the Gulf) indicate special attention by given allies to those areas.

But the imperative of sharing risks implies the need for European participation, even if largely symbolic, in military measures designed for contingencies beyond Europe. Like the loosely coordinated naval deployments during the Iran-Iraq war or French and Italian participation in Lebanese peace-keeping, involvement by the allies can be useful in the region by minimizing images of American intervention. More important, it will serve to diminish the risk of an adverse reaction in American politics which might wash against basic alliance arrangements, such as the presence of American forces in Europe.

SHARED BURDENS, SHARED DECISIONS

The foregoing pages underscore that on many issues the allies will disagree more and more often and with better and better reason. Their interests differ, so do their national capabilities and perspectives, and the claims of domestic politics sharpen the differences or compel them to be pushed forward. Yet at the same time the allies remain central to each others' purposes in foreign affairs. Indeed, in many areas they are more central now than in the past. That reflects the increasing interconnections, especially economic, among them – interdependence, in the modern jargon – and the increasing complexity of the world and of their purposes in it.

For the Europeans this state of affairs is less new. Interdependence has been a fact of life for them throughout the postwar period. If anything is different now, it is that "interdependence" has ensued from the straightforward "dependence" of earlier years; Europeans now are both willing and able to act on their own to advance purposes they feel the United States may not entirely share, or to provide themselves some insulation from what they regard as capricious American policy. German Chancellor Schmidt's interventions with Soviet President Brezhnev in 1980 and 1981 to try to produce movement in the INF talks are a recent example of the former, the European Monetary System (EMS) an attempt at the latter.

It is, rather, for the United States that dependence on the actions of others is unusual, and uncomfortable. The fact of that dependence is becoming clearer and clearer just as an awareness of its implications is more and more resisted. The long-standing desire to be able to go it alone in the world has been reasserting itself in the United States, reflected in increasing impatience with allies. How a recognition of the dependence on actions by allies is worked out in substance by the United States, and worked through its politics, will be critical determinants of the future of the trans-Atlantic alliance.

That need for parallel actions by allies is clearest at the heart of American policy – relations with the Soviet Union. However Americans regard the economic and other links between Western Europe and the Soviet Union, the fact remains that much of what the West has in the way of both "carrots" and "sticks" in dealing with Moscow resides in the hands of the Western European nations. In 1982, for example, total EEC trade with the East totalled $36.9 billion, about 6% of total trade, the same percentage as EEC trade with the United States. By contrast, in the same year American trade with the East reached only $3.9 billion, 0.3% of US imports and 1.6% of exports. Only in 1975 and 1976 did American machinery exports to the Soviet Union exceed a half billion dollars. In 1980 the United States accounted for only 10% of the credit extended to the Soviet Union and Eastern Europe, its allies in Western Europe for most of the rest.[18] (To be sure, as Chapter 3 noted, exactly who has leverage over whom is not always clear, especially in the debt area. By 1984 the Federal Republic alone accounted for $4 billion of Poland's debt.)

American sanctions on specific commodities, grain or high technology may inflict costs on the Soviet Union, but even those American actions can be undercut to some degree if the Europeans do not act in concert. The United States may still be able in specific instances to compel the Europeans to follow suit – for instance through its special leverage in the network of international banking – but those instances are rarer and rarer, their use more and more costly. The bulk of the West's economic relations with the Soviet Union are and will continue to be Western European, not American.

Politically as well, the Soviet Union can to some extent cushion the effect of hard American policies or put pressure on those policies by trying to exploit differences between the United States and its European allies. That was evident in the INF episode. NATO's plans for both missile deployments and arms control were dependent on European agreement; that meant that American actions had to satisfy an interested European audience, and it also gave the Soviet Union room to compete to try to look more reasonable than the United States.

Beyond the central core of relations with the Soviet Union, the Europeans have less to contribute, but, again, their actions can frustrate American policies if the two are at cross purposes. On the positive side, the French and British in particular retain some military assets that are helpful in projecting power into the Persian Gulf region. French and Italian participation in the United Nations force in Lebanon (UNIFIL) has been similarly helpful. Political approaches by the Europeans can complement American policy even if the approaches are not identical; comparative advantage can make for sensible allocations of tasks, even if the allocating is tacit, not explicit. It has been, for example, easier for France to sustain some links to Iraq than for the United States, and broad Western interests probably have been served by it doing so.

On the negative side the effect of European actions is even clearer. With regard to the Arab–Israeli peace process, for example, the Europeans have little influence in pushing the parties toward a settlement, virtually none with Israel, but considerable potential to frustrate American policy. By taking a more forthcoming position on the role of the Palestine Liberation Organization (PLO) in 1980, they embarassed and further exposed Egypt, which found itself lagging behind the Europeans on that issue, and provided additional incentive for Israeli intransigence. A similar pattern ran through policy toward Central America in 1981. There seemed to be some chance that the left in El Salvador would split, with a portion prepared to participate in the March 1982 elections to the Constituent Assembly, elections that were the centerpiece of American policy. That attempt to divide the left collapsed, however, with the Franco-Mexican statement approving a role for the insurgents in the future of politics in El Salvador.

The implications of this interdependence for the alliance are uncomfortable. Logically, if the United States recognizes that its purposes require European cooperation in circumstances where the Europeans may not fully share those purposes or may be tempted by free-riding, then the United States can only induce that cooperation by conceding Europeans a measure of real control over decisions. It must then be prepared to abide by the results even if the decisions that ensue are not those Washington initially sought. For the Europeans the obverse holds. If they want a real share in decision-making, even if only because they fear what America would do if left to act alone, they must be prepared to share responsibility for decisions thus reached. Burdens must be commensurate with control, and vice versa.

Again, the task is hardly new. The alliance has grappled with it for several decades. But it is more necessary now. Old habits, more than procedures, need to change on both sides of the Atlantic. "America decides and Europe complains," as Peter Jay put it, will no longer suffice as a way of taking decisions.[19] No longer can the United States decide, then inform its allies, with American decisions altered only in the light of serious European protests. Equally important, no longer can the Europeans remain aloof, their role limited to a faintly condescending critique of American choices after the fact; they will have to be prepared to propose what should be done, rather than merely analyzing why American proposals are flawed.

Moving in that direction will imply a constraint, and a frustration for American policy-makers. Washington's internal battles over foreign policy often are so intense that the foreign countries that are the ostensible objects of that policy seem scarcely relevant. Imagine a secretary of defense who actually wanted to give European allies a measure of real influence over decisions in American defense budgeting. That secretary would find it hard to do so amidst the tugging of the services, analysts, industry lobbies, Congress and budgeteers in the Executive Branch. Conceding real influence to Europeans will be resisted by those in Congress and elsewhere who will regard it as "being nice" to Europeans for little return. It means, finally, yielding a degree of sovereignty on a number of sensitive issues.

Yet, as chapter one suggested, bargains about control, as well as bargains about burdens, run through the trans-Atlantic alliance. Merely deciding to join in the various alliance arrangements implied for all members, including the Unites States, some cession of sovereignty to the group. The sequence of events before and after the December 1979 decision on INF was illustrative of the change in nuclear decision-making. There were problems with that process, and the jury is not yet in on the outcome. But in both the form of the decision – NATO consensus – and its substance – new missile deployments linked to arms control – the Europeans, and especially the main countries slated to receive missiles, acquired a veto power over deployments and with it important leverage over the US in the INF negotiations. They could not, as in the past, present themselves to their publics as the reluctant objects of American plans embodied in NATO. Rather, for good or ill, they had to take real responsibility for the decision; that, in turn, meant demonstrating at home that they had done everything they could to render the deployments unnecessary through arms control.

The risks and frustrations were clear enough. Arms control was the price the United States paid to elicit European cooperation on deployments. NATO was thus driven into INF arms control negotiations that plainly were unpromising in the extreme. And once embarked on that path, the Europeans became cheerleaders for American concessions. The process was triply frustrating to Americans: not only did it mean consulting with the Europeans on every negotiating detail, but it insured that European publics would be at least as critical in assessing US negotiating positions as in judging Soviet ones. There was, moreover, considerable substance to the

American feeling that it was the Europeans, especially the Germans, who started the whole business in the first place: who were they now to complicate matters? Finally, the issue looked to different parts of the American establishment and for different reasons, much ado about little: to hard-liners 572 missiles more or less was of small consequence, while to those who worried most about NATO, their deployment seemed not worth the candle in light of public opposition it generated.

Yet in the end the degree of shared decision represented by the INF process, if not necessarily the form of that sharing, probably was unavoidable, and necessary. Older forms of decision-making simply could not be sustained against the conditions of the 1980s. Europe's role in the alliance would not permit it, no matter how uncomfortable the newer form was for Europeans. And, from the US perspective, older patterns would not suffice to call forth European cooperation.

Indeed, the INF issue would have been easier, certainly in Britain but perhaps also in the other European states, if the shared control of the missiles once deployed had been more explicit. The "dual-key" system – Europeans controlling the launchers and Americans the nuclear warheads – would have done so. It long had been the practice for much of NATO's nuclear arsenal. It was not followed in the INF instance by the Germans because Chancellor Schmidt reckoned his internal political problems would be eased if there were no German finger even directly on the trigger of missiles that could strike the Soviet Union.

Yet for the other Europeans the overriding consideration was money: under previous NATO dual-key arrangements, Europeans purchased their share of control by paying for the launchers. This time, however, they preferred not to spend defense money in short supply for cruise missile and Pershing launchers. Had a European veto over firing the missiles been explicit through a form of dual key, much of the force of the anti-nuclear movement's argument that the new missiles were part of an American design to fight limited nuclear wars in Europe would have been drained away. So, in retrospect, obscuring the issue of who controlled the missiles merely for reasons of money was unwise. Yet therein also lies the rub: it is far from obvious that an American administration, even had it and the Europeans desired, could have argued Congress into paying the full cost of the systems but then giving the launchers to Europeans. The tradition of sharing money burdens made it harder to sort out the sharing of control. control.

For issues beyond Europe, Europeans have been induced to share burdens, to the extent they have, more for negative than for positive reasons – more to stay in the game than to achieve any real measure of control over decisions. For example, Europeans went along grudgingly with American sanctions against Iran during the hostage crisis, but not necessarily because they accepted the logic of that decision. Rather, they feared that if they did not comply, they would lose all influence over the subsequent course of American action, and might then be confronted with still more worrisome eventualities. In the event they got both sanctions and something more worrisome – the military raid to free the hostages – though the consequences of the latter were less dire than many in Europe (and America) feared.

Europeans felt similar pressures in the aftermath of the Soviet invasion of Afghanistan at the turn of the year 1979–80. The Carter Administration's stern responses – especially economic sanctions against the Soviet Union and a boycott of the Moscow Olympics – became a litmus test of the alliance. It was clear that not to go along was to risk a nasty backlash in the United States. Most Europeans felt that some response was called for, though there was – as outlined in Chapter 4 – an undertone in Europe, never very clear and never clearly argued, that the Soviet invasion did not change things all that much. But most European governments were simply caught unprepared by the American actions. As with US sanctions against Iran, which Europeans heard about on television, the actions were *faits accomplis*.

When President Carter said in an interview that he had learned more about Soviet intentions in the few days of the Afghan crisis than in the previous two years of his Administration, Europeans were bound to take that as confirmation of their fears about the Administration's steadiness of purpose in relations with Moscow. And so Europeans followed suit, in varing degrees, simply because they felt they had to, not because they felt they shared a common approach with the United States, still less because they had participated in the decisions about how to respond.

Yet, other instances at least suggest the possibility of a more positive sharing of burdens and decisions. As the United States built up its Rapid Deployment Force (RDF) for contingencies in the Persian Gulf, both Britain and France decided to sustain, and even modestly increase their own similar forces. In the British case the decision openly followed the logic of Chapter 4: being seen to participate both would minimize the risk of a backlash in the United States against Europeans not doing their share and would give Britain some claim to share in decisions about how forces might be used. The logic was similar in the French case, though much openly argued given French aloofness from military alliance with the United States. When France sent troops to Zaire in 1978, it asked for and received American help in airlifting them there. That reflected more than pure military need; it also reflected a French political interest in implicating the United States in the intervention.

Or the loosely-coordinated naval presence in the Persian Gulf that Britain, France, Australia and the United States put together in 1980 and 1981 as insurance against an expansion of the Iran-Iraq war: apart from symbolism for attentive publics in the United States, the coordination served primarily to reassure local states that the action was not camouflage for other American purposes, for instance an invasion of Iran. But it also provided some parallel assurance to American allies that US purposes would not in fact expand, at least not without some prior consultation. By the same token, French, British and Italian participation in peacekeeping in Lebanon from 1982 to 1984 served primarily to mitigate the image of a dominant American role, but it also gave those countries some claim to a say in future decisions about Lebanon.

It is clearly too much to hope that such bargains about burden and control might be extended through discussions among allied governments. When Germany (or Japan) gives economic aid to Turkey or Pakistan, Americans regard that as no more than discharging their obligations. Washington will see little reason why that should entitle the allies to a share in American decision-making. Yet the logic suggests little alternative to efforts by the allies to assemble packages of approaches more clearly. In the attempt, new forms of cooperation might emerge – for instance, Germany helping Turkey or Egypt refurbish older American aircraft common to the inventories of both. More important, only such attempts will provide Americans enough support and Europeans enough control to make the bargains sustainable.

The United States is not the only ally that faces painful choices about yielding control in order to secure the cooperation of its allies. For instance, Europeans complain, often with reason, about the implications for them of inward-looking American economic management: witness the perennial rows over interest rates and the price of the dollar. Yet, like Americans complaining about wayward European policies, they resist drawing the implications for their own policies. Like Americans, Europeans usually only exhort their partners to behave better.[20]

Also like Americans, when Europeans suggest action, not just exhortation, their first instinct is to seek insulation from the policies of partners. Take the monetary area as an example. European proposals most often run to efforts to insulate European capital markets from American caprice. Yet that insulation, in the form of currency controls, would be likely to fail. It would fragment the European Community's internal capital markets since those countries with tighter controls would seek to avoid leakage through the rest.[21] The opposite approach would mean creating weightier European instruments both for their own sake and as a means of inducing the United States to be more serious about coordinating economic policies. It would imply some decrease in national discretion – in sovereignty – over economic decisions first at the European level and then with the Americans, and thus it is dismissed as too hard. It might mean, for example, creating a European reserve pool to permit the Community to intervene collectively in currency markets, hence to influence American policy. Further expansion of parallel European monetary instruments would then provide further inducement for American cooperation.

Such an alternative is probably impossible in current European circumstances. But the analytics of Chapter 1 suggest it would not necessarily contradict American interests, if a greater degree of European unity led to a greater sense of European responsibility for shared decision. It surely would be uncomfortable in specific instances in American politics, but, plausibly, it could serve on occasion as a constraint national leaders could use against the pleadings of special interests in society. European leaders frequently argue to their publics, in effect, that their hands are tied because "NATO has decided." American leaders might find it useful to do something similar in the economic realm, especially if, however reluctantly, Americans begin to realize that the economic policies of allies, if uncoordinated, can affect their own well-being. So far, however, the most that can be said is that the stakes of allies – for instance with regard to US interest rates – are used as arguments by participants in the debate over "domestic" American economic policy.

It would be helpful, especially in dealing with issues outside Europe, to set discussions in a broader framework, one akin to what the Japanese call "comprehensive national security." That would recognize more explicitly than in the past the different capabilities and different constraints arising from domestic politics in the various allies.[22] Recognizing those differences, it would also permit bargains about burdens and control to be put together over a wider range of issues and contributions. That would not be easy, even if there were the political will, since every ally would have an incentive to try to fit into the bargains actions it intended to take in any case. But at least it would serve as a counterweight to the tendency, natural enough, for every ally and particularly the United States, to judge the contributions of the others by light of its own particular mix of capabilities, politics and perspective.

FRAMEWORK OF ALLIANCE

This discussion of inter-allied bargains over burdens and control is no clarion call for a "new Atlantic charter" or a grand "division of labor." Nor do I conclude with the ritual calls for franker discussion of differences among the allies, better consultation, or more sensitivity on the part of all allied governments to the domestic politics of their partners. Frankness, serious discussion of tasks and sensitivity all would be nice. Doing a little better on any of those scores would help. But doing dramatically better is not about to happen; it is about as unlikely as is a return to the emotional fervor that surrounded European unity and trans-Atlantic partnership in the early postwar years.

For those in all the allied governments charged with policy-making, the task of managing the alliance will be, as in the past, grubby, detailed and plodding. The gap between purposes and principles shared among the allies, on the one hand, and the day-to-day din of specific frictions on the other, will remain frustratingly large. Policy-makers in all the allies, and most notably in the United States, will remain absorbed by claims of their own domestic politics and processes of governance.

Still, my central conclusion about the framework of the alliance in the years ahead is that, for all the apparent changes, the United States and its allies in Western Europe will remain central to each other's purposes across a wide range of issues. Much has changed, but much has not. The famous British commentator, Alistair Buchan, declared that the "Soviet–American strategic deadlock is now unbreakable" in 1958. Eighty percent of the American public was unwilling to contemplate a first use of nuclear weapons in 1949, when the United States had an atomic monopoly. So, too, were differing views of the Soviet threat apparent almost from the beginning. Even Winston Churchill, the author of the "Iron Curtain," was regularly denounced by Americans for his "appeasing gestures" in the early 1950s. The

Europeans were also regularly taken to task for their "parochial" preoccupation with Europe. And sharp disputes over economic issues began as soon as Europe was again on its feet. Present disputes over trade and technology transfer with the East look pallid by comparison to the 1950s, when the American Congress passed the Battle Bill and the Kem Amendment, cutting off any military aid to countries, including Britain and Holland, that continued to trade in strategic commodities with the East.[23]

Even where real change seems clear, its effect is often less than popular commentaries of the present day would have it. The decline in American pre-eminence, and the parallel increase in European willingness to safeguard interests not shared by the United States, seem real enough. But, as perspective, it is worth remembering that in dealings among allies, weakness can be strength. A postwar Western Europe that was down and nearly out could call forth a degree of generosity from the American Congress that is today unimaginable; no amount of European "strength" could bludgeon Congress into parallel attitudes. Even now, the prospect that the Netherlands may be too weak or too embued with pacifist sentiments to accept American cruise missiles calls forth extraordinary attentions from the allies. In the recent past, suggestions that the Italian or French were so unstable as to flirt with inviting domestic communist parties into ruling coalitions called for comparable attentions, at least from the United States. They may well do so again in the future.

Understanding what has changed and what has not, and what both trends mean, should provide a sense of steadiness both to policy-makers and to commentators from outside who need it more. In Virgina Woolf's famous description, journalism is "rain on the surface of the sea." In the instance of the US–European alliance, the waves to which popular accounts allude often are real, and sometimes they reflect changing currents in trans-Atlantic relations. But many are no more than ripples. Some sense for the framework of the relationship provides a perspective on events of the moment, a perspective which is so often lacking.

A similar perspective on current events is the recognition that the United States and its allies have disagreed frequently in the past, sharply and on issues that were ostensibly central to their shared purposes. Not every disagreement is fundamental, still less heralds the final disintegration of the alliance. Indeed, in many areas there is logic to the argument that somewhat different approaches by the various allies may make sense provided broad objectives are the same. Even with regard to policy toward the Soviet Union, varying European and American approaches may not only reflect different perspectives – regional versus global – and different interests – substantial economic and humanitarian stakes versus minimal ones. Some limited differences in approach might also hedge the West's bets given the imponderables of relations with the East. At least the logic to somewhat different approaches should serve as a caution to every ally about maintaining that its approach is the sole repository of good sense.

The framework outlined in these chapters also suggests when the political implications of disagreement among the allies will be acceptable and when they will not. The allies can be expected, for example, to continue to dispute West–West economic issues – trade, international money, and national economic policies. Those disputes have been common in alliance history; they reflect the competition inherent in the international economic arrangements the allies have worked to sustain. And most of the time those disputes have been insulated from basic security arrangements. Not that the disputes are costless; they do have some effect on the ability of the allies to cooperate across the board, and there is always the risk that the steady accumulation of disputes will eventually erode central forms of cooperation. But absent an external shock, the framework suggests that economic disputes can be contained within the alliance.

In other areas, by contrast, different approaches on the two sides of the Atlantic are more dangerous because the risk of a political spillover on basic arrangements is greater. For instance, there is at least as much uncertainty about the nature of the threat to Western interests in the Persian Gulf as there is about what will provoke change in Eastern Europe and the Soviet Union. So, again, somewhat different American and European policies toward the problems of the Gulf could be regarded merely as prudential, a sensible hedging of bets. Yet for all the reasons outlined earlier, policies on the two sides of the Atlantic that diverge too sharply would entail the risk of a political backlash against basic alliance arrangements. For that reason, some visible cooperation between the United States and its allies is imperative. That means enough European support for American purposes to make clear that the Europeans are doing their share, coupled with enough European participation in decisions to make it feasible for them to provide that support.

Along this dimension of the dangers of differing American and European policies, the nuclear issue and policy toward the Soviet

Union in Europe lie between economics and security issues outside Europe. For the nuclear issue, differences in perspecitve can be tolerated because over-arching objectives so clearly are shared; because the alternative to existing arrangements are, for the foreseeable future at any rate, so unattractive; and because the differences are of such long-standing, hence so familiar.

The dangers are greater for issues of policy toward the Soviet Union in Europe – for instance, trade and technology transfer. There, too, a backlash could arise from a perception in the United States that the Europeans were sustaining cozy – and profitable – links to the Soviet Union while the United States was bearing most of the cost – and risk – of containing Soviet military power. Yet that perception should be mitigated because groups in American society with influence over government – farmers and high technology industry, for example – will make arguments of their own, parallel to those of Europeans, why economic interchange with the East is no bad thing. Finally, there will be some residual sympathy in the United States, frequently muted but sometimes more evident, for some measure of European discretion because, after all, it is *their* continent.

There is also the possibility of a political reaction in Europe. On both the nuclear question and policy toward the Soviet Union, Europeans will feel from time to time, as they have throughout the postwar period, that the policies of their ally are nearly as dangerous as those of their adversary. But that reaction is likely to be contained by a recognition, uncomfortable to be sure, that there is no practical alternative to something like existing arrangements with the United States. That recognition will hardly make for inter-allied comity in particular instances, quite the contrary. Nor does the degree of European dependence implied by the recognition mean that Europeans will easily acquiesce in those instances; the increasing political weight of Europe in the relationship, underscored in this book, means they will not. But when they disagree with the United States on these issues, they will continue to have powerful incentives to cast that disagreement in ways that minimize the risk of escalating recriminations across the Atlantic: by rounding off the hard edges of their arguments, by smothering specific disagreements in the rhetoric of shared purposes, and by quickly seeking compromises once they have made their point.

This aspect of the framework directs attention not just to the risks of differences but also to the obverse: how much space do national leaders have, given politics within the allies and among them, to frame policies that reflect their shared interests? For example, the United States and its European allies share "national" interests in more coordinated economic policies; all probably would be better off if all of them yielded a greater measure of national discretion over economic policy. But, given domestic politics, it is not about to happen, surely not soon in any dramatic way. Moreover, history shows that the alliance has been able to contain significant differences on that score in the past, and the framework suggests that it should, with reasonable luck, be able to do so in the future. That does not mean alliance leaders should not try to do better; if leadership means anything it must mean efforts to expand the space of the politically possible. However, recognizing that "domestic" concerns will be over-riding in the making of economic policy should dampen expectations and thus diminish mutual frustrations when disputes among the allies occur.

The gas pipeline issue in 1982 was for the United States at the opposite end of the spectrum with regard to political space. Previous actions had left the European government with little room in which to maneuver: contracts had been made, business and labor constituencies aroused, expectations set loose. Any German government, even a conservative one, would have found it almost impossible to do what Adenauer did in 1963 and annul pipeline contracts already signed. Adenauer found it hard enough two decades before.

Yet the American Administration had considerable space, domestically, to frame the issue as it chose. No domestic economic interests were pressing to extend the embargo; those affected opposed doing so and would have liked to make their own sales in the pipeline project. The main argument for extending the embargo was to send a strong signal to the Soviet Union. That argument was made by elements of the American bureaucracy, notably the Pentagon, but vociferously opposed by the State Department. In the end Mr Reagan could have played the issue any way he chose. He could have chosen to make it an occasion for allied unity, especially since any signal to Moscow was likely to be overshadowed by disarray in the alliance. He decided instead, partly through unhappy circumstance, to make the issue a test of toughness *vis-à-vis* the Soviet Union and of European willingness to join that toughness. That was a mistake, a serious one, but it was not one that arose from the constraint of domestic politics.

In the case of the December 1979 INF decision the space for decision was narrowed by a combination of alliance and domestic politics. In 1979 the Carter Administration was doubly suspect in the eyes of Europeans: in substance because of its handling of the implications for

Europe of the SALT II negotiations and in process by its image of indecisiveness, symbolized in the nuclear realm by the debacle over the neutron bomb in 1977–78. The combination made Washington especially eager to respond to European entreaties that Europe's nuclear interests, in cruise missiles or in limitations on the Soviet SS-20, not be ignored. The US Department of Defense had *its* reasons for responding to the entreaties of its alliance counterparts. In the end, the shadow of the neutron bomb affair also made those charged with the politics of relations – in the State Department and White House – more ready to embrace a strong solution – deploying new "hardware" – than they otherwise might have been. All allied governments, but particularly the American, were keenly aware that they could not be seen to flinch again in the face of Soviet pressure. The urge to appear decisive played into the domestic politics of all the allies, but again particularly into those of the United States.

COPING WITH ALLIANCE POLITICS

The guidance that these comments about the framework of the alliance provide is mostly cautionary, useful understandings for those that make policy and those that analyze it to carry in their heads. But those understandings can only be given effect through the actions of governments – governments that comprise officials and politicians with their stakes, and bureaucratic machines with their perspectives, governments that act, or do not act in light of domestic politics that usually are all-consuming. Those national politics of governing, and their intersection in the alliance, have run through the cases in this book. I draw out here several features of those politics.

The fact of formal alliance in NATO, and the presence of American forces in Europe, affects the politics of decision-making in three ways. First, it elevates decisions into tests of loyalty and cohesion. Once the December 1979 decisions were taken, for example, no European leader – and certainly no German leader – could go back on them. To have done so would have been to confirm the worst American fears of European "unreliability." Heads of government are tempted to leave discussions early on to the parts of their officialdom with direct concern: those leaders are busy, and, after all, nothing is yet decided. Yet once decisions are taken, the fact of alliance makes them hard to adjust in light of changing circumstances. For any government to ask to re-open a decision is to breach the cohesion of the alliance.

Second, the fact of alliance attaches deadlines to issues that national leaders might wish to see deferred. Witness the neutron bomb: the cycle of nuclear modernization in NATO put the weapon on the agenda; to defer the issue became itself a political choice.

Third, national security issues frequently get curiously disconnected from national politics. For American presidents only slightly more than European prime ministers, foreign policy and defense issues are often a relief from the grubbier questions of domestic politics. The former are not so "real" as the latter. Thus, heads of government are tempted to deal with national security questions in technical terms, as framed by their advisors. Those advisors often are disconnected from political advisors. National security questions come to look technical to national leaders; that breeds the illusion that political implications can wait to be dealt with later.

To be sure, issues of international economics are also dealt with along "separate tracks" by specialized, often highly technical advisors. But the difference is that national leaders can have no illusions that economic questions are technical. They are real, directly connected to prices, jobs and political survival. Politics cannot wait. Indeed, for economic issues the domestic political cast usually is overwhelming, crowding out attention to the foreign policy dimension.

The fact of alliance, and the presence of American military forces in Europe encourages politicians to view national security issues in technical terms. Day-to-day cooperation among the allied armed services is strong; the tasks to be performed are concrete, and there are traditions of both staff work and of multinational cooperation. The process keeps the armed services engaged with one another, and it keeps the American services, particularly the Army, absorbed in their European vocation. But the technical "yak" thrown up by that cooperation abets the tendency of politicians to think of security issues as something different, primarily political.

National leaders simply cannot think four or five years hence about their own domestic politics. That is nearly as true of European prime ministers, who may expect to be in office five years hence, as American presidents who may not. But it is a particular problem for decisions about major weapons systems, for which the time lag between decision and implementation, hence political repercussion, often is five years or more. INF is a clear example.

Americans are by nature problem-solvers. That tendency runs deeply into the governmental machine; it is enhanced by the frequent changes of administration, each one bringing to Washington a new set of politicans and their in-and-out-ers, all on the lookout for problems to solve. This American proclivity means that European leaders should beware of raising problems if they do not want them "solved". Doing so was Helmut Schmidt's mistake in INF in October 1977, I judge. His speech in London ended by coalescing the American defense and diplomatic machinery in support of a single objective. The process had a peculiar "knee" in it: it began with Schmidt's speech and other signals of European concern over nuclear deterrence in Europe, with the American administration (though not necessarily its Defense Department) hanging back. Once, however, the Washington machine had convinced itself that new nuclear hardware was required to "solve" the problem, the train had left the station. From then on it became almost impossible, in any government or among them, to pose the question whether Europeans still thought the new deployments necessary.

The INF affair illustrates another feature of alliance politics: institutional memory is weak in the governments of all the allies, and weakest on precisely the nuances outlined here. Bonn had seen the United States operate on a number of questions. Hence it should have been wary about unleashing the American machine on a nuclear problem. Yet that understanding was lost. Or in the instance of the neutron bomb the political center of the American government quite literally was unaware of the weapon, even though it was in the Administration's own budget. Once discovered, it took a long time for the Administration, and Mr Carter in particular, to understand what he could and could not expect from his allies.

In these circumstances, both Americans and Europeans are tempted to look hopefully at the other side. Failing to understand the organizational and political capacity of the other side, both may be tempted to assume that somehow it will all turn out all right when the time comes. National leaders, busy, distracted and preoccupied with domestic politics, make predictions of their allies to suit their own convenience. They seldom ask the more appropriate question: what is the most invonvenient thing my ally could do?[24]

Finally, while most "accidents" in alliance relations are unpredictable, one class is not. Personality differences between major allied leaders are predictable. One major mishap a year is likely to arise from anger or pique. Witness Schmidt's continual back-biting about Carter, or Reagan's anger with Mitterrand over credits and the gas pipeline.

Trying to change these features of national and alliance politics probably is asking too much. They are deeply rooted in the organizations and politics of the allies, and in how those organizations and politics intersect in the alliance. So I return, in conclusion, to policy, not to process. In the end, it may be easier to make adjustments in policy to cope with the demands of alliance politics than to hope that innovations in decision-making or consultation will change those politics.

The principal lesson for policy is the imperative of limiting demands made of allies and simplifying the endeavors that the alliance attempts. The alliance and the governmental machines that comprise it are blunt instruments. Hence the projects in which they engage become perilous if they ask too much of domestic politics, or depend too much on fine-tuned actions by allied governments, or hinge too much on particular circumstances. In Richard Neustadt's words: "Simplicity consists in limiting our claims on other governments to outcomes reachable by them within a wide range of internal politics, under a variety of personalities and circumstances. These are outcomes which do not depend for their achievement on precise conjunctions of particular procedures, men and issues."[25] Neustadt cited the Marshall Plan, despite its scale and sweep, as possessed of such simplicity, in part, it seems, because the requisite officialdom for economic reconstruction already existed in Europe and could readily be put together in America from university and business communities recently experienced by World War II.

Unfortunately, as so often in human affairs, the requisite simplicity is easier to see in retrospect by its absence than to assess for issues on the horizon. German "offset" payments to the United States seemed a simple enough solution in 1961, helpful for the United States, easy for the Federal Republic. So it was in the short run. Yet the politics in which German fulfillment of that American claim would be easy depended on a combination of military need for American weapons and money to pay for them. That conjunction predictably could not last: Germany would complete a cycle of rearmament, or its military leaders would wish to diversify their armory, or budgetary circumstances would bind. Intent on the short-run, no-one made that prediction.

Or in the case of INF the allies made complicated claims on each other, visible as such at the start. A happy outcome required a combination of steadfastness in the three main European governments – Bonn, London and Rome – against varying degrees of domestic opposition and turmoil. How hard it was to be steadfast depended in turn to a considerable degree on domestic perceptions in Europe of the state of INF arms control. And *that* turned on American adroitness in the negotiations or at least in demonstrating a good faith effort.

The need for that difficult combination should at least have counselled caution from the start. It raised uncomfortable questions: how important was the permanence in power of particular European leaders to a successful outcome? How likely was an American administration to bring the requisite adroitness to bear in negotiating? How propitious were the circumstances for negotiation in the absence of SALT II? If they were not propitious, how firmly would the politicians governing in Bonn – regardless of party – wish to find themselves locked into the alternative of deployment by a fixed date? (A glance at Chancellor Erhard's secret discomfort over MLF in 1964 suggests the answer now, and might have done so quite as well in 1979.) This raises one last question: how flexible were Americans likely to be once they had locked onto a position? Every alliance experience since the European Defense Community in 1954 suggests "not very."

In particular, these chapters underline the riskiness of making claims on trans-Atlantic allies and then elevating their fulfillment into tests of alliance solidarity. That is a particularly American temptation, but other allies have succumbed to it as well, most often in wars. Britain and France tried in Suez in 1956 and were deeply disappointed; Britain made the Falklands war in 1982 a similar test, successfully. For the United States, the temptation to make issues into tests of solidarity grows out of America's central place in the alliance. But it is less and less effective as American pre-eminence in the alliance diminishes. Certainly, some issues are in fact real tests of the cohesion of the alliance, but history indicates that most are not. Even many of those that are, such as the December 1979 decision, were elevated into tests by the alliance itself. And for most issues the appeal to solidarity has proved to be both ineffective and irritating to the intended targets of that appeal.

A more specific form of the plea for simplicity is a caution about proceeding with projects over which ostensible experts disagree, quite aside from elevating those issues into tests of the alliance. One form of the problem arises when the allies pursue purposes of one ilk cloaked in the form of another. The classic error of that sort is the multilateral force (MLF). Its purposes were political – reassurance to the Europeans that the American nuclear umbrella was intact plus assurance to the Germans that they would not be forever consigned to second-rank status in allied nuclear arrangements. Yet its military form – medium-range missiles on NATO surface ships – was unconvincing to military experts. At most, they were prepared to say it could be done. That meant, ultimately, that it would be seen as "gimmicky" and labelled so by opponents in and out of government, thus making it inadequate to fulfill its political purpose.

As noted in Chapter 2, comparable dangers ran through the INF episode. Again the primary purposes was political – reassurance to Europeans – and again the mode was military – deployments of new American missiles. Again there were misgivings about the military utility of the deployments – they were too few to matter or too vulnerable, or had no logical targets. Yet, unlike the MLF, the INF deployments were not easy to deride on military grounds, even if there was no set of targets they could cover that could not be covered by other NATO or American nuclear weapons. If the logic of deterrence, as much political as military, suggested the need for more intermediate weapons based in Europe, the cruise missiles and Pershings would fill that bill. Still, their advantage in military terms over the MLF, if significant, was still marginal. Initially, there were few Pentagon enthusiasts for the new weapons, a cautionary sign. At the same time, because these weapons, in and of themselves, were technically respectable, a policy commitment could convert the Pentagon, which once turned on might not then easily be turned off, another cautionary sign.

Two other episodes, both familiar in this book, illustrate the same point. The ostensible purpose of the proposed deployment of neutron (or enhanced radiation) warheads (ERW) in 1977 was military: to better destroy Soviet tank formations once the nuclear threshhold had been crossed. Yet even their military defenders conceded that they would only be a marginal improvement over existing NATO nuclear warheads, and there were experts who doubted even that. More important, once the debate widened to the broader politico–military terrain, there were plenty of eminent NATO military experts, retired officers and civilian analysts, who belived the ERW would lower the threshhold for the use of nuclear weapons, even if only slightly. Their arguments meant that Soviet propaganda against the weapons found a resonance in Western Europe. Given that division of expert opinion, ERW became a marginal military improvement which could only be purchased at enormous political cost. The game was not worth the candle, a fact President Carter recognized in deferring the issue, though that recognition was late in coming.

In the instance of the Soviet gas pipeline the experts disagreed about the leverage provided by both Western technology exports to the Soviet Union and Soviet gas exports to Western Europe.[26] These were unpromising circumstances in the extreme for the US to make demands of its allies, still less to elevate those demands into a test of alliance solidarity. Europeans could cite experts aplenty, and not just Europeans, to support their view that the pipeline would hedge Europe's energy bets in a sensible way, not hand the Soviet Union wherewithal for future blackmail. The United States then only added insult to injury by arguing that its grain sales to Moscow were acceptable because they cost the Soviet Union foreign exchange, hence reduced Soviet economic strength. On that point virtually all the experts agreed: the argument was economic nonsense.[27]

At least it should be possible for the allies to learn from past episodes to dampen their expectations, limit their claims on each other, and simplify the projects in which their alliance engages. But who is to learn those lessons, which Europeans and which Americans? Professional alliance-watchers, like me, in and out of governments, may be more a part of the problem. We are tempted to judge the current state of the alliance by light of past episodes now converted by memory into successes; to define new challenges the trans-Atlantic alliance must meet if it is to survive; and to design elegant, complicted approaches to those challenges. When those approaches then fall short of the grand objectives we harbor for them, another round of handwringing over the fate of the alliance ensues.

Yet the alliance will survive even us. Alliance arrangements have weathered Suez, Vietnam, the French withdrawal, the Year of Europe and the oil crisis. They will not be easily shaken by circumstances that have in fact changed, even though the extent of change is less than is usually thought. Despite the changes the alliance has lasted thirty-five years. It has endured Mr Carter's bumblings and Mr Reagan's ideological reflex. Even if it is managed with only modest adroitness, it should last thirty more in much its present form.

Notes

PREFACE

1. In a review of Jonathan Schell's *The Fate of the Earth* in *The Sunday Times*, London, 20 June 1982.

1 THE NATURE OF THE ALLIANCE

1. From *The Troubled Partnership: a Re-Appraisal of the Atlantic Alliance*, (New York: McGraw-Hill, 1965) pp. 4,9.
2. From *The Wall Street Journal*, cited in Kenneth Adler and Douglas Wertman, "Is NATO in Trouble?: a Survey of European Attitudes," *Public Opinion* (August/September 1981) 8.
3. Josef Joffe, "European-American Relations: The Enduring Crisis," *Foreign Affairs*, (Spring 1981).
4. From the title of A. W. De Porte's book, *Europe Between the Superpowers: The Enduring Balance* (New Haven, Conn: Yale University Press, 1979). His is one of the best of the arguments emphasizing stability.
5. This is Richard Neustadt's classic formulation. See his *Alliance Politics* (New York: Columbia University Press, 1970) esp. pp. 118ff.
6. Herbert Block, "The Planetary Product in 1980," US Department of State, 1981.
7. Joffe, cited above, 841
8. US Central Intelligence Agency, National Foreign Assessments Center, *International Energy Statistical Review* (31 March 1981) 7–8.
9. De Porte, cited above, contains apt discussions of several of the points in this paragraph. See, especially, his discussion of the implications of limited European union, pp. 229ff.
10. Most political science literature on alliances is too theoretical for my purposes, but some of it does stretch thought about categories of alliances and about why alliances form and fall apart. See, for example, "International Alliances: a Survey of Theories and Propositions," ch. 1 of Ole R. Holsti and others, *Unity and Disintegration in International Alliances: Comparative Studies*, (New York: John Wiley, 1973).
11. Quoted in Arnold Wolfers, ed., *Alliance Policy in the Cold War* (Baltimore: Johns Hopkins Press, 1959) p. 184.
12. William Lee Miller, "The American Ethos and the Alliance System," in Wolfers, cited above, pp. 35, 38.
13. Henry Kissinger's criticism of the alliance and of the Reagan Administration in responding to the Polish crisis fell into the error of judging current events in light of

unreal past standards. See his articles in *The New York Times*, 17 and 18 January 1982.

14. This is what Graham Allison, building on the work of many others, labelled the "rational actor" model. See his *Essence of Decision: Explaining the Cuban Missile Crisis* (Boston: Little Brown, 1971).

15. A classic article along these lines is Mancur Olson, Jr and Richard Zeckhauser "An Economic Theory of Alliances," *The Review of Economics and Statistics*, 48, 3 (August 1966) 266–79. See also the recent report to the Trilateral Commission, *Sharing International Responsibilities Among the Trilateral Countries*, (March 1982).

16. This may not be strictly true if, for instance, adding a member to the Alliance means extending the front to be protected with (a given stock of) conventional weapons. It is also possible to imagine circumstances in which more defense spending by one ally would elicit more, not less, from the others – if, for example, the first increment made it possible for the alliance to accomplish a mission hitherto beyond its reach. These circumstances, however, are sufficiently bizarre not to invalidate the basic logic of these paragraphs. See James C. Murdoch and Todd Sandler, "A Theoretical and Empirical Analysis of NATO," *Journal of Conflict Resolution*, 26, 2 (June 1982) 237–63.

17. Olson and Zeckhauser do find such a positive correlation, ibid., using 1960 data. For 1980 the ranklings were: gross domestic product (GDP) – US, Federal Republic, France, Britain, Italy, Canada, Belgium, Denmark, Norway, Turkey, Greece, Portugal, Netherlands, Luxemburg; for defense spending as a percentage of GNP – US, Britain, Greece, Turkey, France, Portugal, Netherlands, Belgium, Federal Republic, Norway, Italy, Denmark, Canada, Luxemburg. From IISS, *The Military Balance, 1981–82* (London: 1981).

18. See his "Alliances in Theory and Practice," in Wolfers, cited above, p. 194.

19. See Olson and Zeckhauser, cited above.

20. See Mancur Olson, *The Logic of Collective Action* (Cambridge, Mass: Harvard University Press, 1965).

21. Some examples from the political season of 1984: "We must take whatever steps we must to see that Americans in the 1980s and 1990s will be buying American products made with American steel" (Senator Edward Kennedy). "We've been running up the white flag when we should be running up the American flag. . . . What do we want our kids to do? Sweep up around Japanese computers" (Vice President Walter Mondale). "The problem that we have gotten into now is that the United States is practicing free trade, period – we are the exclusive practitioner of this ideal" (Senator John Danforth).

2 THE NUCLEAR DILEMMA

1. For instance, Henry Kissinger's comments of two decades ago are an apt description of NATO's current nuclear dilemma: "In the past, the major problem for strategists was to assemble superior strength; in the contemporary period the problem more frequently is how to make the available power relevant to objectives likely to be in dispute. Yet no matter what spectrum of power the major contenders may have at their disposal, the fear of escalation is inescapable. Though states have an

unprecedented capacity to devastate their opponent, their threats to do so have only a limited credibility." Or: "A conventional war confined to Europe must appear in a different light to Americans than to Europeans, on whose territory such a war would be fought. A nuclear exchange which spares their territory may seem to Europeans a more attractive strategy and the threat of nuclear retaliation a more effective deterrent. Although the interests of the Alliance may be indivisible in an ultimate, this does not guarantee that there will not be sharply clashing perceptions about methods to reach common objectives" *The Troubled Partnership*, (New York: McGraw-Hill, 1965) pp. 18,15.

2. For example, in the middle of a rambling answer about nuclear escalation at a press conference in October 1981, President Reagan said: "I could see where you could have the exchange of tactical weapons against troops in the field without it bringing either one of the major powers to pushing the button," *New York Times*, 21 October 1981.

3. On this early history, see Alan K. Henrikson, "The Creation of the North Atlantic Alliance, 1948–1952," *National War College Review*, 22,3 (May–June 1980).

4. North Atlantic Treaty, articles V and VI.

5. The speech is reprinted in *Survival*, 20,1 (January/February 1978) 2–10.

6. On "keys", Alex Gliksman's proposal is innovative but will not do the job. See his "Three Keys for Europe's Bombs," *Foreign Policy*, 39 (Summer 1980) 40–57. More generally, see Pierre Lellouche's argument for a broadening of the role of British and French nuclear forces, in "Europe and Her Defense," *Foreign Affairs*, 54,4 (Spring 1981) 813–34; Hedley Bull's explicit call for more European cooperation, including nuclear, in "European Self-Reliance and the Reform of NATO," *Atlantic Quarterly*, 1, 1 (Spring 1983) 25-43; and a similar though more tentative argument from German Social Democrats, in Wilhelm Bruns and Christian Krause, "Reflections on a European Peace Order," Friedrich Ebert Stiftung, December 1982.

7. W. S. Bennett, R. R. Sandoval and R. G. Shreffler have done the most work on such proposals. See their "A Credible Nuclear-Emphasis Defense for NATO," *Orbis*, 17,2 (Summer 1973).

8. Kent F. Wisner, "Military Aspects of Enhanced Radiation Weapons," *Survival*, 23, 6 (November/December 1981).

9. For a strong argument about the difficulty of controlling nuclear war, see Desmond Ball, *Can Nuclear War Be Controlled?* Adelphi Paper No. 169 (London: IISS, 1981).

10. See, for example, Senator Sam Nunn's report, *NATO: Can the Alliance be Saved?* Report to the Senate Committee on Armed Serivces, 97 Cong., 2 sess. (13 May 1982); and Report of the European Security Study. *Strengthening Conventional Deterrence in Europe: Proposals for the 1980s* (1983).

11. There is only beginning to be good history of NATO TNF. For a summary history, see *The Modernization of NATO's Long-Range Theater Nuclear Forces*, Report for the Subcommittee on Europe and the Middle East of the House Committee on Foreign Affairs, 96 Cong., 2 sess. (31 December 1980). See also David N. Schwartz, *NATO's Nuclear Dilemma* (Washington: The Brookings Institution, 1983); and chapters by Timothy Ireland and Lawrence Freedman in Jeffrey Boutwell, Paul M. Doty and Gregory F. Treverton, eds., *The Nuclear Confrontation in Europe*, forthcoming from Croom Helm, London. For a nice history and summary of the issues, see J. Michael Legge, *Theater Nuclear Weapons and the NATO Strategy of*

Flexible Response, R-2964-FF (Santa Monica, Cal: The Rand Corporation, 1983).

12. For a strong argument on this score, see Uwe Nerlich, "Theater Nuclear Forces in Europe: Is NATO Running Out of Options?," *The Washington Quarterly*, 3, 1 (Winter 1980).

13. The now classic discussion is Albert Wolhstetter, "The Delicate Balance of Terror," *Foreign Affairs* (January 1959).

14. These estimates are from Anthony H. Cordesman, *Deterrence in the 1980s, Part 1: American Strategic Forces and Extended Deterrence*, Adelphi Paper No. 175, (London: IISS, 1982) pp. 35–6.

15. Jeffery Record, "Theatre Nuclear Weapons: Begging the Soviet Union to Pre-empt", *Survival*, 19, 5 (September/October 1977) 208–11.

16. The American Single Integrated Operational Plan (SIOP) divides Soviet nuclear targets into four categories: opposing nuclear forces and other "hard targets"; economic and recovery targets; political control mechanisms; and other military targets (OMT). OMT is the largest of the four categories, some 20 000 comprising half the SIOP targets. See Desmond Ball, "Soviet ICBM Deployment', *Survival*, 22, 4 July/August 1980, pp. 176–70. On the uses of submarine-launched missiles against OMT, see Desmond J. Ball, "The Counterforce Potential of American SLBM systems," *Journal of Peace Research*, 1 (1977) 23–40.

17. See his "NATO Myths," *Foreign Policy*, 45 (Winter 1981–82) 55. This section owes much to Freedman.

18. This point is stressed by Horst Afheldt. See his "Tactical Nuclear Weapons and European Security," ch. 9 of SIPRI, *Tactical Nuclear Weapons: European Perspectives* (London, 1978).

19. See Robert Kennedy, "Soviet Theater-Nuclear Forces: Implications for NATO Defense," *Orbis* (Summer 1981).

20. Alton Frye, "Nuclear Weapons in Europe: No Exit from Ambivalence," *Survival*, 22,3 (May/June 1980) 98–106.

21. See House report, cited above, note 11, p. 22ff.

22. For a summary version of the INF episode, see my "NATO Alliance Politics," ch 13 of Richard K. Betts., ed., *Cruise Missiles: Technology, Strategy, Politics* (Washington: The Brookings Institution, 1981). See also the House report cited above, note 11; and David C. Elliot, *Decision at Brussels: the Politics of Nuclear Forces*, California Seminar Discussion Paper No. 97 (Santa Monica, Cal, 1981).

23. The communiqué of the 11 November 1976 Nuclear Planning Group (NPG) meeting: "The United States is developing a new 8-inch nuclear projectile with greater accuracy and much reduced collateral damage."

24. Walter Pincus, *Washington Post*, 7 June 1977.

25. For a description of the neutron bomb and other recent German-American misadventures on military issues, see Alex A. Vardamis, "German–American Military Fissures," *Foreign Policy* (Spring 1979) 87–106. For a detailed description of the neutron bomb as an issue in Alliance politics, see Lothar Ruehl, "Die Nichtentscheidung ueber die 'Neutronenwaffe',," *Europa Archiv*, 5 (1979) 137–50.

26. Stephen R. Hanmer, Jr, "NATO's Long Range Theatre Nuclear Forces: Modernization in Parallel with Arms Control," *NATO Review*, 28 (February 1980) 1–6. For more detail on the deliberations leading to the December 1979 decision, see Elliot, cited above, note 22.

27. Richard Neustadt's conclusion about the Skybolt affair is even more apt with regard to the MLF: " . . . Macmillan . . . made what seems to me a classic error in high

policy or politics: he pursued objectives, diplomatic and political, designed as something else, a military posture, which was suspect in its own terms, liable to attack or ridicule or both" *Alliance Politics* (New York: Columbia University Press, 1970) p. 147.

28. *Parliamentary Debates*, Commons, 5th Series, vol 977, session 179–80, 24 January 1980 (HMSO 1980) col. 769.

29. For a history of this infelicitously-named principle, see Catherine McArdle Kelleher, *Germany and the Politics of Nuclear Weapons* (New York: Columbia University Press, 1975) pp. 9–59.

30. For a general description of the NPG and its functions, see Richard E. Shearer, "Consulting in NATO on Nuclear Policy", *NATO Review*, (27 October 1979) 25–8.

31. The offer was made in a speech to the National Press Club in Washington and released by the State Department on 18 November 1981.

32. The directive itself remains classified. For Secretary Harold Brown's discussion of it, see his speech reprinted in *Survival*, 23,6 (November/December 1980).

33. See Hans Rattinger's chapter on the Federal Republic in Hans Rattinger and Gregory Flynn, eds, *The Public and Atlantic Defense*, forthcoming from the Atlantic Institute for International Affairs, Paris.

34. See McGeorge Bundy, George F. Kennan, Robert S. McNamara and Gerard Smith, "Nuclear Weapons and the Atlantic Alliance," *Foreign Affairs*, 60,4 (Spring 1982) 753–68.

35. West German Foreign Minister Dietrich Genscher joined his American counterpart Alexander Haig, in criticizing the proposal by Bundy *et al*, in the latter's case before the proposal had even been published. For the German counter-argument, see Karl Kaiser, Georg Leber, Alois Mertes and Franz-Josef Schulze, "Nuclear Weapons and the Preservation of Peace," *Foreign Affairs*, 60,5 (Summer 1982) 1157–70. For background and analysis of the NFU issue, see John D. Steinbruner and Leon V. Sigal, eds, *Alliance Security: NATO and the No-First Use Question* (Washington, The Brookings Institution, 1983).

36. This idea has been suggested earlier by some German and British analysts. For an interesting proposal along those lines, see Lawrence Freedman, "The Dilemma of Theatre Nuclear Arms Control," *Survival*, 23,1 (January/February 1981) 2–10.

37. A number of observers have suggested a more direct role for the Europeans in European arms control negotiations. See, for example, Christoph Bertram, "The Implications of Theater Nuclear Weapons in Europe," *Foreign Affairs*, 60,2 (Winter 1981/82) 323ff.; and Henry Kissinger, "A Plan to Reshape NATO," *Time*, 5 March 1984, pp. 20–4.

3 DEFENSE AND DETENTE IN EUROPE

1. The edited version of Secretary Kissinger's remarks appears in *The Washington Quarterly*, 2, 4 (Fall 1979) and in *Survival*, 21, 6 (November/December 1979).

2. There are many assessments of this period. One good one is Robert E. Hunter, *Security in Europe* (Bloomington: Indiana University Press, 1969) pp. 46ff.

3. See *Crisis in the Atlantic Alliance: Origins and Implications*, Report for the Senate Committee on Foreign Relations, 97 Cong., 2 sess. (March 1982) p. 20.

4. From the German Statistics Bureau, Wiesbaden.

5. Angela E. Stent, *Soviet Energy and Western Europe*, The Washington Papers 90,

(Washington: Georgetown Center for Strategic and International Studies, 1982) p. 24.

6. See, for example, Senator Lugar's comment in *East–West Relations*, Hearing before the Senate Foreign Relations Committee, 97 Cong., 2 sess. (February 2, 1982) p. 20: ". . . in fact if we have any embargo [on trade with the Soviet Union] it is an agricultural embargo, embellished by a few bits and pieces of technological know-how around the edges."

7. For more detail, see Stent, pp. 60ff., and *NATO Today: The Alliance in Evolution*, Report to the Senate Committee on Foreign Relations, 97 Cong., 2 sess. (April 1982) pp. 29ff.

8. The German government's position was set out in a memorandum from its ambassador in Washington to Senator Charles Mathias, reprinted in *Economic Relations with the Soviet Union*, Hearings before the Subcommittee on International Economic Policy of the Senate Foreign Relations Committee, 97 Cong., 2 sess. (30 July, 12, 13 August 1982) pp. 65–7. For an additional German view, see Axel Lebahn, "The Yamal Gas Pipeline from the USSR to Western Europe in the East–West Conflict," *Aussenpolitik*, 3 (1983) 257–81.

9. For a similar view of the effects of the embargo, and for an excellent summary of East–West trade issues, see U.S. Congess Office of Technology Assessment, *Technology and East–West Trade: an Update* (Washington: 1983) esp. pp. 69ff. For a review of the studies agreed at the end of the pipeline affair, see Ellen L. Frost and Angela E. Stent, "NATO's Troubles with East–West Trade," *International Security*, 8, 1 (Summer 1983) 179–200.

10. As *Le Monde* commented editorially, the "embargo . . . had in fact done more damage to what [the President] wanted to strengthen – the cohesion of the Atlantic Alliance – than to the Soviet Union which he wanted to punish," 18 November 1982.

11. For an example of the American argument that the pipeline is bad because it will yield Moscow foreign exchange, hence will increase Soviet military potential, see Undersecretary of State James Buckley's testimony to the Subcommittee on International Economic Policy of the Senate Foreign Relations Committee, cited in Department of State *Bulletin*, September 1982. By contrast, in one analysis, importing an extra one million metric tons of grain in 1982, then worth $160 million, would have saved the Soviet Union enough resources to produce about 2.8 million metric tons of oil, then worth $700 million on world markets. Wharton Econometric Forecasting Associates, *Comparative Advantage in Soviet Grain and Energy Trade* (Washington, 10 September 1982.)

12. Good sources on this episode, similar in most particulars, are Angela Stent, *From Embargo to Ostpolitik: the Political Economy of West German-Soviet Relations 1955–1980*, (Cambridge University Press, 1981) pp. 98ff.; and Robert W. Dean, *West German Trade with the East: The Political Dimension* (New York: Praeger, 1974).

13. Dean, cited above, p. 137.

14. These results are from Hans Rattinger, "The Federal Republic of Germany: Much Ado about (Almost) Nothing," in Gregory Flynn and Hans Rattinger, eds, *The Public and Atlantic Defense*, forthcoming from the Atlantic Insititute for International Affairs. (Hereafter cited as *The Public and Atlantic Defense*.)

15. See Philip Windsor, *Germany and the Western Alliance: Lessons from the 1980 Crises*, Adelphi Paper No. 170 (London: IISS, 1981).

16. Herbert Block, "The Planetary Product in 1980," US Department of State, 1981.

17. A nice summary of these changes is Renata Fritsch-Bournazel, "Germany's Role in

Europe: Historical and Psychological Dimensions," Working Paper No. 44, International Security Studies Program, The Wilson Center, Washington, D.C., August 1982.

18. For a thoughtful discussion of this and other issues in Germany's role in the alliance, see Windsor, cited above.

19. See Christoph Bertram, "European Security and the German Problem," *International Security*, 4 (Winter 1979–80).

20. For an expanded argument along these lines, see my "The Federal Republic in the NATO Alliance," in Peter H. Merkl, ed., *West German Foreign Policy: Dilemmas and Directions* (Chicago Council on Foreign Relations, 1982.) See also Gabriel Robin, "The German Problem Revisited," *Atlantic Quarterly*, 1,3 (Autumn 1983) 191–200. Robin argues for dramatic change, but his evidence also underscores why it is so unlikely.

21. "The most urgent crisis is the impending collapse of NATO. In all of Western Europe, a wave of public opinion that favors unilateral nuclear disarmament is gathering force. The governments oppose it, but ever more feebly and ineffectually. We deplore it, while consoling ourselves that it is a passing spasm of the kind we have lived through before. But it is not a spasm. It is a tidal wave that will sweep all before it, leaving NATO in ruins." The words are Irving Kristol's in the *Wall Street Journal*, cited in Kenneth Adler and Douglas Wertman, "Is NATO in Trouble?: A Survey of European Attitudes," *Public Opinion* (August/September 1981) 8.

22. These polling data are from an Enmid poll in West Germany, sponsored by *Der Spiegel* and conducted in the fall of 1981; from a Gallup poll of February 1982 reported in *Newsweek*, 15 March 1982; and various USICA (now USIA) polls. The last are summarized and analyzed in Adler and Wertman, cited above.

23. Adler and Wertman, cited above, pp. 10–11.

24. See Stephen F. Szabo, "The Successor Generation," in Alan Platt, ed., *The Atlantic Alliance: Perspectives from the Successor Generation*, R-3100-NIS/USIA/DOS/FF/RC (Santa Monica: Rand Corporation, 1983). This issue merits more study than it has received.

25. See Stephen F. Szabo, ed., *The Successor Generation: International Perspectives of Postwar Europeans* (London: Butterworths, 1983) p. 172.

26. John E. Rielly, ed., *American Public Opinion and U.S. Foreign Policy 1983* (The Chicago Council on Foreign Relations, 1983) pp. 21,31.

27. James O. Goldsborough argues that the root problem in US policy toward Europe is the "total lack of American homogeneity. American is not a melting pot, but a pot that wouldn't melt." See his *Rebel Europe*, (New York: Macmillan, 1982) p. 181.

28. Rielly, cited above, p. 11.

29. This and the following paragraph owe much to Catherine McArdle Kelleher, "America looks at Europe: Change and Continuity in the 1980s," in Lawrence Freedman, ed., *The Troubled Alliance: Atlantic Relations in the 1980s*, Joint Studies in Public Policy 8 (London: Heineman, 1983).

30. See Stephen J. Artner, "Detente Policy Before and After Afghanistan," *Aussenpolitik*, 2 (1980) 134–146.

31. The emphasis, of course, is on *relatively*. The US government estimated during the pipeline affair that controls on oil and gas equipment and technology sales to the Soviet Union would cost US firms between $300 million and $600 million in lost exports over three years. That is small for the entire economy; it is not for particular industries or firms, and so, as discussed earlier, the political effect of sanctions at home may be out of all relation to aggregate economic impact. Caterpillar Tractor,

for example, estimated that before 1978 it had captured 85% of the lucrative Soviet market for pipelaying machines, while its Japanese competitor, Komatsu, had 15%. After two rounds of sanctions, Caterpillar estimated that the shares had been reversed. US Congress Office of Technology Assessment, cited above, pp. 57–8.

32. The following formulation is typical; "Among Western European governmental leaders, there has hardly ever been any question as to whether economic relations with Eastern Europe should be pursued and cultivated in order to create a basis for communication which could be used to take steps in the direction of reducing confrontations and mistrust in Europe." Friedemann Mueller, "East–West Trade and Security Policy," *Aussenpolitik* (1979) 182–3.

33. See Peter Wiles, "Is an Anti-Soviet Embargo Desirable or Possible? in *The Conduct of East–West Relations in the 1980s, Part II*, Adelphi Paper No. 190 (London: IISS, 1984).

34. For a brief version of this argument, see Charles Wolf's testimony, based on a longer RAND study, in *The Premises of East–West Commercial Relations*, Workshop sponsored by the Senate Foreign Relations Committee, 97 Cong., 2 Sess. (December 1982) pp. 142ff. For a broad treatment of East–West economic issues from a variety of German perspectives, see Friedemann Mueller and others, *Zur Frage von Wirtschaftssanktionen in den Ost-West Beziehungen: Rahmenbeding-ungen und Modalitaeten* (Ebenhausen: Stiftung Wissenschaft und Politik, August 1983).

35. See, for example, the conclusions of US Congress Office of Technology Assessment, cited above, pp. 70–1.

36. To some extent, European governments lack the authority to implement sanctions comparable to that granted to the American President in the Export Administration Act of 1979. That act (section 3B) confers wide authority to invoke sanctions in order to "further significantly the foreign policy of the United States or to fulfill its international obligations." See *ibid.*, p. 201.

37. Rielly, cited above, p. 30.

4   DEFENSE BEYOND EUROPE

1. This limitation is in article 6 of the North Atlantic Treaty.

2. Alfred Grosser, *The Western Alliance: European–American Relations Since 1945* (London: Macmillan, 1980) pp. 91–3.

3. For the Lovett quote and more detail, see Alan K. Henrikson, "The Creation of the North Atlantic Alliance, 1948–1952," *Naval War College Review*, 32, 3 (May/June 1980).

4. André Fontaine, *L'alliance atlantique à l'heure de dégel* (Paris: Clamann-Lévy, 1959) p. 73.

5. Konrad Adenauer, *Errinerungen 1955–1959*, vol III (Stuttgart: Deutsche Verlangs-Anstalt, 1965) pp. 159, 163, 166, 320, 334–6,cited in Theodore Draper, "The Western Misalliance," *The Washington Quarterly*, 4, 1 (Winter, 1981) 28.

6. John Newhouse, *De Gaulle and the Anglo-Saxons* (London: Andre Deutsch, 1970) pp. 66ff.

7. *The Atlantic Alliance*, Hearings before the Senate Subcommittee on National

Security and International Operations, 89 Cong., 2 sess., Part 7 (Supplement) (15 August 1966) pp. 230–1.

8. Charles de Gaulle, *Discours et Messages*, vol III (Paris: Plon, 1970) pp. 247–8, cited in Draper, cited above, p. 30.

9. These figures are from Melvin A. Conant, *The Oil Factor in U.S. Foreign Policy, 1980–90* (Lexington, Mass.: D. C. Heath and Co., 1982) pp. 3,20.

10. For more discussion, see Robert J. Lieber, "Economics, Energy and Security in Alliance Perspective," *International Security*, 4, 4 (Spring 1980) 139–63.

11. These data are from IISS, *The Military Balance, 1983–84* (London, 1983); *NATO Today: The Alliance in Evolution*, Report to the Senate Committee on Foreign Relations, 97 Cong., 2 sess. (9 June 1982) pp. 37–8: and from Dominique Moisi, "France: The Limits of Consensus," *Atlantic Quarterly*, 1, 2 (Summer 1983) 149–62.

12. See, for example, the writings of Theo Sommer in *Die Zeit*, 22 and 29 February 1980, and 27 June 1980.

13. For a variety of perspectives on the RDF and its possible mission, see Jeffrey Record, *The RDF and U.S. Military Intervention in the Persian Gulf* (Cambridge, Mass: Institute for Foreign Policy Analysis, 1981); Congressional Budget Office, *RDF: Policy and Budgetary Implications*, (Washington, 1983); Joshua M. Epstein, "Soviet Vulnerabilities in Iran and the RDF Deterrent," *International Security*, 6, 2 (Fall 1981) 126–58; and Kenneth N. Waltz, "A Strategy for the RDF," *International Security*, 5, 4 (Spring 1981) 49–73.

14. David Capitanchik and Richard C. Eichenberg, *Defence and Public Opinion*, Chatham House Papers, 20 (London: Royal Institute of International Affairs, 1983) pp. 84–5.

15. John E. Rielly, ed., *American Public Opinion and U.S. Foreign Policy 1983* (Chicago: Chicago Council on Foreign Relations, 1983) pp. 12, 31.

16. The report is officially titled *Report of the National Bipartisan Commission on Central America* (Washington, January 1984).

17. For a brief summary of the German Social Democratic view, see Friedrich Ebert Stiftung, "The Central American Crisis and Western Europe: Perceptions and Reactions," Bonn, 1982.

18. See Lieber, cited above.

19. 1977 is the last year for which reliable figures are available. See United Nations, *1981 Yearbook of International Trade Statistics*.

20. *The Times* (London) 30 July 1981.

21. See my *The Dollar Drain and American Forces in Germany: Managing the Political Economics of Alliance* (Ohio University Press, 1978) pp. 106ff.

22. On the earlier period, see Phil Williams, "Puzzles, Paradoxes and Ambiguities: U.S. Commitment to Western Europe," *RUSI Journal* (December 1980) 29–33.

23. In October 1982 the Senate Appropriations Committee, at the behest of Senator Stevens' subcommittee on defense, called for a cap on the number of US forces in Europe. It also reported that it was "greatly disturbed that the US commitment to European security in terms of force levels and defense expenditures continues to escalate while our NATO allies' share of defense steadily declines." Reported in *Congressional Quarterly*, 9 October 1982, p. 2650. For a selection of neoconservative views on the alliance, see Irving Kristol, "What's Wrong with NATO?" *New York Times Magazine*, 25 September 1983; Norman Podhoretz, "The Present Danger," *Commentary*, March 1980; and Walter Laqueur, "Euro-Neutralism," *Commentary*, June 1980.

24. *NATO Today*, cited above, p. 39.
25. See, for example, the communiqué of the Defense Planning Committee Ministerial Session, Brussels, 12–13 May 1981.
26. On this episode, see André Fontaine, "Trans-Atlantic Doubts and Dreams," *Foreign Affairs*, 59, 3 (1981) 584ff.
27. For a suggestion along a similar line, see Larl Kaiser, Winston Lord, Thierry de Montbrial and David Watt, *Western Security: What has Changed? What Is to be Done?* (New York: Council on Foreign Relations, 1981).
28. The summit is described in the memoirs of both President Carter and his National Security Advisor, Zbigniew Brzezinski. See respectively, *Keeping Faith: Memoirs of a President* (New York: Bantam Books, 1982) p. 235; and *Power and Principle: Memoirs of the National Security Advisor* (New York: Farrar, Straus, Giroux, 1983) pp. 294–5.
29. The classic account of the Skybolt affair is Richard E. Neustadt's. See his *Alliance Politics* (New York: Columbia University Press, 1970).
30. The letter was leaked to the German weekly *Stern*. For the American reaction to Schmidt's comments and for an account of how the letter came to be sent, see Brzezinski, *Power and Principle*, cited above, p. 309.
31. See Nicholas Bayne, Robert Putnam, *Hanging Together: The Seven-Power Summits*, (Cambridge, Mass.: Harvard University Press, 1984).

5 THE IMPACT OF ECONOMICS

1. This speech was published in *The New York Times*, 24 April, 1973.
2. This is a point made by Francis Bator in his "The Politics of Alliance: The United States and Western Europe," in Kermit Gordon, ed., *Agenda for the Nation* (Washington: The Brookings Instutition, 1968).
3. See Elizabeth Stabler, "The Dollar Devaluations of 1971 and 1973," in "Appendix H: Case Studies on U.S. Foreign Economic Policy, 1965–1974," to *Report of the Commission on the Organization of Government for the Conduct of Foreign Policy* (Washington, 1975) p.154. (Hereafter cited as *COG Economic Cases*.)
4. This argument was made strongly by Robert O. Keohane and Joseph S. Nye, *Power and Interdependence* (Boston: Little Brown, 1977) pp. 39ff.
5. Journalistic accounts and my own conversations suggest this. Poll results provide some confirming evidence. See, for example, *Eurobarometre*, (June 1980) p.20, cited in Bruce Russet and Donald R. DeLuca, "Theater Nuclear Forces: Public Opinion in Western Europe," *Political Science Quarterly*, 98, 2 (Summer 1983) 180.
6. See, for example, the column by Flora Lewis in *The New York Times*, 6 May, 1983.
7. The richest set of cases, now somewhat long in the tooth, is contained in *COG Economic Cases*, cited above.
8. For example, Peter Katzenstein, ed., *Between Power and Plenty: Foreign Economic Policies of Advanced Industrial States* (Madison: University of Wisconsin Press, 1977); Keohane and Nye, cited above; or David P. Calleo and Benjamin M. Rowland, *America and the World Political Economy* (Bloomington: Indiana University Press, 1973).
9. Bela Balassa, "The United States in the World Economy," in Christian Stoffaes, ed., *The Political Economy of the United States* (New York: North-Holland, 1983) p. 451.

10. See The Atlantic Institute for International Affairs – International Herald Tribune–Louis Harris Poll, 20 October 1982.
11. See Stephen D. Krasner, "United States Commercial and Monetary Policy: Unravelling the Paradox of External Strength and Internal Weakness," in Katzenstein, cited above, pp. 67–71.
12. *Ibid.*, pp.66–7.
13. John E. Rielly, ed., *American Public Opinion and U.S. Foreign Policy 1983* (Chicago: The Chicago Council on Foreign Relations, 1983) p.24.
14. "Trade Act of 1974," Public Law 93–618, 93 Cong., H.R. 10710, Sec. 301.
15. These are points made by Raymond Vernon in his "International Trade Policy in the 1980s: Prospects and Problems," *International Studies Quarterly*, 26, 4 (December 1982) 483–510.
16. For a more detailed discussion of these circumstances, see Raymond Vernon, "Old Rules and New Players: GATT in the World Trading System," paper prepared for the 25th Anniversary of the Center for International Affairs, Harvard University, 11 May 1983, forthcoming in an edited volume.
17. Albert Bressand, ed., *The State of the World Economy, 1982*, Annual Report by the French Institute for International Relations (Cambridge, Mass.: Ballinger Publishing Company, 1982) p. 131.
18. Raymond A. Bauer, Ithiel de Sola Pool, and Lewis Anthony Dexter, *American Business and Public Policy: The Politics of Foreign Trade* (New York: Atherton Press, 1963)
19. These are Robert Pastor's conclusions. See his *Congress and the Politics of U.S. Foreign Economic Policy, 1929–1976* (Berkeley, Cal: University of California Press, 1980) pp.329ff.
20. For a discussion of those risks, see Bressand, cited above, pp. 129–34.
21. Raymond Vernon, *Two Hungry Giants: The United States and Japan in the Quest for oil and Ores* (Cambridge: Harvard University Press, 1983) p. 124.
22. The fullest treatment of this case is in I.M. Destler and others, *Managing an Alliance: The Politics of the U.S.–Japanese Relationship* (Washington: The Brookings Institution, 1976) pp. 8ff.
23. For a brief history of offset, see my *The "Dollar Drain" and American Forces in Germany: Managing the Political Economics of Alliance* (Ohio University Press, 1978) pp. 31–51.
24. Their statement was more-than-usually frank. It said: "Given recently introduced changes in the international monetary area, specifically flexible exchange rates, as well as the notably improved strength of the dollar, the President and Chancellor consider that the traditional offset arrangement has lost its relevance," see ibid., p. 51.
25. For example, in 1982, the US Administration successfully pressed the Federal Republic to sign a Wartime Host Nation Support Agreement under which Germany would form a force of 93 000 reservists to provide support for reinforcing US forces in time of tension.
26. Reported in *Congressional Quarterly*, 9 October 1982, p. 2650.
27. The summit is described in the memoirs of both President Carter and his National Security Advisor, Zbigniew Brzezinski. See, respectively, *Keeping Faith: Memoirs of a President* (New York: Bantam Books, 1982) p. 235; and *Power and Principle: Memoirs of the National Security Advisor* (New York: Farrar, Straus, Giroux, 1983) pp. 294–5.

28. See Edward F. Graziano, "Commodity Export Controls: The Soybean Case, 1973," in *COG Economic Cases*.
29. See the cases by Stabler, cited above, and by Linda S. Graebner, "The New Economic Policy, 1971," both in *COG Economic Cases*.
30. Quoted in Graebner, ibid., p.172.
31. This observation derives mostly from my own experience working for the National Security Council during 1977–78. Notice that the table of contents to Brzezinski's memoirs, cited above, contains not a single reference to economics.
32. There is no good single account of this episode. This account is compiled from Department of Commerce press releases, 10 June and 25 August 1982 and from newspaper accounts.
33. See Vernon, "Old Rules and New Players," cited above.
34. The problem of early warning is discussed at length in Chapter 6 of Treverton, cited above.
35. This approach was outlined in "An Analysis of Export Control of U.S. Technology – A Department of Defense Perspective," generally referred to as the Bucy Report after the task force chairman, J. Fred Bucy, Jr. See Richard Perle, "The Strategic Implications of West–East Technology Transfer," in *The Conduct of East–West Relations in the 1980s, Part II*, Adelphi Paper No. 190 (London: IISS, 1984).
36. Robert E. Klitgaard's conclusions of a decade ago are still apt. See his analysis in *National Security and Export Controls*, R–1432–1–ARPA/CIEP (Santa Monica, Cal: The Rand Corporation, April 1974)

6   MANAGING ALLIANCE POLITICS

1. See Samuel P. Huntington, "Conventional Deterrence and Conventional Retaliation in Europe," *International Security*, 8, 3 (Winter 1983–4) 32–56.
2. For interesting evidence on this point, see Philip P. Evert, "Public Opinion on Nuclear Weapons, Defense and Security: the Case of the Netherlands," in Gregory Flynn and Hans Rattinger, eds, *The Public and Atlantic Defense*, forthcoming from the Atlantic Institute for International Affairs. (Hereafter cited as *The Public and Atlantic Defense*.)
3. See Hans Rattinger, "The Federal Republic of Germany: Much Ado About (Almost) Nothing," in *The Public and Atlantic Defense*.
4. See the conclusions in ibid.
5. See *Report of the President's Commission on Strategic Forces* (Washington, April 1983).
6. These data are from Rattinger, cited above.
7. John E. Rielly, ed., *American Public Opinion and U.S. Foreign Policy, 1983* (The Chicago Council on Foreign Relations, 1983) pp. 8–9, 13.
8. On this point, see Stephen Woolcock's chapter in Lawrence Freedman, ed., *The Troubled Alliance: Atlantic Relations in the 1980s*, Joint Studies in Public Policy 8 (London: Heinemann, 1983). Hereafter cited as *The Troubled Alliance*.
9. For example, Robert Reich, *The New American Frontier* (New York Times Books, 1983)
10. This and other aspects of tacit bargaining among the allies have parallels to the process of tacit and informal arms control between adversaries that Thomas Schelling suggested more than two decades ago. In the alliance context, the process

usually takes the form of implicit (American) threats to do something if the allies do not act. But it might – and sometimes has – been the reverse: implicit commitments to act positively if the allies reciprocate in some way. Allies should find it easier to communicate directly than do adversaries, but formal bargains still may founder on domestic politics, or the complexity of the "bargain." And since allies give signals to each other in a larger number of ways than do adversaries – through parliaments, or commerce, or public opinion – implicit threats may be more likely and tacit commitments even harder to make credible. See Schelling's "Reciprocal Measures for Arms Stabilization," in Donald G. Brennan, ed., *Arms Control, Disarmament and National Security* (New York: George Braziller, 1961).

11. Lloyd Free and William Watts, "Internationalism Comes of Age . . . Again," *Public Opinion*, 3 (April/May 1980) 45–50.
12. Rielly, cited above, p.21.
13. See Stephen F. Szabo, ed., *The Successor Generation: International Perspectives of Postwar Europeans* (London: Butterworth, 1983) esp. the chapters on Germany and Italy, and the conclusions.
14. This paragraph owes much to Catherine McArdle Kelleher, "America Looks at Europe: Change and Continuity in the 1980s," in *The Troubled Alliance*.
15. This sounds a lot like Charles Lindblom's famous description of policy formulation by "successive limited comparisons." See his "The Science of 'Muddling Through'", *Public Administration Review*, 19 (Spring 1959) 79–88. People – or in this case, allies – may be able to agree on the broad outlines of policy even though they disagree on specific analyses and do not fully share (and could not specify) over-arching objectives or values.
16. Rielly, cited above, pp. 17–18.
17. See "Britain's Grenada Shut-Out," *The Economist*, 10 March 1984.
18. Trade figures are from International Monetary Fund, *Direction of Trade Statistics Yearbook 1983*. The credit figures are from the US State Department, Exim Bank and Commodity Credit Corporation.
19. "Europe's Ostrich and America's Eagle," *The Economist*, 8 March 1980.
20. See, for example, Helmut Schmidt, "The World Economy at Stake: The Inevitable Need for American Leadership," *The Economist*, 26 February 1983, pp. 23–4, 30.
21. See John Pinder's chapter in *The Troubled Alliance*.
22. One explicit formulation of such a broad bargain, which also serves to illustrate how difficult it would be to assemble, is John Montgomery, "Leadership for Peace: Japan's Way," *Soka Gakkai News*, 8, 167 (February 1983) 2–11.
23. I am indebted to Derek Leebaert for reminding me of these pieces of history.
24. This question, the one right to ask in thinking not just about allies but about adversaries as well, is my colleague Ernest May's formulation.
25. Richard E. Neustadt, *Alliance Politics* (New York: Columbia University Press, 1970) p. 149.
26. For a summary discussion of these issues, see the chapter by Marshall Goldman and Raymond Vernon in Joseph S. Nye, ed., *The Making of America's Soviet Policy* (New Haven, Conn: Yale University Press, for the Council on Foreign Relations, 1984).
27. The real issue is resources, not foreign exchange. If the Soviets are at all adept at calculating their interests, they will buy grain from the United States if it costs fewer resources than to grow it in the Soviet Union. Then, in principle, the resources thus "saved" could be put to any purpose from making hosiery to building nuclear warheads.

Index

A-6 nuclear-capable aircraft, 37
A-7 nuclear-capable aircraft, 37
Adenauer, Konrad, 117
  on NATO, 94
Afghanistan, Soviet invasion of, 1979, 6,
    52, 71–2, 79, 86, 87, 94, 96, 100,
    105, 109, 111, 118, 178
  boycott of Moscow Olympics, 87, 178
  Western economic sanctions against
      Soviet Union, 86, 87, 110, 178
air-launched cruise missiles (ALCMS), *see*
    cruise missiles
anti-nuclear movements in Europe 7, 14, 26,
    53–5, 125, 157, 159, 160
  German "Greens," 73
Azores summit, 147

Barre, Raymond, 118
Battle Bill, 182
Brandt, Willy, 72
Brezhnev, Leonid, 4, 173
  summit talks with Helmut Schmidt,
      1980, 71
Brzezinski, Zbigniew, 147, 151
Buchan, Alistair, 181
Burns, Arthur, 146

Camp David agreements on Middle East,
    104, 112
Camp David economic decisions, August
    1971, 146, 148
Carter, Jimmy, 192
  December 1979 NATO decisions, 120
  Iranian hostage crisis, 117
  neutron bomb, 45, 188, 191
  Presidential Directive (PD) 59, 52
  Soviet invasion of Afghanistan, 178
Central America, 106–9, *see also* public
    opinion polls *and* Grenada
  American intervention in Grenada, 1983,
      108
  as American "backyard," 108
  European activities in, 108–9
  European criticisms of American policy
      toward, 108

Kissinger Commission on, 107
trans-Atlantic differences over, 106–7,
    109
Churchill, Winston, 181
COCOM, 66, 151–3
command, control, communications and
    intelligence (C31), 36–7
Commerce, US Department of, 148, 151
Common Agricultural Policy (CAP), *see*
    European Economic Community (EEC)
Conference on Security and Cooperation in
    Europe (CSCE), 23, 90
Connally, John, 146–7
Council of Economic Advisors (CEA), 146
cruise missiles, *see also* intermediate
    nuclear forces (INF)
  air-launched (ALCMS), 43
  deployed in Europe, 68, 161
  Dutch position toward, 182
  ground-launched (GLCMS), 43
  NATO's December 1979 decision to
      deploy, 25, 31, 37, 42–4, 46, 48, 50,
      56–7, 68, 90, 142, 149, 177,
      186, 191
  sea-launched (SLCMs), 43
Czechoslovakia, Soviet Invasion of,
    1968, 12

detente, 4, 69, 82–3, 90, 100, 170
  in Europe, 6, 60, 69, 72, 82, 100,
      113–4, 170
  German role in, 68
  Kissinger comment on, 59
dual key, 23-4, 32, 34, 48–9, 177, *see also*
    theater nuclear forces (TNF)
Dulles, John Foster, 94
Dunkirk, Treaty of, 1947, 27

European Economic Community (EEC), 68,
    118–19, 133
  Common Agricultural Policy (CAP),
      129, 135
  Conference on Security and Cooperation
      in Europe (CSCE), role in, 23
  declarations on Middle East, 110, 119

207